Medievalism in Europe II

Studies in Medievalism VIII

1996

Studies in Medievalism

Edited by Leslie J. Workman

Volume I

1. Medievalism in England. Edited by Leslie J. Workman. Spring 1979.
2. Medievalism in America. Edited by Leslie J. Workman. Spring 1982.

Volume II

1. Twentieth Century Medievalism. Edited by Jane Chance. Fall 1982. *(Out of print)*
2. Medievalism in France. Edited by Heather Arden. Spring 1983.
3. Dante in the Modern World. Edited by Kathleen Verduin. Summer 1983.
4. Modern Arthurian Literature. Edited by Veronica M. S. Kennedy and Kathleen Verduin. Fall 1983. *(Out of print)*

Volume III

1. Medievalism in France 1500-1750. Edited by Heather Arden. Fall 1987.
2. Architecture and Design. Edited by John R. Zukowsky. Fall 1990.
3. Inklings and Others. Edited by Jane Chance. Winter 1991.
4. German Medievalism. Edited by Francis G. Gentry. Spring 1991.

   Note: Volume III, Numbers 3 and 4, are bound together and cannot be ordered separately.

IV Medievalism in England. Edited by Leslie J. Workman. 1992.

V Medievalism in Europe. Edited by Leslie J. Workman. 1993.

VI Medievalism in North America. Edited by Kathleen Verduin. 1994.

VII Medievalism in England II. Edited by Leslie J. Workman and Kathleen Verduin. 1995.

Medievalism in Europe II

Edited by

Leslie J. Workman

Kathleen Verduin

Studies in Medievalism VIII 1996

Cambridge

D. S. Brewer

Copyright © Studies in Medievalism 1997

All Rights Reserved. Except as permitted under current legislation
no part of this work may be photocopied, stored in a retrieval system,
published, performed in public, adapted, broadcast,
transmitted, recorded or reproduced in any form or by any means,
without the prior permission of the copyright owner

First published 1997
D. S. Brewer, Cambridge

ISBN 0 85991 432 1

ISSN 0738–7164

D. S. Brewer is an imprint of Boydell & Brewer Ltd
PO Box 9, Woodbridge, Suffolk IP12 3DF, UK
and of Boydell & Brewer Inc.
PO Box 41026, Rochester, NY 14604–4126, USA

A catalogue record for this book is available
from the British Library

Library of Congress Cataloguing-in-Publication
Card Number: 97–28791

This publication is printed on acid-free paper

Printed in the United States of America

Studies in Medievalism

Editor	Leslie J. Workman
Associate Editor	Kathleen Verduin (Hope)
Editorial Assistant	Angella Huddleston (Hope)
Corresponding Editors	Geraldine Barnes (Sydney)
	Ulrich Müller (Salzburg)
	Domenico Pietropaolo (Toronto)
	Toshiyuki Takamiya (Keio)
	Andrew Wawn (Leeds)
Advisors	Norman F. Cantor (New York)
	Alice Chandler (Princeton, New Jersey)
	Otto Gründler (Western Michigan)
	Paul Szarmach (Western Michigan)

Studies in Medievalism provides an interdisciplinary medium of exchange for scholars in all fields, including the visual and other arts, concerned with any aspect of the post-medieval idea and study of the Middle Ages and the influence, both scholarly and popular, of this study on Western society after 1500.

Studies in Medievalism is published by Boydell and Brewer, Ltd., P. O. Box 9, Woodbridge, Suffolk IP12 3DF, UK; Boydell and Brewer, Inc., P. O. Box 41026, Rochester, NY 14604, USA. Orders and inquiries about back issues should be addressed to Boydell and Brewer at the appropriate office.

Submissions and inquiries regarding future volumes should be addressed to the Editor, **Studies in Medievalism**, Department of English, Hope College, Holland, MI 49423 USA, tel. (616) 394-7626, fax (616) 395-7134, e-mail workman@hope.edu. Contributors should submit the original manuscript and one copy with an abstract: unsolicited manuscripts should be accompanied by a stamped self-addressed envelope. When a manuscript is accepted for publication, copy on an IBM-compatible disk will be required.

Acknowledgments

The Editors make grateful acknowledgment for financial and other assistance to the Department of English at Hope College.

The device on the title page comes from the title page of **Des Knaben Wunderhorn: Alte deutsche Lieder**, edited by L. Achim von Arnim and Clemens Brentano (Heidelberg and Frankfurt, 1806).

The epigraph is from an unpublished paper by Lord Acton written about 1859, printed in Herbert Butterfield, **Man On His Past** (Cambridge University Press, 1955), 212.

Studies in Medievalism

Medievalism in Europe II

Preface	1
Editorial	3

Germany

Inventing German(ic) Chaucer: Ideology and Philology in German Anglistics before 1945	Richard J. Utz	5
Hermann Hesse's Approaches to Medieval Literature	Albrecht Classen	27
Jeschute, or, How to Arrange the Taming of a Hero: The Myth of Parzival from Chrétien to Adolf Muschg	Otfrid Ehrismann	46

Scandinavia

King and Marshal: Ballad and Liturgy in a Danish Music Drama	Nils Holger Petersen	72
Medievalism in the Service of the Swedish Proletariat: Jan Fridegård's Viking Trilogy	Robert E. Bjork	86

France

The Cradle and the Crucible: Envisioning the Middle Ages in French Romanticism	Michael Glencross	100

Medievalism in the Midi: Inventing the Medieval House in Nineteenth-Century France	Martha L. MacFarlane	125
Saint Louis and French Political Culture	Adam Knobler	156
Saint Louis in French Epic and Drama	William Chester Jordan	174
Asceticism, Masochism, and Female Autonomy: Catherine of Siena and *The Story of O*	Suzy Beemer	195
Closing the Circle: Medievalism in Today's Occitan (Provençal) Literature	William Calin	210
From *The Song of Roland* to the Songs of Arnaut Daniel: Chapbooks and Transcreations in Modern Brazilian Poetry	Roy Rosenstein	223
Notes on Contributors		241

Volume VIII 1996

Two great principles divide the world, and contend for the mastery, antiquity and the middle ages. These are the two civilizations that have preceded us, the two elements of which ours is composed. All political as well as religious questions reduce themselves practically to this. This is the great dualism that runs through our society.

Lord Acton

IN MEMORIAM

Veronica M. S. Kennedy

We greatly regret to announce the death of Veronica M. S. Kennedy on July 4, 1996, in Manhattan. Professor Kennedy was a graduate of St. Hilda's College, Oxford, where she read with C. S. Lewis and J. R. R. Tolkien, and of Kings College, London. She taught at City College of New York and was a member of the Department of English at St. John's University, New York. Author of a number of studies in modern and popular literature, she was a founding member of the Editorial Board of *Studies in Medievalism* and co-editor of Volume 4, Number 4, *Modern Arthurian Literature*. Veronica was a tireless organizer of conference sessions on medievalism and other topics for *Studies in Medievalism* and at meetings of the International Congress on Medieval Studies, the Northeast Modern Language Association, the Popular Culture Association, the Plymouth Medieval Conference, and elsewhere. She was a stimulating and imaginative contributor to these sessions. Her wit, often devastating but never unkind, was an unfailing delight on these and all other occasions. Veronica Kennedy was a scholar of unusual insights: she was a courageous and loving spirit and will be very sorely missed.

Forthcoming Volumes
Volumes IX and X will be devoted to *Medievalism and the Academy*. In view of the rapid changes in the field and the long lead time for the volumes of *Studies in Medievalism* we are unwilling to commit ourselves to the topics of further volumes at this time. Watch our web page for further information:

http://www.macatawa.org/ ~ simnet/

The Year's Work in Medievalism
Volume V has been published, as announced in our Newsletter; the Delaware volume (VI) and the Bozeman volume (IX) are in press, and we hope gradually to overtake our backlog in this series.

Newsletter
Studies in Medievalism is currently seeking to set up a Listserv to replace the annual Newsletter. Subscribers are asked to notify the Editor of their e-mail address; those without electronic access should send a mailing or fax address in order to receive an abbreviated Newsletter and other announcements.

Preface

Medievalism is the continuing process of creating the Middle Ages. Nobody, I think, would now disagree with this very simple definition, and it could well be asked why I have not said it before instead of the more rhetorical definitions which I have offered from time to time. One reason certainly is that twenty years ago, when I set about launching *Studies in Medievalism*, the word *process* was not in my critical vocabulary and hardly, I think, in anybody else's: we thought in terms of conclusions. Historical scholarship, and I must emphasize yet again that medievalism is fundamentally an historical subject, had at the beginning of the twentieth century painfully and reluctantly surrendered its faith in nineteenth-century positivism, but it was still felt that scholarship could achieve a kind of certainty on particular questions in humane studies. As Norman Cantor described the conventional procedure in *Inventing the Middle Ages*, in the course of academic debate between differing views "hypotheses are tested, ideas refined, and ultimately a consensus is reached."

At the time when I founded *Studies in Medievalism* I was concerned to distinguish medievalism very carefully from "the province of medieval scholarship" and said only that it was "time to begin the interdisciplinary study of medievalism as a comprehensive phenomenon analogous to classicism or romanticism." The distinction was then important because of the confusion which surrounded the word *medievalism*; and since our introduction of medievalism as a scholarly topic began and has continued in the context of medieval conferences, it scarcely seemed necessary to emphasize their mutual dependence. I had learned in graduate school the importance of recognizing subjective and personal factors in scholarship and the importance of imagination in scholarly hypotheses. I thought that the study of medievalism would cast light in these dark places and thus enrich our understanding of medieval studies. This was an early recognition of the importance of what we now call "process."

In 1992, when *Studies in Medievalism* became an annual volume published by the progressive house of Boydell & Brewer, my editorial noted that we were still "constrained by what we have been offered," and I remarked on the continuing indifference of medieval scholars to medievalism. As a very small journal creating in effect an entirely new field, we were not simply constrained by what we were offered: we were still hoping in fact that our field, our terms of reference, would be defined by the traditional process I have described. As for the continuing indifference of medieval scholars to medievalism, I must of course except a few, such as Otto Gründler, Paul Szarmach, and Norman Cantor, who had the vision and imagination to support our activities, and those who contributed to our Conferences and publications. I now first dared to challenge the vast and imposing edifice of medieval studies, quoting Ernst Curtius to the effect that "the Middle Ages for which I had been searching did not exist": but nobody rose to the bait. Unwisely, as I now see, I still felt that it was not for me as an editor to offer direction but to see what would emerge from the field.

In our first European volume (1993), I noted that medievalism was still a new field in which the basic exploration remained to be done before we could adopt "a real critical and philosophical appreciation." By 1995, however, I felt that "the previous volumes have established a framework for the historical consideration of medievalism and we may now turn to different questions. The theory, method, and philosophy of medievalism are long overdue for exploration."

Meanwhile, in 1994, after we had been publishing and conducting a very active program of conference activity for fifteen years without apparent effect, everybody suddenly discovered medievalism. Conferences sprang up, there were graduate courses and books on medieval historiography, to which Norman Cantor had given a lead with his *Inventing the Middle Ages* (1991), and there began to be increasing debate on the future of medieval studies, in which we have actively engaged as a natural part of our province. With all these things in mind we announced in 1995 a new issue, *Medievalism and the Academy* (now to be two issues), to take cognizance of all these questions.

In the course of these changes we have progressively abandoned our view of medievalism as modestly ancillary to medieval studies. As Kathleen Verduin points out below, their relations are "clearly reciprocal," or, as I remarked in a recent book review, quoting Yeats, "how do you separate the dancer from the dance?" Critical scholarship in general, having reeled back on the very brink of deconstruction, has not only supplied a large inventory of sophisticated critical tools, but an unmistakable emphasis on process: and the natural development of our own work has similarly led us to emphasize the process of creating the Middle Ages, which is medievalism.

This present issue of *Studies in Medievalism*, then, like our previous European issue, exemplifies what *Studies in Medievalism* has long proclaimed, the universal, pervasive, and comprehensive nature of medievalism in modern western civilization, progressively building upon our chosen epigraph from Acton.

Leslie J. Workman
Holland, Michigan

Editorial

The twelve essays in this collection extend the work of our previous volume on *Medievalism in Europe*, published in 1993, by bringing forward significant examples of postmedieval engagement with the Middle Ages in literature and the other arts. In a wide-ranging study, Otfrid Ehrismann traces successive constructions of the Jeschute-Parzival encounter from Chrétien to Adolf Muschg as an implement for tracking western society's shifting notions of nature, civilization, and the feminine; similarly broad in scope is William Chester Jordan's survey of literary and dramatic representations of St. Louis from LeMoyne's epic poem in 1658 to exoticist novels of the twentieth century. As Albrecht Classen shows, Hermann Hesse's attraction to the spirituality and moral virtue he discovered in the life of St. Francis and the *Gesta Romanorum* informed his own work and helped popularize medieval texts; Nils Holger Petersen's study (the first we have published by a Scandinavian scholar) presents Heise's 1878 music drama *King and Marshal* as a culmination of Denmark's longterm cultural involvement with an incident from the thirteenth century; Robert E. Bjork outlines the motives and development of Jan Fridegård's twentieth-century Holme trilogy, now available to an English-speaking audience through Professor Bjork's authoritative translation. Martha MacFarlane's study of restorations of the medieval houses of Cordes analyzes French attention to the architectural past; Roy Rosenstein documents the surprising transmission of Provençal texts to the literary culture of contemporary Brazil.

More pronounced in this second European collection, however, is the relation between medievalism and a variety of ideologies. Fridegård's fiction, as Bjork points out, rewrites Viking history through the lens of Fridegård's anarchist socialism; the restorations of Cordes strengthened communal mythologies by proposing aristocratic origins. The political uses even of sainthood are amply demonstrated in Adam Knobler's account, in an essay complementary to Jordan's work, of how post-Revolutionary parties shuttled St. Louis from royalist to colonialist campaigns; William Calin finds in the contemporary Occitan revival both a cultural minority's need for roots and an appropriation of the language of the troubadours by an intellectual elite. Michael Glencross, whose new book *Reconstructing Camelot* offers a long overdue revaluation of French medievalism, traces a correlation between genre and conflicting representations of the medieval in historiography, philology, and literature of the Romantic decades. Considerations of national and ethnic self-definition figure prominently in several of these essays: we read of Provençal assertions of cultural continuity with ancient Rome and of scholarly efforts to legitimate the *langue d'oc* in Glencross, of French efforts to repossess North Africa in an ostensible replay of the Crusades in Knobler, of romantic Scandinavian claims to Viking vitality in

Bjork, and we are at a loss to explain the attraction to the poetry of the troubadours in the racial melange of contemporary Brazil. Most politically disturbing of all, perhaps, is Suzy Beemer's connection between extremist medieval asceticism and modern sexual masochism, Catherine of Siena dissolving into *The Story of O* in a common orgy of female self-annihilation.

Where does medievalism end and medieval studies begin? What are the boundaries between the two disciplines, the one still new, the other well established in the bastion of the academy? Undeniably, artistic and popular medievalism remains dependent on the discoveries of scholarship: Hesse's interest in medieval legends, as Classen points out, was facilitated by newly available editions and anthologies, and Petersen documents how Heise's opera drew on recent scholarship on the ballad tradition, primarily the famous work of Grundtvig; the Holme trilogy, similarly, made use of archaeological as well as cultural studies, and MacFarlane shows how restoration of medieval dwellings may be traced to nineteenth-century historiography. Yet the influence emerges as clearly reciprocal as well. Glencross, for example, considers Romantic philology and historiography in parallel with literary events like Hugo's (newly famous, *grace à* Disney) *Notre-Dame de Paris,* reminding us of the generic interplay, after Walter Scott, between the writing of history and the writing of novels. More directly, Richard J. Utz breaks apart the myth of apolitical scholarship by his masterful exposé of Nazi-inspired racism in the still respected Chaucer studies of Will Héraucourt—a pathological end result of the "philological arms race" (to which Glencross refers) of a previous generation, a generation entranced by romantic myths of ancestral forest heroes.

As Leslie J. Workman asserted in his editorial to our last volume, "Medievalism and medieval studies might well be defined as the Middle Ages in the contemplation of contempory society." Centuries of study and artistic recreation have succeeded in elevating the Middle Ages—or, more properly, "the Middle Ages," a constantly shifting swirl of images and meanings—to the position of cultural icon, an authoritative presence for whose possession we continue to wrangle in often transparent bids for ideological superiority. To what extent has the academy participated in this struggle, and how has academic medievalism taken on the coloration of its successive times? In our next volume, *Medievalism and the Academy,* we hope to confront these questions head on.

Kathleen Verduin
Hope College

Inventing German(ic) Chaucer: Ideology and Philology in German Anglistics before 1945

Richard J. Utz

> L'important ne me paraît pas de parfaire, sur tel ou tel point, une réhabilitation de ce "Moyen Age," et pas plus d'évoquer, par choix personnel, une sorte d'âge d'or où tout aurait été d'une autre qualité humaine dans une société plus sereine. Mais bien d'affirmer que ce Moyen Age, en réalité, n'a pas existé; qu'il s'agit d'une notion abstraite forgée à dessein, pour différentes commodités ou raisons, à laquelle a été sciemment appliquée cette sorte d'opprobe.
>
> Jacques Heers, *Le Moyen Age, Une Imposture*

It is one of the most persistent myths in the history of modern academic thought that philological positivism can avoid subjectivity, metaphysics, and religion by deducing laws of development from the facts of history and literary texts. The main cause for the attempt of nineteenth-century positivism in the humanities to utilize scientific methodology was its competition with the success and progress of the natural sciences and the older, already institutionalized Classical Philology. It was in such a climate of emulation that German scholars in the "New Philologies" developed a "science of literature" ("Literaturwissenschaft") to assert the relevance of their fields. Confining themselves to editing, collections of factual detail, historical background studies, lexicography, indices of motifs, etc., professors were also reacting to the political situation in Germany after 1848. As Jost Hermand has noted,

> Ideologically speaking, this positivism . . . is the faithful reflection of the saturated bourgeoisie in the second half of the nine-

Studies in Medievalism VIII, 1996

teenth century which has given up on the idealism of the 1848 generation and which is satisfied with the leisurely consolidation of the power already gained. Audacious thoughts, political perspectives or social reform are no longer in the foreground, but a sedulous collecting of tiny and tiniest pieces to build an imposing tower of mere facts which was furnished with everything except an idealistic structural frame.[1]

However, it would be much too easy to characterize the nineteenth-century philological positivism as apolitical merely because it abstained from overt activity. Recently, Renate Haas has provided ample evidence that, despite ubiquitous claims about the incompatibility of philological positivism and ideology, there are illustrative examples of the fruitful interplay of ideology and philology even in the early periods of academic Chaucer criticism in Germany. As early as the 1840s, Haas points out, Eduard Fiedler reinvented the medieval poet according to his own liberal *Vormärz* ("Pre-March," i. e., the years before the Frankfurt parliament in 1848) ideology. Although quite thorough in his philological substantiation of Chaucer's biography, Fiedler emphasized the parallels to his own time so much, Haas writes, "that his criticism of fourteenth-century misuses indirectly criticized the same misuses of the present and that, on the other hand, he revealed some possibilities of remedying them." In typical *Vormärz* manner, Fiedler underlined the role of parliament (and the middle class represented in it) against the unjust trespasses of the English kings and hailed Chaucer as a literary Wycliffite who tried to undermine respect for the pope and the corrupt medieval clergy. Interestingly enough, Haas also notes that "in several places, Fiedler betrayed quite strong pro-Germanic and anti-Romance feelings (e. g., contrasting Romance pathos with true Germanic 'Gemüth')."[2]

Only some years after the dreams of intellectuals like Fiedler had come to naught, a new reading commenced with Wilhelm Hertzberg, who accentuated Chaucer's loyalty as a court poet and his disinterestedness in political and religious extremism. Haas shows that for Hertzberg, the medieval poet thus embodied the ideal intellectual of his own time, the philologist, the—supposedly—neutral and apolitical observer. As in Fiedler's case, however, Hertzberg's philology waxed nationalistic when he depicted Chaucer as a "divided personality with a Janus-face, one side a courtly and chivalrous Frenchman, the other a robust, earthy Anglo-Saxon." Since Hertzberg was certainly aware of the popularity of the French fabliaux, his characterization of Chaucer's predilection of sturdy folk char-

Inventing German(ic) Chaucer

acters as "Low German and Anglo-Saxon" can be understood only as an intentional Germanicizing of the English poet.[3]

Despite these and numerous other obvious examples of overt symbioses between ideology and philology (with temporary excursions into the nationalistic mode of Germanicizing), the myth of philology as objective, neutral, and politically innocuous endured. Joerg Fichte, in his concise essay "Chaucer's Work in German Literary Scholarship to 1914," demonstrates how some German philologists forged their own uncompromising use of philological methods into an intellectual tool to distinguish themselves from the predominantly essayistic British critics who centered on such potentially "political" topics as the aesthetic features of Chaucer's poetry or Chaucer's personality.[4] Philological positivism dominated the German academic scene when—very late in comparison with the more liberal Switzerland—English philology was finally institutionalized at German and Austrian universities in the 1870s and 1880s. In 1872, Julius Zupitza, a German, was hired at the University of Vienna to fill what was considered an obvious lack at Austrian universities in lectures and seminars on Nordic law, the Eddas, the older English poets, and Shakespeare. The government document promoting Zupitza's hiring mentioned that since no qualified Austrian candidate was available a foreign national had to be hired, a young man who, according to credible sources, "abstains from all political activity and lives only for his philological studies."[5] If the recommending voice of this Austrian document thought Zupitza's "philological" qualifications equivalent to "politically inactive" and hoped for an academic who would not cause any trouble at the university, the decision of the newly victorious imperial German government to create the first chair of English Philology in Strasbourg/Straßburg in the same year also demonstrates the political aspect of philology. Before 1872, there had been no chairs of English Philology independent of Romance Philology. Even if the new chairholder, Bernhard ten Brink, thought of himself and his work as philological and apolitical, the acceptance of the innovation by Bismarck and his ministry and its positioning at the newly Germanized university of Straßburg was a conspicuous political act.

According to Joerg Fichte's observations, philological studies ruled supreme among the first generations of German Chaucerians. From the beginnings in the nineteenth century until 1914, Fichte counts two hundred-fifty studies on Chaucer's language and meter as well as about one hundred twenty-five books, dissertations, articles, and notes dealing with Chaucer's poetry, its sources, analogues, manuscripts, and reception:

This distribution in itself is of great significance because it demonstrates that medieval texts were mainly regarded as mere source material for study by historical grammarians. As a matter of fact, the designations "German" and "Germanic" were not differentiated for a long time, so that Anglo-Saxon studies were a domain of the German departments, which were established during the first half of the 19th century.[6]

A look at the general history of English studies in Germany substantiates Fichte's observations. I would like to caution, though, that neither the combination of Nordic and German(ic) studies nor the concentration of the first English philologists on early (i. e., Anglo-Saxon), Middle English, and Renaissance literature should be necessarily construed as a conscious political choice of German academics. At least in most cases, both features would have been due to the special history of English as a discipline within the specific German cultural history. From what has been said, it also emerges, however, that philological positivism was cultivated in Germany as something particularly German and, in some cases, of a higher degree of scholarliness than academic production in neighboring countries. It was exactly this reputation of the superiority of German philology to all other methods of academic research in the humanities which thoroughly impressed and influenced American methodology during the first thirty years of the twentieth century and which, as we shall see, still has a remarkable impact on the American reception history of German Chaucer scholarship.

The unification of Germany in the wake of the Franco-Prussian War not only helped institutionalize English Philology, it also produced a forceful ideological framework for many Germans, including university professors: racial nationalism. As racial nationalism—not only in Germany—elevated loyalty to the nation-state above all other allegiances, persecuted minorities at home, and stirred up hatred against other nations, the new philologies were under pressure to produce—on the basis of their texts—the characteristics which distinguished the spirit of one people from that of all others. In Germany, *Völkisch* thought denounced the liberal-humanist tradition of the West as alien to the German soul and attacked the Enlightenment and parliamentary democracy as foreign ideas that corrupted the German soul. With fanatical devotion, *Völkisch* thinkers embraced all things German—the medieval past, the German landscape, the simple peasant—and claimed that the German race was superior to all other races. As the apolitical methodology *par excellence*, philological positivism should have been recalcitrant, if not diametrically opposed to such myth-driven racist assertions. In practice, however, even the pioneering nine-

Inventing German(ic) Chaucer

teenth-century studies of British scientist J. C. Prichard provide ample evidence for the high compatibility of both methods of investigation, racist ethnography and nationalistic philology. Prichard (and others) did not simply collect and compare cultural phenomena but implicitly ranked them in a hierarchy of degrees of civilization. This resulted in a potential politicization of all disciplines involved in such investigations, including nationalistic philology.[7]

A look at Thomas Finckenstaedt's 1983 survey *Kleine Geschichte der Anglistik in Deutschland* shows that in the specific cultural situation in Germany between 1870 and 1918, philology and nationalist/racist thought go hand in hand in their fight against making the teaching of modern foreign languages part of the university and Gymnasium curricula. Not only is the inclusion of language teaching regarded as an attack against the scientific status of the new philologies, but the full mastery of the foreign language is also seen as detrimental to full perfection in one's own, more important, national idiom. During World War I, English Studies had not been spared from the consequences of extreme nationalism and xenophobia against anything connected with the Entente powers. Chaucer studies do not seem to be involved in the widespread attacks against British imperialism among German anglicists. Hans Hecht's statement at the 1915 meeting of the German Shakespeare Society that the Germans should be seen as more faithful preservers of Shakespeare's spirit than the poet's own fellow countrymen confirms that racial nationalism and the heated atmosphere of the war could sway even the most philologically-minded scholars.[8]

After World War I, English Philology came under attack for not having provided sufficient linguistic and cultural knowledge about contemporary Great Britain and the emerging United States. This development and the increasing importance of English as the language of international trade and diplomacy adds the subjects of "Kulturkunde" und "Auslandswissenschaft" (science of foreign cultures) to existing school and university curricula. The changes were partly influenced by Wilhelm Dilthey's philosophy, Eduard Spranger's pedagogy, and an essential paradigm shift in history which postulated the unity of cultural periods, a notion which directly challenged the tenets of philological positivism among scholars in literature. The political changes in the New Philologies occurring in the wake of the Nazi takeover in 1933 marginalized positivism even more; as one triumphant essay declares as early as May 1933, "Positivism did not want to have anything to do with revolution. That is why today's revolution does not want to have anything to do with positivism."[9] The effects of the new state ideology are mostly visible in a dramatic rise in university courses taught on English culture ("Englandkunde"). Moreover, a variety of classes in literature, language, and didactics reveal the coeval political developments: "The English Way of Thinking as an Expression of *Völkisch* Spirit"; "Democracy and the Idea of Leadership/ Führership"; "Poetry as *Völkisch* Leadership/ Führership;" "History of the English Language as Reflected in Culture and Race"; "Readings at School in the Service of *Völkisch* Education."[10] It is interesting to see how the density of such topics is not the same throughout all German universities. The vast majority of English professors want to stay apolitical and carry on with their mostly philological studies. Not unlike many post-1848 academics, the majority of German anglicists in this period seek to avoid the danger of confrontation with the government and achieve a state of Stoic inner emigration. As Finkenstaedt underlines, many an important study was penned during the years of the Third Reich in the private offices of these scholars.

However, some individuals and their programs collaborated early and efficiently with the new Nazi powers, demonstrating anew the compatibility of philological methodology and ideology. An especially high concentration of the new spirit was visible in the capital, Berlin, and at the University of Marburg. English studies at the latter institution were strongly impacted by a unique paradigm of investigation which seems to have been shaped as a compromise among the older philological positivism, the new politically minded "cultural science," and recent findings in synchronic (Saussurean) linguistics. The paradigm was called the "national-psychological method" ("nationalpsychologische Methode"), and it promised an overview of contemporary English on the basis of analogies drawn between specific linguistic traits and individual constituents of the English national character. Despite its "pseudoscientific" methodology, the "nationalpsychologische Methode" was little more than a reassertion of the traditional clichés about the British "other." Max Deutschbein, the method's founder, claimed that the Englishman in general lacked one particular German character trait, the urge to strive for knowledge and the curiosity necessary to engage in research.[11] Although the general paradigm had been developed well before 1933, it is easy to comprehend how it was reinforced by and could actively reinforce the objectives promoted by the new cultural ideology of the Third Reich.[12] Also in 1933, Deutschbein published an essay entitled "Die Aufgaben der Englischen Philologie im Neuen Staat" ("The Tasks of English Philology in the New State") in which he celebrated Goethe, Shakespeare, and Milton as "representatives of the German spirit."[13] One of Deutschbein's eager students, Will Héraucourt, felt obliged to add the father of English poetry to his teacher's list of prestigious "German" writers. In his extensive study *Die Wertwelt Chaucers* (1939), Héraucourt set out to invent Chaucer as a truly German(ic) poet.[14]

Inventing German(ic) Chaucer

A first glance at *Die Wertwelt Chaucers* might easily underline the impression which most post-1945 scholars had (and still have) of the study as a thorough—because philological—academic enterprise. Its table of contents shows a short introductory chapter on theoretical issues and objectives, followed by an historical introduction. Then, a survey of Chaucer's adherence to the traditional medieval tenets of courtly ideals, the poet's "world of values" (a literal translation of *Wertwelt*), is divided into four major categories, the cardinal virtues of *Prudentia, Justitia, Fortitudo*, and *Temperantia*, each of which is subdivided into discussions of the respective corresponding subvirtues. A comprehensive index of all Greek, Latin, French, Italian, Provençal, German, and English words, a name index, a textual index, and a bibliography complete the solid philological surface. If one only used Héraucourt's book as many scholars have done, namely as a quarry for solving specific philological inquiries into, e. g., Chaucer's use of "Knowen," "trouthe," "debonairtee," "fredom," "honour," or "corage," its ideological bias might never even come to light. However, there is evidence that *Die Wertwelt Chaucers*, despite its positivistic, philological appearance, is the most blatant example of a dangerous symbiosis of philology and ideology in the history of German Chaucer scholarship. It is thoroughly informed (1) by the strong ethnographic (nationalist/racist) streak of late nineteenth- and early twentieth-century philology as propagated by Deutschbein and his students in the "nationalpsychologische Methode," and (2) by the ideological mentality of an Anglophilic but often pro-Nazi German upper-class intelligentsia.

Héraucourt bases all his later observations about Chaucer as exemplifying the (Germanic) English national spirit on the poet Rudolf G. Binding's notion that "the thoughts of a people, of a time, only enter into indestructibility via the power of a poet's words. Poetry is the expression, the voice, and the conscience of a people" (2).[15] Therefore, the investigation of Chaucer's values is for Héraucourt not simply a search into something past. He strongly believes Chaucer's terminology still contains a significant metaphysical message for his own times. Héraucourt's short historical survey, then, places Chaucer in a calamitous fourteenth century (this is the "Zeitwende" the book's subtitle indicates) which witnesses the destruction of the static high-medieval mentality and the beginning of the emancipation of the individual. He situates the medieval writer in this unstable period as shifting from the world of bourgeois common sense into the sophistication of the court poet. Within this picture of the historical background, in a short paragraph which seems strangely out of place, Héraucourt defends Chaucer against some French scholars who have dared to claim the German(ic) poet for France:

Chaucer's early literary dependence on France is conspicuous. However, to construct him as a French genius, as has been done (pro domo) by some French criticism, is absolutely wrong and presents an attempt at spiritual piracy. According to his whole personality, Chaucer is an Englishman. J. N. Manly has shown, how little importance should be placed on the French origin of Chaucer's name. Chaucer's forefathers can be verified as living in England well over 150 years before his birth. Even the fact that Chaucer transforms English into a poetic language proves him to be an Englishman. A serious French scholar such as Cazamian acknowledges this entirely. (29f.)[16]

This outburst comes out of the blue and also contradicts the philological premise of the study, since the alleged French nationalist "pirates" remain mysteriously anonymous and without any bibliographical reference.

Shortly after this remark, a pattern begins to establish itself: Héraucourt attempts a description of central European knighthood and its most cherished values. Since most studies—in his view—overestimate the importance of the French courts for the development of European court culture, he adds a one-page footnote which, once again, is only faintly relevant to his chosen philological objective but is meant to set the national record straight:

Thorough investigations into military history . . . have proven conclusively that it was the mounted Germanic comitatus which is at the origin of western knighthood; this is true not only for Germany and England, but also for France, even if the idea might have been stylized there somewhat earlier and might have exerted influence on the Germanic countries of origin. (Let us not forget that many of the French expressions in military history are of German origin!). (33, note 1)[17]

About the education of the courtly page, the "Junker," Héraucourt adds:

At the age of seven commences a strictly planned educational program to learn the *courtoisie*, the refined behavior, the faultless courtly conversation, attitudes which according to general agreement were mastered exclusively at the French court. However, the institution of this program of education seems to originate from a German(ic) custom. . . . In Anglo-Saxon England, Scandinavia, and Ireland it was customary for the sons of noble families

Inventing German(ic) Chaucer 13

(usually from the age of seven onwards) to be handed over to foreign housholds for their education. . . . A comparison with the modern English public-school education seems obvious. (33-34, note 1)[18]

Next, Héraucourt introduces the division of his study into the four cardinal virtues of medieval theology. Here again, without any necessity for the philological goals of his investigation, he makes it abundantly clear that, even if the medieval system of virtues can be tracked back to antiquity as an abstract system, all of these virtues already exist of old in German(ic) heritage, e. g., in *Beowulf*, as far as the individual virtues and their terminology are concerned (39).[19]

In his discussion of "Goodnesse, bountee, and good entente," Héraucourt observes how Chaucer always stresses the good intention with all his positive, noble characters. Héraucourt sees this as as a "truly German(ic)" ("echt germanisch[en]") attitude which has not yet been "mollified" ("angekränkelt[en]") by pragmatism (60). In the corresponding footnote, he compares the justice system under Edward III, which punished even the intent of killing the king, with the German system after 1933 which—more generally—punished no longer only according to the actual success of premeditated crimes but penalized premeditation and dangerous intent as such. In this chapter, Chaucer emerges as a German(ic) writer who attributes high value to punishing sinful intentions such as *luxurie* ("Wollust") in the "Man of Law's Tale." When Héraucourt encounters examples of unmistakably ironic use of the word "entente" (cf. "Merchant's Tale" [E 2375] or "Nun's Priest's Tale" [B 4613]) which cannot be attributed to a German(ic) and moral Chaucer, he reads these passages as illustrations of the poet's "typically Germanic humor" (62).[20]

Perhaps the most conspicuous example of Héraucourt's Germani(ci)-zing of Geoffrey Chaucer is his explication of the terms "trouthe" and "sooth." He nicely attributes the gradual supersession of "sooth" by "trouth" to the emergence of a new kind of psychological "verity" which is based on the individual's experience, an earthly "trouthe" which needs to be distinguished from the metaphysical "sooth," the revealed truth of the gospel. Moreover, he explains this development in late medieval mentality by comparing it to the separation of truth by William of Ockham and the nominalist movement of thought.[21] However, his valuable philological and historical observations do not remain without some ideological ornamentation either. Rather, this part of his study turns again into an occasion for Héraucourt to embark upon an extensive explanatory footnote which presents the Nazi understanding of "truth" as exemplified in the new Code of Civil Procedure ("Zivilprozeßordnung," "ZPO") as a typically German(ic) development and in correspondence with Chaucer's usage.[22] For this "original" observation Héraucourt acknowledges himself indebted to a certain Hans Möller-Hamburg whom he describes as a "comrade from the Dozentenlager" (152). The "Dozentenlager" (literally, camp for young university professors) was one of the principal means of indoctrination for German postgraduates of all disciplines. It is this footnote which seduced even the otherwise cautious Finkenstaedt, in the *Kleine Geschichte*, to wonder whether this and many other contemporary parallels in footnotes of studies between 1933 and 1945 were only "compulsory exercises."[23] However, in Héraucourt's case, the footnotes only add to the glaring prejudice which informs the main body of his text.

The discussion of "honor" establishes the dominating binary opposition Héraucourt constructs between the French and the German(ic) national psychologies and their respective systems of values. He ascribes all instances where Chaucer's characters are worried about their social reputation ("saving his honour," E 1766; "honour and renoun save," F 530) to the general externalization of honor in French medieval culture.[24] Including his audience in his judgmental vision, he elaborates that "we" sense honor as it is presented in the *Chanson de Roland* or in the texts of Chrétien de Troyes immediately "as ungermanic on the one hand and expressly French on the other."[25] The true kind of honor, honor internalized, is deeply rooted in "Germanic ethos." Consequently, for Héraucourt, Chaucer exemplifies it only in his morally sound characters, such as Griselda, who lacks all the outward traits of courtliness and nobility but who is nevertheless "honourable" in the highest degree.

A similar binary judgment informs the discussion of Chaucer's use of "freedom, franchise, and largesse." Here again, the German(ic) "free" is regarded as a generosity grounded in an internalized, positive stystem of values, a sort of Germanic "frankness" ("Freimut"), whereas its French other, the word "large," is supposedly exclusively concerned with the external impression which a public generosity wants to create in the recipient of gifts (230).

Chaucer is also said to utilize German(ic) words whenever he wants to express moral stability and steadfastness. Héraucourt summarizes Chaucerian usage in the following "Nota Bene" which also contains a call for new research objectives:

> He [Chaucer] reaches for Germanic words; *perseveraunce* is much too bland and, in addition, it is being used in a disparaging sense; Chaucer uses it unwillingly and rarely. The same is true for the

romance word *constaunce*. One should be less surprised about Chaucer's use and introduction of so many words from Romance languages and more about how rarely he uses these words. (251)[26]

The latter assertion is bolstered by the observation that Chaucer prefers the German(ic) "sikernesse" to the French "seuretee" (254).

In the final summary of his study, Héraucourt's celebration of everything German or Germanic and his disparagement of everything that reeks of a French or a Romance background becomes almost pathological, especially when one considers the origins of the family name Héraucourt.[27] *Die Wertwelt Chaucers* presents the late medieval poet as deeply concerned about the values of his times. Chaucer is shown to be interested in promoting "wisdom," "justice," gaiety," and "religious emotion"; as much as he likes a manly joke, he appreciates "chastity," dislikes "incest," and is deeply involved in furthering humanistic ideals. Héraucourt is particularly delighted with Chaucer's "typically Germanic sense of justice," as exemplified by "the poetic justice within even the grossest of stories"; the critic also celebrates the poet's "deep moral sensibility" which informs, for example, the *Legend of Good Women*, a text which defies the "frivolity of the French combination of erotic and religious notions." Finally, Héraucourt praises Chaucer's "good-natured gaiety" ("gutmütige Fröhlichkeit") which keeps the "cold laugh of the Frenchman" at bay (361). One recalls, of course, Fiedler's *Vormärz* distinction between Romance pathos and true German(ic) "Gemüth" ("mentality"?). However, Héraucourt seems to have come to his national-psychological judgment without the benefit of Fiedler's study. Thus, the ideological intertextuality between the two scholars' opinions demonstrates how easily the nationalism of the *Vormärz* liberal could coincide with the more dangerous nationalism of the philological promoter of Nazi ideology.

All the values selected are sustained—according to Héraucourt—by the poet's healthy balance between his commonsensical bourgeois origins and his education and close contact with courtly ideals. Chaucer critically investigates and deepens the courtly world of values. The attitude which allows him to do this is an "inner willingness" which is described in terms of genetics; it is due to his "blood" and "morals" (354).[28]

> The essential consequence of this inner rebirth [of courtly values] is: the moral vocation of the nobility is not questioned, but it is no longer seen as exclusive; the ideal based on class becomes a national ideal based on the general dignity of humankind—for we

recognize in Chaucer's work clear signs of an awakening national spirit.[29]

In his closing arguments, Héraucourt provides an ingenious philosophical explanation for his interesting binary oppositions between the influence on Chaucer of Romance and Germanic vocabulary. He maintains that the Romance expressions used in Chaucer's texts to describe values mainly belong to the sphere of the court, describe chiefly external things, customary behavior, mere accidents in the philosophical sense of the word (358). The ethical and spiritual substances of the individual human being, however, are always expressed through German(ic) vocabulary, an observation which he substantiates statistically. However, once again Héraucourt does not abstain from an ideological interpretation of his philological research:

> As a rule, the German(ic) expressions signify the hereditary, but always freshly lived and realistically-felt paternal property, the healthy, living power of the people. In contrast, the Romance expressions signify, above all, the courtly, external, fashionable world of formality, or expressions used by the church, or abstract terms. (360f.)[30]

He ends by reminding the reader how strongly the Germanic heritage is ingrained in Chaucer's general "Wertwelt":

> The basic stock of ethical notions of German(ic) origin was so firmly rooted and strong that it developed on its own—despite the French tendrils—a powerful new life and maintained its own main branches true to its German(ic) kind. (361)[31]

After what has been said, it comes as quite a surprise that Will Héraucourt's *Die Wertwelt Chaucers* is cherished today as one of the classical investigations in Chaucer scholarship. Muriel Bowden, in her 1949 *Commentary on the General Prologue to the Canterbury Tales*, admiringly called the book "exhaustive." F. N. Robinson's revised edition of *The Works of Geoffrey Chaucer* (1957) ensured that the study would gain general acceptance as an essential source for explanatory and textual notes. Robinson mentioned it as one of only twenty-seven titles under the category "General Criticism," together with famous names such as Kittredge, Manly, Lewis, and Mossé. John H. Fisher listed it—in one breath with Margaret Schlauch and Sheila Delany—as an important social interpretation of Chaucer in his essay "Scala Chauceriensis," included in Joseph Gibaldi's widely distributed

MLA volume *Approaches to Teaching Chaucer's Canterbury Tales*; and finally, today's most widely used scholarly edition of Chaucer's texts, Houghton Mifflin's *Riverside Chaucer*, includes the title among the book-length studies and collections of essays which are "frequently cited" in its explanatory notes.[32]

As a scholarly study, then, *Die Wertwelt Chaucers* was recognized and categorized as one of those typically reliable, because philological and positivistic, German studies. The reputation of German philology, established and defended as typically German in the nineteenth and early twentieth centuries and greatly influential across the Atlantic, secured Héraucourt his place among the classical authorities of Chaucer studies. It was (and still is) utilized mainly to answer the questions which are thought to be answered especially well by the philological approach to literature and language: questions concerning word study, sources and analogues, etymology, topoi, and motifs. However, once acknowledged by its users as a typical example of philological "Quellen- und Einfluß-forschung," the study also acquired the concomitant reputation of objectivity and political neutrality. The title of Héraucourt's study should have prevented such a thorough underestimation. Although based upon the massive authenticating power of sound philological detail, any investigation into Chaucer's "etymology of values," as Robert Ackerman quite tellingly translated the book's title, was bound to include value-driven readings of writer and period.[33] Postmodern critical theory has made it abundantly clear that value judgments, whether in literature or in criticism, are historically variable and usually bear close relations to social—and sometimes racial—ideologies. Value judgments thus, in the words of Terry Eagleton, "refer in the end not simply to private taste, but to the assumptions by which certain social groups exercise and maintain power over others."[34]

The reception history of Héraucourt's study substantiates how recalcitrant the myth of an allegedly non-ideological philological positivism remains against such recent critical insights. Numerous Chaucerians who used *Die Wertwelt Chaucers* must have chosen to read the book for some of its praiseworthy philological detail and neglected to notice its conspicuous ideological premise. One illustrative example, published nine years after Héraucourt, must suffice for the purposes of this essay. Muriel Bowden, in her philological commentary on the "General Prologue," raises the question of which sources Chaucer used to describe his Knight: "Did the poet draw upon general knowledge of what a knight should be, or did he use a living model, or did he go to some literary source?" Bowden's discussion centers on the parallels between Chaucer's character description and Watriquet de Couvin's celebration of his knightly patron, Gauchier de

Chatillion, in the *Dit du Connestable de France*, an elegy of some three hundred lines. Although she is very cautious about postulating Chaucer's direct dependence on Watriquet (one of the most famous poets of the Hainault, Queen Philippa's home), she strongly suggests that both poets share the very same etymology of values, an opinion which she supports by selecting—out of all available scholarship—Héraucourt's observations on Chaucer's employment of the word "honour:"

> Watriquet's preud'omme and Chaucer's Knight both prize "honour": that is, both have a fine awareness of and strict allegiance to righteousness. Dr. Héraucourt . . . in *Die Wertwelt Chaucers*, calls attention to the change which is manifest in the poet's use of the word *honour* after he had translated Boethius; after Chaucer had written "And therfore it is thus that honour . . . cometh to dignyte for cause of vertu," he unquestionably employed *honour* to mean much more than "distinction" or "reputation." "Honour" in in such high moral sense would obviously be a *sine qua non* for true knighthood, and both Watriquet and Chaucer stress this quality in their respective heroes.[35]

Bowden's reading of the concise subchapter on "honour" in *Die Wertwelt Chaucers* (64-71) must have been fairly selective, because the post-*Boece* meaning of *honour*, which she also wants to see in Watriquet's *preud'omme*, is presented by Héraucourt as an innovation of Chaucer's mature years, after he had finally freed himself from the externalization of knightly values in French court culture and redefined *honour* in its more internalized, noble, and German(ic) sense. That Bowden should have been diametrically opposed to Héraucourt's ideological reading becomes even more evident when—only one page later—she likens Chaucer's use of "worthy" and "wys" for his Knight to similar descriptions of Beowulf on the one hand and of Roland and Oliver on the other, an opinion entirely incompatible with Héraucourt, who regards the world of values in the *Song of Roland* as "expressly French," "ungermanic" (68), hence unChaucerian.

At a first glance, then, Bowden's *faux pas* seems surprising. However, it represents a fairly typical attitude towards studies which profess to follow in the wake of traditional German scholarship in philology. I am convinced that Bowden chose to look up Héraucourt's discussion of *honour* in the inclusive index of his study and that she read only the lines following the discussion of Boethius on page 69 of *Die Wertwelt Chaucers*, trusting that all the other pages would be just as philological and nonideological as those three pages seem. It is exactly this petrified myth of the

Inventing German(ic) Chaucer

possible objectivity and superiority of philological positivism, cultivated by German scholarship as part of its establishing a national identity in higher education, which still shields too many investigations from the necessary *Trauerarbeit* of post-nationalist literary historians.

In her study *Midwives to Nazism*, Alice Gallin sums up her findings on the role of university professors in the transitional phase from the Weimar Republic to the Third Reich:

> The lesson one can learn . . . from the German experience is that academia and politics cannot be divorced that easily. It is impossible in the twentieth century—given our dependence on institutional structures—for an institution to be politically neutral. Silence has its own price, and both personal and social ethics require moral decision.[36]

Many a university professor's decision to attempt hibernating Nazism in silence, far above all the breathing human passions of politics and in the realms of the inner emigration presumedly guaranteed by philological positivism, deserves to be understood individually. It should be clear by now, however, that Will Héraucourt, at least with his book on Chaucer, should not be counted among those who—for a variety of reasons—simply chose to stay silent. In a speech given on March 25, 1933, Joseph Goebbels announced to his audience that Germany had not lost the first World War "because our cannons failed, but rather because our spiritual weapons didn't fire."[37] According to this reading of *Die Wertwelt Chaucers*, Héraucourt consciously chose to be part of the spiritual mobilization ("geistige Mobilmachung") of the German(ic) race which the leaders of the Third Reich propagated. Encouraged by his teacher Max Deutschbein, he easily assimilated the "nationalpsychologische Methode" not only to his philological training but also to the ideological program of spiritual mobilization in an effort to secure Geoffrey Chaucer a place of honor in the racially defined Valhalla of genial German(ic) writers.[38] His book may be a far cry from more decidedly Nazist publications such as, e. g., "Carlyle und der Nationalsozialismus," a 1937 Bonn dissertation.[39] Perhaps Héraucourt cherished the vague hope that his study would contribute—on the academic level—to avoiding another devastating confrontation between the two alleged "Aryan/ Nordic/ Germanic" peoples, England and Germany.[40] Perhaps, like the historian Percy Ernst Schramm, who according to Norman F. Cantor may have had visions of a book pointing out the close family ties between the medieval Plantagenet rulers of England like Henry II and the Guelph dukes of Saxony, Héraucourt would have liked to see

20 Studies in Medievalism

materialize a New European Order which would have divided world power peacefully between Germany and Britain at the expense of other countries. As Cantor remarks, "This is what Hitler indeed offered Churchill in June 1940 after he let the beaten British army escape—without its weapons—at Dunkirk. Peace with honor and pieces of the French Empire is what Hitler offered the new British prime minister, Winston Churchill."[41] Héraucourt's obvious marginalization of any French influence on Chaucer and his centering on and celebration of everything he can possibly construe as German(ic) in the poet's texts can be seen in correspondence with such political goals.

As we have seen, other German Chaucerians before the Third Reich had appropriated Chaucer via philology for their ideological purposes. However, it is with Will Héraucourt's study that the invention of a German(ic) Chaucer, born out of the interplay of philological positivism and nationalist/racist ideology, reached its most inglorious stage.[42] How anyone who appears to have read the entire book may be bold enough to recommend *Die Wertwelt Chaucers* without any reservation as "a model for further studies" is extremely difficult to comprehend.[43]

NOTES

A preliminary version of this essay, entitled "Inventing German(ic) Chaucer: The Political Background of Linguistic Analysis in Will Héraucourt's *Die Wertwelt Chaucers* (1939)," was presented in the session on "Postmedieval Chaucer Reception" at the Twenty-Ninth International Congress on Medieval Studies at Western Michigan University in May 1994. For the completion of this essay I am indebted for help and advice to Joerg Fichte (University of Tübingen), Norbert Gross (University of Regensburg), Renate Haas (University of Kiel), Anke Janssen (University of Regensburg), and William H. Watts (Butler University). I am very grateful to my friend Kay Stensrud (University of Northern Iowa) for reading and commenting on a draft version of this essay.

1. Jost Hermand, *Synthetisches Interpretieren*, 4th ed. (München: Nymphenburger Verlag, 1973), 23. (If not indicated otherwise, all translations of German sources are mine.)
2. Renate Haas, "From the 'Vormärz' to the Empire," *Poetica* 29/30 (1989), 105-106. It is interesting to see that a picture of the medieval church and nobility very similar to that of Fiedler also governs post-Revolutionary France. See Jacques Heers' provocative study *Le Moyen Age, Une Imposture* (Paris: Perrin, 1992), especially 103-256.
3. Haas, 107. Haas's final judgment on philological Chaucer studies in Germany before 1871 is deftly critical: "Thus, much—perhaps most—of this Ger-

Inventing German(ic) Chaucer   21

man research may seem a waste of energy, especially if we picture it in its socio-political context: an extremely high percentage of scholars and future school teachers of English, instead of furthering the communication with the much more advanced United Kingdom and United States and the understanding of their progressive literature or such moments in the older English literature, pedantically collecting trifling data of the early stages of the language and styling themselves strict scientists—aloof from the crowd and superior to the unscholarly British amateurs—, thinking their work unpolitical and value-free, while they upheld an economically, socially and politically outdated system" (114).

4.   Joerg Fichte, "Chaucer's Work in Literary Scholarship in Germany to 1914" *Poetica* 29/30 (1989), 96. Fichte discusses Ludwig Lemcke's review (*Jahrbuch für romanische und englische Literatur* 8 [1867], 96) of Thomas Wright's six-volume Chaucer edition of 1867.

5.   Quoted in Gunta Haenicke, *Zur Geschichte der Anglistik an deutschsprachigen Universitäten 1850-1925*, Augsburger I- & I-Schriften 8 (Augsburg, 1979), 120f.

6.   Fichte, 94.

7.   Cf. George W. Stocking, Jr., who explains in his introduction to James Cowles Prichard's 1813 *Researches into the Physical History of Man* (Chicago: University of Chicago Press, 1973) that for Prichard "anatomy, physiology, zoology, physical geography, history, archeology, and philology were among the departments of knowledge that 'contributed to the cultivation of ethnology'" (xcviii). For another interesting example, cf. the following entry in the *Prentice Hall Guide to English Literature*, ed. Marion Wynne-Davis (New York: Prentice Hall, 1990): "*Aryan*. A linguistic term derived from the Sanskrit *arya* or noble, coined by the early philologists. It was applied to the group of languages which includes Sanskrit, Zend, Persian, Greek, Latin, Celtic, Teutonic and Slavonic. Although apparently a convenience of classification, its root-meaning shows how it played a part in creating a hierarchy of languages. Cultural nationalists were quick to appropriate the term and use it to assert that speakers of these languages had a common biological identity. It is now recognized that there is no such thing as common genetic origin within any group, owing to tribal migrations and intermarriages, but the myth of racial purity under the banner of Aryanism promoted the mass killing of Jews under Hitler."

8.   Cf. Thomas Finkenstaedt, *Kleine Geschichte der Anglistik in Deutschland. Eine Einführung* (Darmstadt: Wissenschaftliche Buchgesellschaft, 1983), 90f., 127.

9.   Quoted in Finckenstaedt, 141.

10.   See Finckenstaedt, 164f. For an investigation of the contemporary English missionary spirit in political texts which combines information about England ("Kulturkunde") with nationalist/racist undercurrents, see, e. g., Hans Galinski's "Das Sendungsbewußtsein der politischen Führungsschicht im heutigen Britentum," *Anglia* 64 (1940): 296-336.

11.   Cf. Deutschbein's essay "Englisches Volkstum und englische Sprache," *Handbuch der Englandkunde*, ed. Paul Hartig and W. Schellberg (Frankfurt a.M.: Diesterweg, 1928), 1:49: "Freilich hängt die Neugierde, die Wissbegier des

Deutschen mit dem Forschungstrieb des einzelnen, mit dem Bildungsbedürfnis des ganzen Volkes zusammen, während der Engländer es leichter hat, sich in dieser Hinsicht Zurückhaltung aufzuerlegen, da es vielfach bei ihm an geistiger Regsamkeit fehlt." It is fairly astonishing that Hermann Klitscher, who revised Deutschbein's essay for the 1955 edition of the *Handbuch*, reprinted this passage almost unchanged (340).

12. Deutschbein seems to have embraced the new policies of 1933 as fast as he collaborated with the Soviet occupational policies in 1946. Cf. Finkenstaedt, 161 and 174; Finkenstaedt is unsure whether to call Deutschbein a convinced follower of Nazism or simply an opportunist. Biographical research on Deutschbein is difficult since it has been almost exclusively in the hands of eulogizing students. Cf., e. g., Will Héraucourt's entry on his scholarly mentor in the influential *Neue Deutsche Biographie*, ed. Historische Kommission bei der Bayerischen Akademie der Wissenschaften (Berlin: Duncker & Humblodt, 1957), 3:642: "Kinderlos, ist er ein väterlicher Freund seiner Studenten gewesen, mit denen er edle Geselligkeit pflegte. Durch seine hohe ethische Menschlichkeit fesselte er nicht weniger als durch seinen lebendigen Vortrag."

13. *Die Neueren Sprachen* 41 (1933), 323. The appropriation of Shakespeare for the common German(ic) heritage seems to have been quite a common occurrence in the 1930s; cf. Leonhard Röttenbacher and Siegmund Speyerer, *Englisches Lehrbuch für realistische Knaben- und Mädchenschulen*, II. Teil: Mittelstufe (Bamberg: C.C. Buchners Verlag, 1937), 29: "Shakespeare is the greatest dramatic genius not only of England but of all countries and of all times—the great representative poet of German(ic) Europe."

14. Will Héraucourt, *Die Wertwelt Chaucers. Die Wertwelt einer Zeitwende*; further citations in text. Héraucourt's study was published as vol. 1 of the new series, entitled "Kulturgeschichtliche Bibliothek," with Heidelberg's prestigious Carl Winter Universitätsverlag in 1939. The general editor of the series, Kurt Stegmann von Pritzwald, published Edgar Glässer's racist schoolbook, *Einführung in die rassenkundliche Sprachforschung*, in the same year and series. In his preface (viii) Héraucourt indicates that Deutschbein actually suggested the idea for his study. In 1936 Héraucourt edited the Festschrift für Max Deutschbein, entitled *Englische Kultur in Sprachwissenschaftlicher Deutung (English Culture in Linguistic Interpretation)* (Leipzig: Quelle & Meyer). His essay in this volume, "What is trouthe and soothfastnesse," became a prerequisite for the subchapter on "trouthe" in *Die Wertwelt Chaucers*. For a contemporary national-psychological reading of post-sixteenth-century English sermons, see Rudolf Kapp, "Können wir aus der Englischen Predigt Volkstypologische Rückschlüsse ziehen?" *Anglia* 60 (1936): 211-33. The essay presents another example of the symbiosis between philology and ideology in English studies in Germany during the Third Reich. The wish for a 'scientific' (i. e., philological) basis of national literatures, however, was very powerful even among the "apolitical" Anglicists. In his essay "Beiträge zur Geschichte und Aufgabe der Englischen Studien in Deutschland," *(Anglia* 60 [1936]: 1-19), Theodor Spira asks future studies to establish Herder's "Volksgeist," the "historical

Inventing German(ic) Chaucer

binding force of a people, in which language, literature, and culture form a unity" (18-19).

15. Héraucourt chose Binding (1867-1938) for obvious reasons: on the one hand, Binding had a reputation of being anglophilic; on the other hand, he was known to represent the German post-World War I ethos in his diary *Aus dem Kriege* (1925; the English translation, *A Fatalist at War*, appeared 1932) and his poetry (cf. *Stolz und Trauer*, 1922), an ethos he expressed in numerous public speeches, such as the one at the University of Marburg on 1 November 1937 from which Héraucourt takes his quotations. Cf. Dieter Helmuth Stolz's entry on Binding in Volume 2 of *Neue Deutsche Biographie* (1955), 245f.

16. "Chaucers frühe literarische Abhängigkeit von Frankreich ist unverkennbar, ihn aber als einen französischen Genius hinstellen zu wollen, wie dies (pro domo) die französische Kritik teilweise tut, ist ganz verfehlt und der Versuch eines geistigen Raubes. Seiner ganzen Persönlichkeit nach ist Chaucer Engländer. J. N. Manly hat gezeigt, wie wenig Gewicht auf den französischen Ursprung von Chaucer's Namen in diesem Zusammenhang gelegt werden sollte. Chaucers Vorfahren sind volle 150 Jahre vor seiner Geburt in England nachgewiesen. Daß Chaucer das Englische zur dichterischen Sprache erhebt, allein zeigt ihn schon durch und durch als Engländer. Dies erkennt ein ernster französischer Forscher wie Cazamian auch durchaus an" (29f.).

17. "Eingehende Spezialuntersuchungen zur Entwicklung des Heerwesens . . . . haben ganz klar bewiesen, daß es die beritten gemachte germanische Gefolgschaft ist, aus der letzten Endes das abendländische Rittertum seinen Ursprung nimmt; dies gilt nicht nur für Deutschland und England, sondern auch für Frankreich, wenn es dort wohl auch früher zu einer gewissen Stilisierung gekommen sein mag, die dann auf die germanischen Ursprungsländer zurückwirkte. (Vergessen wir nicht, daß sehr viele der französischen Ausdrücke, die das Heerwesen betreffen, germanischen Ursprungs sind.)" (33, note 1). Michel Rouche, "Eclatement et Mue de l'Occident (V^e-VIIe siècle)" (in *Le Moyen Age*, ed. Robert Fossier [Paris: Armand Colin, 1982], 1:77-122, especially 101-104), indicates that Héraucourt's opinion conforms with the results of recent research in which the realm of military life is presented as the only one in which the early medieval settlement of Germanic tribes in France left recognizable linguistic traits. Therefore, my objection is not to Héraucourt's statement as such but to its ideological partisanship as an unsubstantiated remark.

18. "Mit dem 7. Lebensjahre beginnt eine scharf geregelte Zucht zur Erlernung der courtoisie, des feinen Schliffs, des tadellosen Verkehrstons, wie ihn nach allgemeiner Ansicht der damaligen Zeit einzig und allein der französische Hof beherrschte. Doch scheint diese Erziehungseinrichtung auf eine germanische Sitte zurückzugehen. . . . Es war im angelsächsischen England wie in Skandinavien und Irland allgemein üblich, daß die Söhne von Adligen (meist vom siebten Jahr an) zur Erziehung in fremde Häuser gegeben wurden. . . . Ein Vergleich mit der modernen englischen public school-Erziehung liegt nahe" (33-34, note 1).

19. See also 208: "Bravery and loyalty between lord and vassal are undoubtedly original virtues of the Germanic warrior. Both are supported by a feeling of

honor. They are only reasserted during the middle ages by the principles of *fortitudo* and *iustitia* from classical antiquity."

20. The complete sentence (bottom of 62) is even more illustrative of Héraucourt's nationalist rhetoric: "In beiden Fällen ist die beabsichtigte Wirkung komisch, echt Chaucer, echt germanischer Humor: Pessimistisches im optimistischen Gewande."

21. With this opinion, Héraucourt anticipates a more recent paradigm in Chaucer criticism since the 1970s which sees Chaucer's texts in analogy with late medieval nominalism. See William H. Watts and Richard J. Utz, "Nominalist Perspectives on Chaucer's Poetry: A Bibliographical Essay," *Medievalia et Humanistica*, n. s. 23 (1993): 147-173, and Richard J. Utz, *Literarischer Nominalismus im Spätmittelalter. Eine Untersuchung zu Sprache, Charakterzeichnung und Struktur in Chaucers Troilus and Criseyde*, Regensburger Arbeiten zur Anglistik und Amerikanistik 31 (Frankfurt a.M.: Peter Lang, 1991). Cf., most recently, *Literary Nominalism and the Theory of Rereading Late Medieval Texts: A New Research Paradigm*, ed. Richard J. Utz (Lewiston, New York: Edwin Mellen, 1995).

22. Cf. Héraucourt's praise of developments since 1933 in the same footnote: "Seit der nationalsozialistischen Revolution ist unsere 'deutsche' Vorstellung von der Wahrheit im juristischen Sinne im Begriff, sich von Grund aus zu wandeln and zwar im Sinne von *triuwe unt wârheit*." As in this case, Héraucourt's terminology is often based upon the *Nibelungenlied*, one of the principal German(ic) texts abused by Third Reich ideologues for their purposes.

23. Finckenstaedt, 293, note 124.

24. See also his statement on the French *curteisye* which he calls "the exterior garment of the *honestum*, the moral attitude, which is based upon the knowledge of evil" (71).

25. "Immerhin sei hier angedeutet, daß uns eine Ehrvorstellung, wie wir sie im Rolandslied oder bei Kristian von Troyes finden, als einerseits ungermanisch, andererseits als ausgesprochen französisch erscheint" (68). As usual, Héraucourt uses "ungermanisch" instead of "undeutsch." By identifying "ungermanisch" with "uns" (i. e., his German contemporaries), he not only invents a common German(ic) identity but also construes everything French—whether medieval or contemporary—as "other."

26. "N.B.! Er greift zu den germanischen Wörtern; *perseveraunce* ist viel zu farblos, es wird auch in abfälligem Sinn gebraucht; Chaucer braucht es ungern und sehr selten. Dasselbe gilt für das romanische *constaunce*. Man sollte sich nicht verwundern, daß Chaucer so viele romanische Wörter gebraucht und eingeführt hat, sondern vielmehr darüber, daß er diese romanischen Wörter so selten gebraucht."

27. Cf. Héraucourt's own *Genealogie auf wissenschaftlicher Grundlage der Familien Haraucourt—Herancourt—Héraucourt* (Marburg: Im Selbstverlag des Autors, 1964), where he provides evidence for his family's background in "Lothringen, Elsaß, den Rheinischen Marken und Frankreich."

28. The German original reads: "Notwendig dazu war eine gesunde innere Bereitschaft blutmäßig-sittlicher Art." Finkenstaedt believes that the use of expres-

Inventing German(ic) Chaucer

sions such as "Blut," "Boden," and "Rasse" does not necessarily mean a scholar's agreement with Nazi ideology but that these expressions may have their origin in pre-1930 usage (163).

29. "Das hauptsächliche Ereignis dieser inneren Wiedergeburt (scil. höfischer Werte) ist folgendes: die sittliche Berufung des Adels wird nicht in Frage gestellt, aber sie wird nicht mehr exklusiv gesehen; aus dem Standesideal wird ein von allgemeiner Menschenwürde getragenes Volksideal—denn wir erkennen in Chaucers Werk deutlich Zeichen eines erwachten Nationalgefühls" (354). Later (360), Héraucourt also equates the evaluative adjectives "warm" with German(ic) and "cold" with Romance vocabulary.

30. "Die germanischen Adjektive bezeichnen also in der Regel das von den Vätern ererbte, immer neu erlebte und lebensnah empfundene ethische Gut, die gesunde lebendige Kraft des Volkes. Die romanischen Ausdrücke bezeichnen dagegen meist nur eine höfische, äußerliche, modische Formenwelt, oder kirchliche bzw. abstrakte Begriffe" (360f.). Cf. also 359: "In diesem Zusammenhang sei ganz besonders darauf hingewiesen, daß die Abstrakta, die das Gute, Wahre, Rechte, also die 'inneren' überpersonalen Werte bezeichnen, germanisch sind: *good*; *sooth*; *trouthe*; *right*; während die Abstraktvorstellungen des äußeren Wertes Schönheit bereits romanisch ist: *beautee*."

31. "Der Grundstamm der ethischen Vorstellungen germanischer Herkunft war so innerlich fest verwurzelt und stark, daß er trotz des französischen Rankenwerks aus sich selbst heraus starkes neues Leben trieb und seine Hauptzweige in germanischer Art behauptete" (361). Cf. Deutschbein, "Englisches Volkstum und englische Sprache," 67f., where the dichotomy between French and German(ic) influence on the English language is already very strong: "Ich überlasse es dem Leser, zu entscheiden, ob die englische Sprache mehr germanischen oder romanischen Charakter aufweist. Wer sich aber eingehend mit dem Studium des germanischen Volkstums und der germanischen Kultur befaßt hat, wird ohne weiteres zugeben, daß die besonderen Eigentümlichkeiten des englischen Volks-charakters—und diese prägen auch der Sprache und dem Stil den Stempel auf—gerade diejenigen sind, die wir den alten Germanen zuschreiben müssen; und Dibelius . . . trifft wohl das Richtige, wenn er in dem Engländer im wesentlichen die Charakterzüge des niedersächsisch-friesischen Bauern wiederfindet. Allerdings dürfen wir nicht as den Augen verlieren, daß der germanische Grundstock des angelsächsischen Volkes wesentlich verstärkt worden ist durch die starke Besiedlung Nord-ud Ostenglands durch Norweger und Dänen; ebenso müssen wir die Stärkung bzw. Modifizierung des anglo-skandinavischen Volksgeistes durch die Normannen, die selbst ursprünglich Wikinger gewesen waren, in Rechnung stellen."

32. Muriel Bowden, *A Commentary on the General Prologue to the Canterbury Tales* (New York: Macmillan, 1948), 46;42; Frederick N. Robinson, *The Works of Geoffrey Chaucer*, The Riverside Chaucer, 2nd ed. (Boston: Houghton Mifflin, 1957); *Approaches to Teaching Chaucer's Canterbury Tales*, ed. Joseph Gibaldi (New York: Modern Language Association of America, 1980) 40; Larry D. Benson, ed., *The Riverside Chaucer*, 3rd. ed. (Boston: Houghton Mifflin, 1987), 790-93. Similarly, Barry A. Windeatt's critical edition of *Troilus and Criseyde* (London: Longman,

1984), mentions *Die Wertwelt Chaucers* in its selected bibliography under rubric no. 10, "Some Feelings and Values: The 'World' of 'Troilus'" (580).

33. Robert Ackerman, "Chaucer, the Church, and Religion," in *Companion to Chaucer Studies*, ed. Beryl Rowland (New York: Oxford University Press, 1979), 34.

34. Terry Eagleton, *Literary Theory: An Introduction* (Minneapolis: University of Minnesota Press, 1983), 16.

35. Bowden, 46, 48.

36. Alice Gallin, *Midwives to Nazism: University Professors in Weimar Germany 1925-1933* (Macon, Ga.: Mercer University Press, 1986), 113.

37. Quoted in Jeffrey Herf, *Reactionary Modernism: Technology, Culture, and Politics in Weimar and the Third Reich* (Cambridge: Cambridge University Press, 1984), 195.

38. About the possible dangers of the "nationalpsychologische Methode," although without reference to its use during the Third Reich, see Ernst Leisi's *Das heutige Englisch. Wesenszüge und Probleme* (Heidelberg: Carl Winter, 1986), 15.

39. Cf. Finkenstaedt, 163ff., for more examples.

40. How deeply World War I had disturbed many German Anglicists is documented by Finkenstaedt, 127. It is possible that pre-World War II Anglicists had inherited some of their older colleagues' fears.

41. Norman F. Cantor, *Inventing the Middle Ages: The Lives, Works, and Ideas of the Great Medievalists of the Twentieth Century* (New York: William Morrow, 1991), 92. The disappointment of German scholars was widespread and especially strong among Anglicists. Cf. Wolfgang Schmidt's "Dokumente englischer 'Friedensbereitschaft,'" *Neuphilologische Monatsschrift* 11 (1940): 1-9. Schmidt denounces the German hopes for a close collaboration between Germany and England as "die alte Krankheit der Anglophilie" and blames the British ruling class for the war.

42. It should be mentioned that Héraucourt's long essay "Chaucers Vorstellung von den Geistig-Seelischen Kräften des Menschen," published in *Anglia* 65 (1941): 255-302, although strongly influenced by the "nationalpsychologische Methode," is free from any obvious ideological interference. The same is true for two of his other essays: "Das Hendiadyoin als Mittel zur Hervorhebung des Werthaften bei Chaucer," *Englische Studien* 73 (1940): 190-201, and "Das sprachliche Feld der *goodes* und seine Gliederung bei Chaucer," *Neuphilologische Monatsschrift* 11 (1940): 9-21. It almost seems as if Héraucourt felt obliged to add a fair amount of ideology in his book publication, an effort unneccessary for essay publications in journals of Anglistics.

43. This recommendation was made by Larry D. Benson in his essay "A Reader's Guide to Writings on Chaucer," published in *Geoffrey Chaucer*, ed. Derek Brewer (London: Bell, 1974, rpt. 1990), 329, where he praises Héraucourt's study as considering Chaucer's language "from the standpoint of a semantic field."

Hermann Hesse's Approaches to Medieval Literature

Albrecht Classen

There is no longer any question that the Middle Ages represent an important cultural period which established the foundation for the emergence of the modern world.[1] For a number of years now scholarship has eagerly traced the impact of medieval thinking on us today, as is indicated with regard to the German-speaking countries by Siegfried Grosse and Ursula Rautenberg's impressive and highly useful bibliography of translations and rewritings of medieval German literature.[2] This excellent reference work allows us to investigate the extent to which literary connections exist between the modern world—here defined as beginning ca. 1800—and the literary past—here defined as beginning ca. 800 A. D. But Grosse and Rautenberg's primary interest is not focused on medieval motifs, themes, and *Stoffe* in modern literary texts. Their bibliography informs us, rather, which medieval texts have survived throughout the centuries and found their translators or retellers, and in this sense it is primarily concerned with the medieval writers and the question of which of their texts enjoyed an actual "afterlife" in the modern age.

To use the opposite approach but with a similar purpose, an analysis of Hermann Hesse's various treatments of medieval authors and their works will allow us to see what relevance the Middle Ages had for one of the major twentieth-century writers in Germany—that is, to what extent his examination of medieval texts influenced his own thinking and then his literary and essayistic writing. Although many attempts have been made by medievalist scholars in the last ten years to trace the connections between the medieval and the modern world, as is richly documented by a number of major international conferences and their subsequently published proceedings, Hesse's fascination with the Middle Ages has not

Studies in Medievalism VIII, 1996

found adequate attention, although he made important contributions as translator, editor, and interpreter.[3]

Fritz Wagner has been one of the few scholars to have noticed Hesse's serious orientation towards the Renaissance and the Middle Ages: Wagner has pointed out, above all, Hesse's fascination with the writings of St. Francis of Assisi and Boccaccio, and he has also reedited some of the most important texts by Hesse which demonstrate the author's knowledge of the medieval and Renaissance world. Yet Wagner's work, valuable in its own terms, does not answer all the questions regarding Hesse's rather intense study of the pre-modern period, because his primary focus rests on those essays and translations by Hesse which concern the Franciscan order and its founder or the Italian Renaissance.[4] Joseph Mileck argues along the same lines, but largely ignores Hesse's considerable familiarity with medieval literature, as if it played nothing but a minor role in the author's fiction and essays.[5]

The following analysis will address this *desideratum* by focusing on Hesse's detailed study of medieval German and Latin literature and his personal reactions to the messages it contains. Wagner's investigations, despite their different emphasis, will offer an important reference point for the examination of how far Hesse can be included in the movement of "medievalism" and thus of how far his *oeuvre* was significant for the popularization of the Middle Ages in the early twentieth century.[6]

Wagner has sensitively observed that Hesse's idealistic purpose was to develop, by means of his responses to medieval and Renaissance voices, an alternative value system to that prevalent during his own days. By pointing out what authors such as St. Francis and Boccaccio had to say about their society, Hesse hoped to rescue the intellectual heritage of Europe for the future, and this at a time of cultural chaos in the wake the First, and then of the Second World War. His disgruntlement with the present led Hesse, like so many other cultural critics of that time, on a search backwards into the past.[7] Hesse claimed, for instance, in the introduction to his collection *Geschichten aus dem Mittelalter* (*Tales from the Middle Ages*):

> Heute nun, wo unsre Kultur erschüttert erscheint und ihre geistigen Fundamente von vielen Seiten her einer neuen Kritik unterzogen werden, regen sich . . . bei uns viele Stimmen zu Gunsten jenes vergessenen und verachteten Mittelalters.[8]

> (Today, as our culture seems to be in crisis and its spiritual foundations are criticized from many sides, there are many

voices among us in favor of the forgotten and despised Middle Ages.)

Although this new movement was also very promising for medieval philology, Hesse was faced, in the first place, with the many obstacles to gaining access to the literature from the period, because it was generally still popularly considered a dark phase in the history of Western culture and therefore had previously been neglected both by editors and publishers. For that reason Hesse's first project was to reedit and translate some of the relevant medieval texts; the second step was to evaluate them critically.

In his 1929 essay "Eine Bibliothek der Weltliteratur" ("A Library of World Literature"), Hesse emphasizes: "so kommt es, daß wir von der lateinischen Literatur jener Jahrhunderte wenig moderne Ausgaben und Übersetzungen besitzen" (the consequence is that we have few modern editions and translations of the Latin literature from those centuries).[9] Notwithstanding these difficulties, Hesse's essay reveals that he had acquired a considerable knowledge of medieval texts, as he reports in his recommendations regarding the reading of world literature. With respect to Italy he mentions, first of all, Dante's *Divina Commedia*, then Boccaccio's *Decamerone*, Ariosto's *Orlando furioso*, Petrarch's sonnets, Michelangelo's poems, and Cellini's *Vita*.[10] With his discussion of Goldoni and Leopardi (348), among others, he crossed (without pointing this out) the limits of the Middle Ages and the Renaissance, however we might define those periods, and moved into modern Italian literature.[11]

This essay also shows that Hesse knew and appreciated the following medieval literary texts composed north of the Alps: the Arthurian epics, the *Nibelungenlied*, the *Kudrun*, the poems by the troubadours and Walther von der Vogelweide, then Gottfried of Strassburg's romance *Tristan* and Wolfram von Eschenbach's *Parzival*. From French literature Hesse recommends Villon, Montaigne, Rabelais, Pascal, and Corneille (349), which takes him, of course, again by far beyond the period normally defined as the Middle Ages. When he refers his reader to England, he mentions Chaucer, then jumps to Shakespeare and briefly lists Milton, Chesterfield, Swift, Defoe, and others (351). With respect to other languages Hesse refers to the *Lieder der alten Edda*, the Icelandic sagas, and the *Isländerbuch* by Bonus (353). The list does not exhaust the range of his own intellectual horizons, because in this essay he had only laid down general recommendations.

It is interesting to observe how Hesse seems to have acquired his familiarity with the courtly epics, because he obviously never read them in their original, and not even in modern German translations. Instead he learned about them via the so-called "Volksbücher" (chapbooks) from the fifteenth and sixteenth centuries which he found in Richard Benz's anthology *Deutsche Volksbücher*. These chapbooks, however, represented considerably changed versions and do not really provide authentic access to the medieval "originals." Here the twelfth- and thirteenth-century romances were rendered into prose and often abbreviated, amplified, or otherwise drastically altered to adapt to the taste of a post-feudal age.[12]

It seems highly questionable to place these "Volksbücher," as Hesse does—and he was apparently quite ignorant of the complexities involving this late medieval reading material—directly next to heroic epics such as the *Kudrun* and the *Nibelungenlied*, because these poems represent an entirely different generic orientation, value system, and ethical outlook. Today we know that Hesse equated, without being able to make objective distinctions, apples with oranges, and also ignored vast differences between the High Middle Ages and the literary world of the fifteenth century.

On the other hand, Hesse was self-critical enough to observe how idiosyncratic and individualistic his selection was, and he made efforts to counteract this uncertainty factor by pointing out in "Eine Bibliothek" the timelessness of great literary texts: "alles Geistesgut, das einmal über eine gewisse Frist hinaus gewirkt und sich bewährt hat, gehört dem Bestand der Menschheit an und kann jederzeit wieder hervorgeholt, nachgeprüft und zu neuem Leben erweckt werden" (every intellectual work which has had some effects over a certain period of time and has proven its value belongs to the history of humanity and can be pulled out [of the bookshelf] at any time, be examined and revived [361]).

It is somewhat curious that Hesse concludes his account, after having sung a song of praise on the German classics from the turn of the eighteenth century, with an examination of the Christian Middle Ages, that is, especially of the "mönchische Kunst und Dichtung" (monkish art and poetry), because "die Orden und Klöster mir als Freistätten eines fromm-beschaulichen Lebens beneidenswert, und als Stätten der Kultur und Bildung höchst vorbildlich erschienen" (the orders and monasteries appeared to me as enviable locations of freedom destined for a life filled with piety and meditation, and as highly exemplary places of culture and education [371f.]).

Without doubt this fascination with the religious and intellectual culture of the medieval convents represents one of the important sources for Hesse's 1943 *Glasperlenspiel* (*The Glass Bead Game*), although many other inspirations and concepts would have to be considered to fully understand this magisterial novel.[13] First of all, we need to take into

Hesse and Medieval Literature

account that the monastic life in Mariafels exerts a noteworthy influence on Josef Knecht because only there is he thoroughly familiarized with the basic principles of history as taught by Pater Jakobus, an expert scholar and philosopher particularly dedicated to the Middle Ages—recognizably modeled after Jacob Burckhardt, whom Hesse admired deeply.[14]

Secondly, the outstanding features of this monastery are its "gewaltige . . . Bibliothek der mittelalterliche[n] Theologie" (majestic library of medieval theology) and its musical practice. Knecht also learns much about the entire tradition of the Benedictine order, the history of which can be traced back to late antiquity.[15] Certainly Hesse's enthusiasm for the intellectual world of the Middle Ages and even its scholarly treatment manifests itself here. As soon as Knecht's private lessons with the Pater begin, they quickly expand beyond a simple and naive discussion of Benedictine history and confront instead the question of how to examine critically the documentary sources for the early Middle Ages and the relevance of medieval chronicles for historical studies (200). The monk teaches Knecht that "Geschichte" (history) has to be understood "nicht als Wissensgebiet, sondern als Wirklichkeit, als Leben" (not as a study area, but as reality, as life), "und dazu gehört als Entsprechung die Wandlung und Steigerung des eigenen, persönlichen Lebens zu Geschichte" (to this pertains, correspondingly, the transformation and intensification of the personal life with respect to history [206]).

Pater Jakobus considers the Middle Ages, and especially the monastic orders, as his favorite subject of research, and he does not allow his student Knecht to get away with a superficial knowledge of that past when Knecht wants to judge the library and the cultural period it represents at first sight. It is very likely that in this scene Hesse intended to develop a literary discussion about the close relationship between a factual but superficial knowledge of the Middle Ages on the one hand—misleading the spectator—and the individual development of the modern reader confronted with this "foreign" world on the other hand, since he emphasizes this repeatedly in different contexts in the novel. For the Pater the continuity of the monastic order throughout the centuries represents "das merkwürdigste und ehrwürdigste Phänomen der Geschichte" (the most noteworthy and honorable phenomenon of history [182]), and it will be this orientation towards the past as a living organism which will incite Knecht at the end of his career to break the barrier of his own glass bead game order and embark on a short but meaningful journey into "real" life as the tutor of a young and insubordinate student.

To be sure, for Hesse the medieval monastery does not symbolize the crucial ideal which he wants to advocate; his concern is rather the transcendental unification of man with his environment and finally with God. For that reason, in the *Glasperlenspiel* Knecht must go through the entire institution of the monastic order of the Glass Bead Game, and he must leave it again at the end and enter the secular world, where he will, however, meet his own death.[16] In this sense he reenacts through the progressive steps of his own life the historical development of the Western world and also that of the Orient from the Middle Ages until the present time as reflected in the concept of various types of convents. From this point of view we begin to understand how much the *Glasperlenspiel* formed a mirror of medieval culture, literature, and theology, although Hesse perceived the study of that age only as a springboard for reaching a higher level of understanding. The study of the medieval Benedictine order turns out to be a catalyst, both for the protagonist Knecht and his creator, Hesse.

But let us return to Hesse's statements about the medieval period in his essays. Hesse had no hesitation about appropriating specific ideological values from the Middle Ages which conformed with his own political orientation. He stresses, for instance, "[wir] finden dort, ebenso wie in der frommen und innigen Kunst jener Epoche, denselben Himmel gewölbt, finden dieselbe Centrierung der ganzen Welt um einen göttlichen Mittelpunkt, dieselbe hierarchische Stufung der menschlichen Eigenschaften und Charaktere" (there [we] find, like in the pious and introspective art from that period, the same arching sky, the same centralization of the entire world on a divine focal point, the same hierarchical structure of human properties and characters).[17] This highly conservative value system that Hesse propagates could be pursued further in detail if we looked at his entire *oeuvre*, but suffice it here to point out that Hesse felt a natural inclination to admire the Middle Ages because of its strong religiosity, authoritarian structure, and spiritual value system. Both the *Glasperlenspiel* and other texts by Hesse confirm this observation.

Kyung Yang Cheong has pointed out the extent to which Hesse was also influenced by mysticism, whether derived from medieval or early modern writers, whether they came from a European or an Oriental background.[18] Hesse reviewed many publications, but showed preference for those which dealt with medieval mystics. He had great praise for Meister Eckhart ("Zu den grossen Gestalten des deutschen Mittelalters" ["among the great personalities of the German Middle Ages"]), Heinrich Seuse, and Johannes Tauler. And in his review of *Deutsche Mystikerbriefe* (1932) he emphasized that this collection was a "Kleinod, es ist uns in ihnen ein Strom geistigen Lebens zugänglich gemacht, der bisher nur wenigen bekannt war" (a gem; in [the letters] there is a stream of spiritual life made accessible which has been known so far only to few).[19] Moreover, for our purposes it is important to know that Hesse was also closely familiar with many Middle High German texts and that he considered them as important a key for a supra-rational, perhaps transcendental, explanation of this world as were the fundamental texts of Indian Buddhism.[20]

Overall we can now definitely confirm that Hesse had studied an unspecified number of medieval voices, though in many cases he had gained access to them only indirectly through early modern versions. Perhaps in this sense we may argue that Hesse was a Neoromanticist who relied extensively on secondary literature and created a picture of the Middle Ages for himself without always consulting the primary sources. Fritz Wagner emphasizes explicitly that the Romantics A. W. Schlegel, Tieck, and Novalis, later also Wackenroder, played a major role for Hesse. In particular, Wackenroder's *Herzensergießungen eines kunstliebenden Klosterbruders* became an important model for Hesse, who strongly recommended that other writers copy it.[21]

At a second look, however, we discover that Hesse was deeply fascinated by medieval Latin legends and other types of tales, which he had studied meticulously during his youth. Whereas Boccaccio provided him with the novella as a particular narrative genre, his reading of Latin miracle accounts by Caesarius of Heisterbach filled him with important impulses for his own creative interaction with the Middle Ages.[22] As early as in 1900 Hesse conceived the plan to translate a selection from the *Dialogus miraculorum* of Heisterbach and to bring it to print: "Um später auch einmal eine schöne Probe von alten, unbekannten Schätzen zu bringen, habe ich vor, dieses Jahr einige Stücke aus dem famosen Mönchslatein des alten Caesarius von Heisterbach zu übersetzen" (I intend, in order later to put into print a nice sample of ancient, unknown treasures, this year to translate some pieces of fabulous monkish Latin by the old Caesarius of Heisterbach).[23] This plan he realized a year later, in March 1901, when he published samples of his translations in the journal *März*, for which he was the coeditor.[24]

We can credit Hesse with having accomplished not only the important task of conveying these medieval tales of miracles to the modern reader, but at the same time with having rescued from total oblivion the scholar and writer Caesarius, for whom he felt strong admiration and respect. To quote Fritz Wagner, "in der Literaturgeschichte [ist] bisher kaum mit so viel nachtastendem Spürsinn, innerem Aufnahmevermögen und zugleich mit so viel interpretatorischer Sensibilität über die Erzählkunst des Zisterzienserpriors geschrieben [worden]" (so far in literary history hardly ever anybody has written with such an investigative understanding, spiritual receptivity, and interpretive sensibility about the narrative art of the Cistercian prior).[25] In other words, Hesse acknowledged not only the religious foundation of the Middle Ages as something of relevance for the modern word, but recognized, in particular, in the narrative art of that time a model for his own creative work.

The highly popular *Gesta Romanorum*, an anonymous collection of around three hundred short narratives of various types which had been transcribed in England around 1330 and were quickly disseminated all over Europe, appears to have held a particular appeal for Hesse, as we can tell from a translated selection which he published in 1914 in Leipzig.[26] At the same time, Hesse's introduction indicates that he was well aware that a naive and uncritical presentation of such tales could produce a highly stereotypical understanding of the Middle Ages. To read in the *Gesta Romanorum* without the proper introduction could easily mislead readers into assuming that the tales confirmed their preconceived notion of the Middle Ages as a period when the Church dominated all aspects of life and the phenomena of witchcraft and witch hunts were rampant. In other words, even the most sympathetic reading of these moral tales could invite the assumption that the Middle Ages were an era full of ignorance, superstition, and fear.[27]

To go the other way and to call the Middle Ages a time of gaiety and fun, however, would also constitute a too simplistic and contrasting picture which Hesse also did not aspire to paint. Nevertheless, he endeavored to free the Middle Ages from its traditional stigma as a repressive and barbaric period filled with endless suffering. In order to balance the religious viewpoint expressed in Caesarius' tales and those taken from the *Gesta*, he also searched for secular narratives in which basic human qualities and concerns would be discussed. For this purpose, in 1918 he published four other novellas taken from Leo Greiner's recent translation of Middle High German tales, together with six narratives from Johann Graesse's translation of the *Gesta Romanorum*, under the general title *Geschichten aus dem Mittelalter*.[28] The four novellas Hesse selected for inclusion were Wernher the Gardener's "Helmbrecht," the Freundenleere's "Die Wiener Meerfahrt," the Stricker's "Die drei Wünsche," and Konrad von Würzburg's "Der Welt Lohn."[29] The collection is embellished with attractive late-medieval woodcuts, which all together make this edition to a bibliophile art work in itself.

Why did Hesse fall back on these four texts only? Why was he concerned with these moralistic tales, which he tried to make palatable to a modern readership? We have no direct comment available, but in a

Hesse and Medieval Literature

35

fleeting reference in "Eine Bibliothek" to Dante's *Divina Commedia*, Hesse offers an interesting note which might be read as an indication of his general attitude towards the Middle Ages and towards these short narratives in particular: "aber immer wieder tiefe Wirkungen ausstrahlend, eines der paar großen Jahrtausendbücher der Menschheit" (one of the few millennium books of humanity, always exerting deep influence again [348]). The selection of the four "novellas," as well as Hesse's other literary responses towards and interactions with the Middle Ages, might have to be explained in a similar fashion. Even though he did not discuss it in detail, we may conclude that here we can identify a fundamental concept in Hesse's thinking which he found realized in the great world literature—the latter defined of course according to his own perception. This idealistic program, in his view, had been ignored and lost in modern times, which also would explain the reason for what he considered the crisis of the twentieth century. Hesse noticed that the texts he had made available again and which he also had discussed extensively in journals and other publications received little attention among general readers. Consequently for Hesse there was a need to remind the public of the valuable texts handed down from the Middle Ages, and the necessity of translating them into the modern vernacular.

Let us consider for a moment the content and messages of the four Middle High German texts edited by Hesse. Wernher's novella treats the rebellion of a farmer's son against his family and against society. Young Helmbrecht propels his upward move on the social ladder against his father's wishes, but then he only manages to join a group of robber knights and will, at the end, be punished with amputations; a year later, apprehended by peasants he had previously maltreated, he will die by hanging. The "Wiener Meerfahrt" describes the foolishness of a group of drinkers whose behavior leads to serious injury of one of their fellows. "Die drei Wünsche" demonstrates the ignorance of a peasant couple when they receive three free wishes which their jealousy and cantankerousness will render useless. "Der Welt Lohn" illustrates the transitoriness of this world's glory with the allegorical figure of Lady World, who has a very attractive frontal surface and a horribly rotten and festered back. Moral teachings can be easily learned from all four narratives, which proffer examples of bad behavior, arrogance, stupidity, self-delusion, lack of respect for other people, and absolute materialism.

Although these tales project a negative image of the medieval world, they nevertheless indicate that these very ills were directly attacked by these various authors, who used the literary statement as a powerful instrument in their moral crusade. It seems that Hesse would also have applied these criticisms to his own time. In this sense the Middle High German writers became meaningful again for the modern reader and might be used, as Hesse indirectly suggests, as warning signals against wrongful behavior and foolish pride.

Despite the negative connotations evolving from these counterexamples, Hesse idealized the Middle Ages with the following words:

> Dort finden wir alles, was uns heute fehlt: Glaube, Moral, Ordnung, Seelenkultur. Und dort, nirgends anders müssen wir anknüpfen, um das Neue zu erreichen, das wir suchen. Das christliche Mittelalter ist, ebenso wie der Geist Asiens, eine der Urquellen, zu denen wir auf verschütteten, mit Druckerschwärze und Professorengerede zugeschütteten Wegen wieder hinsuchen.[30]

> (There we find everything we are missing today: belief, morality, order, spiritual culture. And that is the point where we have to reconnect, nowhere else, to reach new shores on our quest. The Christian Middle Ages are, like the spirit of Asia, one of the ur-sources to which we have to return on paths which have been made inaccessible through printer's ink and idle professorial talk.)

As we can tell today, the very novellas which Hesse had selected indicate the degree to which the traditional order of thirteenth-century society was undermined and threatened with collapse.[31] Of course, Hesse was not so naive not to have noticed those societal problems, because even in the miracle tales recounted by Caesarius of Heisterbach we constantly hear of human frailty. Nevertheless, these very narratives attracted Hesse above all because in them he encountered the medieval combination "aus innig-edlem Streben und wilder Verwahrlosung, das nahe Beieinander von Teuflischem und Himmlischem" (of spiritual-noble striving and uncouth neglect, the close proximity of the devilish and the heavenly). Nevertheless, even Caesarius could not become a model case for Hesse's twentieth-century readers, although Hesse deeply admired this man as a writer: "denn Cäsarius [war] ohne Zweifel ein abhängiger und verbohrter, doch heißer und edler Geist . . . in dessen Äußerungen und Irrwegen wir mit Teilnahme ein typisches Stück deutschen, mittelalterlichen Wesens erkennen" (because Caesarius was, without doubt, a dependent and obstinate, yet warm-hearted and noble spirit, in whose statements and errors, full of compassion, we recognize a typical piece of German medieval life).[32]

Hesse and Medieval Literature 37

Hesse always pursued those very human foibles and recognized in them the basic conditions of human existence: his interest in the Middle Ages was therefore not a romantic obsession, although he was well acquainted with Romanticism as such.[33] By contrast, his true objective was to gain a profound understanding of human life, to teach his readers about human weakness, and to explore both good and evil within man.

In his discussion of the *Dialogus miraculorum* by Caesarius of Heisterbach, he made the following comment: "Es ist das Werk eines heiteren Plauderers, eines fabulierenden Einsamen, die Schöpfung eines Dichters, der Spiegel einer lebhaft bewegten Zeit und zugleich eines reinen, guten Menschen" (it is the work of a pleasant narrator, a lonely story teller; it is the creation of a poet, the mirror of a lively and agitated time and, at the same time, the mirror of a pure, good man). He admired Caesarius for having "eine feine, dichterische Innigkeit, die schlechthin ergreifend ist" (a fine, poetic inner life, which is simply moving), which would connect him, in a way, with the Romantic poet Johann Peter Hebel (1760-1826) and his calendar stories. Moreover, for Hesse the *Dialogus* turns out to be "ein Schatzkästlein von Erfahrungen, Einfällen und Spruchweisheit" (a treasure box full with experiences, ideas, and proverbial wisdom) because of Caesarius's masterly control of Latin and profound understanding of human nature.[34]

Though lauding Caesarius as free of any dogmatic thinking, Hesse openly admits that this figure certainly belonged to a world foreign to modern man; nevertheless he perceived in him a kindred spirit who like himself went his own way and thus gained insights worthwhile even for the modern reader: "Er hatte Freude am Stillsitzen und am Zurechtlegen und Ausdenken von Fabeln und Geschichten, seine Weltbetrachtung ging von dem Begehren aus, das Vielerlei des täglichen Geschehens nicht in Theorie aufzulösen, sondern es unverändert mit den Grundsätzen seines Glaubens in Einklang zu bringen" (He enjoyed a quiet sitting and imagining and writing of fables and stories. His meditations on the world were conditioned by the desire not to dissolve the many aspects of daily events into theory, but to bring it into conformity with the basic principles of his belief).[35]

It comes as no surprise that St. Francis of Assisi acquired a great importance for Hesse, if we consider the conclusions to be drawn from his comments on Caesarius. As documented in his autobiographical narrative *Hermann Lauscher* (1900), Hesse seems to have become familiar with this saint first around 1899 when he read Burckhardt's *Zur Cultur der Renaissance in Italien* (1860) and when he occupied himself with the tradition of fourteenth- and fifteenth-century novellas and legendary literature. In 1901 Hesse traveled to Italy and searched for traces of St. Francis, studying his life and visiting the locations of his religious activities. This search finds its reflections in Hesse's 1904 novel *Peter Camenzind*—another important indication of Hesse's interaction with the Middle Ages.[36] Fritz Wagner emphasizes: "Auf seiner Italienreise erlebt Peter Camenzind, wie es Hesse selbst schon 1901 in Italien widerfahren war, die Vergangenheit des heiligen Franziskus unmittelbar als Gegenwart" (on his trip to Italy Peter Camenzind experiences, just as it happened to Hesse in Italy in 1901, the past life of St. Francis as an immediate presence).[37]

Hesse saw in this saint, as he notes in the introduction to his biographical study *Franz von Assisi* (1904), a model human being, a person who had exerted a "gewaltige Wirkung . . . auf ganze Völker und Zeiten" (a gigantic impact on entire peoples and periods). The admirable aspect of St. Francis was, according to Wagner, that he lived, like many people before and after him, the life of a "Träumer und Heldenseele" (dreamer and heroic soul), and whose existence was in conformity with the ancient sources of human life, even though he was first decried as a "Narr" (fool). The accomplishments of Francis resembled those of other saints insofar as he had "allen anderen Menschen Gott nähergebracht und das Geheimnis der Schöpfung aufs neue wert und teuer gemacht" (had brought God close to all other people, and invigorated and given new relevance to the secret of creation). The relationship between St. Francis and the world of the twentieth century consists in the fact, as Hesse sees it, that the Middle Ages, just like modern times, moved towards absolute chaos: "Unter den geängsteten Völkern aber entstand tiefe Not" (among the frightened peoples arose deep suffering).[38] With his retelling of St. Francis' life he intends to transport the hope for rescue from abyss, which Francis had engendered, to his own time. Over many years Hesse expressed his deep admiration for this medieval saint in a large number of newspaper articles, reviews of translations by other writers, and narratives of his own. The medieval biographical accounts and poetic treatments of St. Francis' life had become a sort of spiritual revelation for Hesse, a source of inspiration and new faith for the future.[39]

Hesse's own engagement with St. Francis includes, in addition to the biography, a collection of critical reflections, the result of a number of book reviews, published in 1905 under the title "Der Blütenkranz des heiligen Franziskus von Assisi" (The Flower Wreath of St. Francis of Assisi); and a pious tale, "Das Blumenspiel: Aus der Kindheit des Heiligen Franziskus von Assisi" (The Flower Game: A Tale from St. Francis of Assisi's Childhood) from 1919.[40]

Hesse and Medieval Literature

In his letters from the 1930s and 1940s Hesse openly acknowledged that he considered this idealistic figure a model to be emulated during the terrible times of the Second World War and afterwards. Hesse was realistic enough, though, to understand why his appeals fell on deaf ears. Nevertheless, responding in a sense to the horrors of the Holocaust, Hesse formulated the following sentence: "Wenn ein heutiger Franziskus das Bedürfnis hätte, sich mit aller Menschennot der Welt möglichst innig zu verbinden, so müßte er sich mit einer Cernowitzer Jüdin verheiraten" (If a present-day St. Francis felt the need to connect as intensely as possible with all the human suffering, he would have to marry a Jewish woman from Cernowitz).[41]

We do not need to discuss in detail the impact of the legendary tales of St. Francis' life on Hesse's poetic *oeuvre*, but it is worthwhile to point out his novel *Demian* (1919), where we can identify important parallels with the youth of the Italian saint. On many other occasions Hesse indicated quite openly that texts about Francis played a major role for him: "Die Fioretti, trotz ihres frommen Inhalts ein Vorläufer der italienischen Novellenliteratur, sind das schönste und unvergänglichste Denkmal, das je ein großer Mensch in der Literatur seines Volkes gefunden hat" (The Fioretti, despite their pious content being the precursors of the Italian novella literature, are the most beautiful and immortal monument which ever a great person found in the literature of his people).[42] Although Hesse clearly distanced himself from the religious component of these medieval tales, he turned into a strong admirer of this saint, in whose life work he recognized one of the most important sources for his own thinking. St. Francis and Caesarius of Heisterbach wrote more about the simple life of the people than about God, and this very model Hesse tried to capture in his literary works as well.[43]

As old-fashioned this approach to the Middle Ages might appear today, Hesse certainly deserves credit not only for having revived important literary texts from the Middle Ages, but, more important, also for having built significant bridges between twentieth-century culture and the world of the twelfth and thirteenth centuries.[44] This represents an important contribution to medieval studies as well, because the general enthusiasm among the public today for that past world found an early spokesperson in Hesse, who knew well how to demonstrate the relevance of medieval literature for modern culture. Hesse's literary reputation does not need any further elaboration here, but we now add that some of his major ideas were based on his readings of the *Gesta Romanorum*, on Caesarius of Heisterbach's miracle tales, and on the life of St. Francis. Moreover, he knew many of the important Middle High German texts, even if only indirectly, and thus had a fairly good idea of medieval literature.

It is quite reasonable to assume, as Bozhidar Peytscheff has argued, that Hesse's *Glasperlenspiel*, in particular the chapter "Zwei Orden," exerted an influence on Umberto Eco's *Il nome di rosa*.[45] Eco, himself an expert in medieval semiotics, theology, and philosophy, presented the medieval library as a metaphor for the human quest. Its labyrinthine qualities pose difficult challenges which only the highly trained intellectual can master, but which eventually lead to ultimate insights into human existence. In Hesse's *Glasperlenspiel* the narrator does not paint the library as such a dangerous place as Eco does in his novel, but even there the quest motif plays a major role. The secret of life rests in the medieval library, in the manuscripts and illuminated books. The confrontation with these documents turns into a catharsis for those willing and able to read them. Both Josef Knecht and William of Baskerville prove to be such capable readers because they can look backwards and forwards in the literary-intellectual time-continuum, and the outcome of their reading is the transformation of themselves. If the thesis might hold that Hesse's *Glasperlenspiel* inspired Eco to write his *Il nome di rosa*, then we might also be justified in arguing that Hesse was indeed highly influential in contributing to the present popularity of the Middle Ages in movies, novels, and many other forms of public entertainment, including medieval festivals, comic strips, medieval concerts, and other manifestations.

Are we now in a position to determine whether Hesse was a serious philologist or simply a lay enthusiast for the Middle Ages? Can we place him among the ranks of academically trained medievalists, as a scholar and researcher? He knew enough Latin to read medieval texts in the original, and he was certainly well aware of cultural, historical, religious, and social conditions dominating the twelfth and thirteenth centuries. Yet the answer would have to be a clear "no," as indicated both by his confession in a note on Caesarius of Heisterbach and his criticism against the professorial world at the universities.[46] There is a certain naïvité in Hesse's attitude and thinking, and his approach to the epoch was more one of inspiration, feeling, and intuition than of critical discourse and rational interpretation.

Nevertheless, in many respects Hesse made important contributions to the study of the Middle Ages which opened the public's eye toward a past age and familiarized it with some of the most important literary texts from that period. Moreover, his deliberately subjective reading made it possible to rediscover the timelessness of some of the fundamental ideas and notions prevalent in the Middle Ages. This subjective factor, as

Hesse and Medieval Literature 41

unscholarly as it might appear, was a crucial vehicle in bringing medieval life and literature out of the "dark" corner of world history and illuminating it as an essential root of modern life. Praising the new interest in Roman Catholicism, he also commented: "Es wird sich . . . zeigen, daß mit zum Guten und Bleibenden an dieser Geisteswelle die erneute Liebe und Aufmerksamkeit für die Kunst und die Dichtung des Mittelalters gehört" (it will turn out that the positive and lasting effect of this intellectual movement will be the renewed love and attention for the art and poetry from the Middle Ages).[47]

Hesse was not the first to inspire interest in the medieval culture in Germany, because philology had for some time been well established at the universities and even at the *Gymnasium* level. Other writers such as Thomas Mann and Robert Musil had also reflected on medieval literature and expressed their respect, whether for the documents left behind by the mystical writers or for courtly narratives.[48] Nevertheless, Hesse assumed an independent and even idiosyncratic position among the many medievalist enthusiasts of the first half of the twentieth century. If Hesse's familiarity with some of the most important literary works of the medieval period was impressive, even more impressive proves to be his ability to incorporate this information into his own novels and narratives and to apply medieval learning and ideas to questions of the modern world.

NOTES

I have written on the same material in a related article, "Herman Hesse als Mediävist? Ein Essay," forthcoming in *Michigan Germanic Studies*. The present study builds on my previous findings and expands on them both in detail and in terms of primary material documenting Hesse's interest in the Middle Ages.

1. See Evelyn S. Firchow, "Mittelalter und Moderne: Ein Interview mit Dieter Kühn," *German Quarterly* 67.4 (1994): 455-62 (461). I myself have taught a course at the University of Arizona with the title "Medieval Answers to Modern Questions," in which my students and I read texts such as Boethius's *Consolation of Philosophy*, *Beowulf*, Wolfram von Eschenbach's *Willehalm*, and Mechthild von Magdeburg's *The Flowing Light of the Godhead*, each time asking ourselves what the poets' messages might have been in terms of modern human problems.

2. Siegfried Grosse and Ursula Rautenberg, *Die Rezeption mittelalterlicher deutscher Dichtung. Eine Bibliograpie ihrer Übersetzungen und Bearbeitungen seit der Mitte des 18. Jahrhunderts* (Tübingen: Niemeyer, 1989).

3. See Francis G. Gentry and Ulrich Müller, "The Reception of the Middle Ages in Germany: An Overview," *Studies in Medievalism* 3.4 (Spring 1991): 399-422; *Das Weiterleben des Mittelalters in der deutschen Literatur*, ed. James F. Poag

and Gerhild Scholz-Williams (Königstein: Athenäum, 1983); Ulrich Müller, "Das Nachleben der mittelalterlichen Stoffe," *Epische Stoff des Mittelalters*, ed. V. Mertens and U. Müller (Stuttgart: Kröner, 1984), 424-48; *Mittelalter-Rezeption. Ein Symposion*. Germanistische Symposion, ed. Peter Wapnewski, Berichtbände 6 (Stuttgart: Metzler, 1986); *Forum. Materialen und Beiträge zur Mittelalter-Rezeption*, Vol. III, ed. Rüdiger Krohn, GAG 540 (Göppingen: Kümmerle, 1988); and volumes in the occasional series *Mittelalter-Rezeption*, ed. Ulrich Müller et al. (GAG 286, 358, 479). Proceedings of the Fifth Symposium on Mittelalter-Rezeption and the Fifth International Conference on Medievalism, sponsored by *Studies in Medievalism*, are forthcoming as a joint volume.

4. See the following studies by Fritz Wagner: "Franz von Assisi und Hermann Hesse," *Franziskanische Studien* (1986): 285-307; "Herman Hesse and the Middle Ages," *Modern Language Review* 77.2 (1982): 378-86); "Franz von Assisi und Hermann Hesse," in H[ermann]. H[esse]., *Franz von Assisi* (1904; Frankfurt a. M: Insel, 1988), 98-128; "Dante, Boccaccio e Petrarca nella prospettiva di Hermann Hesse," *Atti e Memorie dell'Arcadia*, serie 3a, 8.2/3 (1983-85): 135-173.

5. Joseph Mileck, *Hermann Hesse: Life and Art* (Berkeley: University of California Press, 1978), 54.

6. See also the introductory article by Barbara Völker-Hezel, "Hermann Hesse und die Welt des Mittelalters," *Festschrift für Kurt Herbert Halbach zum 70. Geburtstag*, GAG 70 (Göppingen: Kümmerle, 1972), 307-25.

7. Recently both historians and anthropologists, consciously or not, have followed Hesse's model, building bridges between the past and the present; see Hans-Dietrich Kahl, "Was bedeutet 'Mittelalter'?" *Saeculum* 40.1 (1989): 15-38; Otto Gerhard Oexle, "Das Bild der Moderne vom Mittelalter und die moderne Mittelalterforschung," *Frühmittelalterliche Studien* 24 (1990): 1-22; Peter Moraw, "Die Wiederentdeckung des Mittelalters," *Interesse an der Geschichte*, ed. Frank Niess (Frankfurt a. M.: Campus, 1989), 9-99, 138; *Modernes Mittelalter. Neue Bilder einer populären Epoche*, ed. Joachim Heinzle (Frankfurt a. M.: Insel, 1994).

8. *Geschichten aus dem Mittelalter*, ed. Hermann Hesse, trans. Hermann Hesse and J. G. Th. Graesse (Frankfurt a. M.: Suhrkamp, 1976), 10.

9. "Eine Bibliothek der Weltliteratur," in *Schriften zur Literatur 1*, Vol. 11 of Hermann Hesse, *Gesammelte Werke* (Frankfurt a. M.: Suhrkamp, 1970), 347; further citations in text.

10. Regarding Italian literature and its impact on Hesse, especially regarding his fascination with Boccaccio, see Fritz Wagner, "Boccaccio aus der Sicht Hermann Hesses," *Sprache und Literatur der Romania. Tradition und Wirkung. Festschrift für Horst Heintze*, ed. I. Osols-Wehden, G. Staccioli, and B. Hesse (Berlin: Spitz, 1993), 224-43; also Mileck, 53f.

11. See also Fritz Wagner, "Hermann Hesse und die italienische Renaissance," *Come l'uom s'etterna. Beiträge zur Literatur-, Sprach- und Kunstgeschichte Italiens und der Romania. Festschrift für Erich Loos zum 80. Geburtstag*, ed. G. Staccioli and I. Osols-Wehden (Berlin: Spitz, 1994), 295-312.

Hesse and Medieval Literature

12. Regarding the study of *Volksbücher* and their history of adaptation, see my study *The German Volksbuch*, German Language and Literature 15 (Lewiston, New York: Edwin Mellen, 1995).

13. See Christian Immo Schneider, *Hermann Hesse*, Beck'sche Reihe 620, Autorenbücher (München: Beck, 1991), 96-104.

14. Mileck, 27.

15. Hermann Hesse, *Das Glasperlenspiel*, Vol. 9 of *Gesammelte Werke*, 164; further citations in text.

16. See Sunlil Bansal, *Das mönchische Leben im Erzählwerk Hermann Hesses*. Europäische Hochschulschriften, Reihe I. Deutsche Sprache und Literatur 1304 (Frankfurt a. M.: Lang, 1992), 180.

17. Hesse, "Zur Einführung," *Geschichten aus dem Mittelalter*, 10.

18. Kyung Yang Cheong, *Mystische Element aus West und Ost im Werk Hermann Hesses*, Europäischer Hochschulschriften, Reihe 1. Deutsche Sprache und Literatur 1217 (Frankfurt a. M.: Lang, 1991). Hesse was certainly quite familiar with the most important names of German mysticism, such as Meister Eckhart, Seuse, and Tauler, and in general he preferred to talk about mysticism as a broad term for all world religions (see Cheong, 25f.).

19. *Schriften zur Literatur* 2, Vol. 12 of *Gesammelte Werke*, 72-74, 12, 90.

20. Cheong, 40-43.

21. Wagner, Afterword to Hesse, *Geschichten aus dem Mittelalter*, 219f. See also Hesse's essay "Romantik und Neuromantik," *Schriften zur Literatur* 1, 105-113.

22. M. Pfeifer, *Hesse-Kommentar zu sämtlichen Werken* (München: Winkler, 1980), 74.

23. Hermann Hesse, *Gesammelte Briefe*, ed. U. and V. Michels, 4 vols. (Frankfurt a. M.: Suhrkamp, 1973), 1:138.

24. Detailed information on Caesarius's afterlife and the impact his work had on the late Middle Ages can be found in Wagner, Afterword, 221f.

25. Wagner, Afterword, 225.

26. Hermann Hesse, *Gesta Romanorum. Das älteste Märchen- und Legendenbuch des christlichen Mittelalters* (Leipzig: Insel, 1914).

27. Hesse, *Gesta Romanorum*, 7f.

28. The earlier volumes are Leo Greiner, *Altdeutsche Novellen. Nach dem Mittelhochdeutschen*, 2 vols. (Berlin: Reiß, 1912); J. G. Th. Graesse, *Gesta Romanorum, das älteste Mährchen* [sic] *und Legendenbuch des Christlichen Mittelalters* (Dresden, 1842).

29. These creative summaries are here edited as anonymous tales from the Middle Ages, although they can be identified rather easily. Neither Greiner nor Hesse—nor even Fritz Wagner—made an effort to discover the authors. Any Germany philologist would be able to carry out this task, but Hesse did not operate within the parameters of scholarly philology. Moreover, the label "Legendenstoffe" is not quite appropriate; the term "novella" would be more fitting, although this is also fraught with problems (see Wagner, Afterword, 229). Otfrid Ehrismann knows the translation of "Die drei Wünsche" by Leo Greiner, but he is unaware of Hesse's interest in this writer and subsequent quasi-scholarly

44 Studies in Medievalism

contribution; see Ehrismann's *Der Stricker. Erzählungen, Fabeln, Reden.*, ed. and trans. Ehrismann (Stuttgart: Reclam, 1992), 223f. Ehrismann does not know Hesse's translation.

30. Quoted in Wagner, Afterword, 219; see also *Gesammelte Werke* 12: 238.

31. For a general introduction, see Joachim Heinzle, *Wandlungen und Neuansätze im 13. Jahrhundert (1220/30-1280/90), Geschichten der deutschen Literatur von den Anfängen bis zu Beginn der Neuzeit. Vom hohen Mittelalter bis zum späten Mittelalter* (Königstein/Ts.: Athenäum, 1984), 2.

32. *Geschichten aus dem Mittelalter*, 10.

33. Wagner, Afterword, 219; Reso Karalaschwili, *Hermann Hesse—Charakter und Weltbild. Studien*, suhrkamp taschenbuch 2150 (Frankfurt a. M: Suhrkamp, 1993), 50-56.

34. Hesse, "Caesarius von Heisterbach," *Geschichten aus dem Mittelalter*, 61-65. See also Hesse's review of Hebel's "Kalendergeschichten," *Gesammelte Werke* 12: 200f.

35. Hesse, "Caesarius von Heisterbach," 59. On Caesarius, see Fritz Wagner, "Caesarius von Heisterbach," *Lexikon des Mittelalters*, Vol. 2 (München-Zürich: Artemis, 1983), 1363-66.

36. Mileck, 54f.

37. Wagner, "Franz von Assisi," *Franziskanische Studien*, 101.

38. Hesse, Franz von Assisi, 9-12.

39. Wagner, "Franz von Assisi," *Franziskanische Studien*, 127ff.

40. Wagner, "Franz von Assisi," in Hesse, *Franz von Assisi*, 121f.

41. Hesse, *Gesammelte Briefe*, 3: 192. In this letter Hesse is actually talking about his wife Ninon, as Rudolf Koester has pointed out to me.

42. Quoted in Wagner, "Franz von Assisi," *Franziskanische Studien*, 120; see also Hesse, "Der Blütenkranz des heiligen Franziskus von Assisi," *Gesammelte Werke* 11: 113-22.

43. Winfried Frey ("The Messiah of the Jews in German Medieval Literature," *Canon and Canon Transgression in Medieval Literatur*, ed. Albrecht Classen, GAG 573 [Göppingen: Kümmerle, 1993], 175-93) has pointed out the not so subliminal form of antisemitism in the tradition of the "false Messiah," which was handed down far into the nineteenth century and used again and again to denigrate Jews. We cannot determine with any guarantee whether Hesse even noticed the problematic nature of this piece when seen in this light. Even if we give him the benefit of the doubt, Hesse's tale serves as another example of how deepseated and pervasive antisemitism was, as well as how it found a spokesperson even among humanistic thinkers such as Hesse.

44. Mileck, 56f.

45. Bozhidar Peytscheff, "Die Klosterbibliothek. Vom 'Glasperlenspiel' zu 'Il nome dell rosa,'" in *Hermann Hesses Glasperlenspiel. 4. Internationales Hermann-Hesse-Kolloquium in Calw 1986*, ed. Friedrich Bran and Martin Pfeiffer (Bad Liebenzell: Gengenbach, 1986), 64-67.

46. Hesse, "Caesarius von Heisterbach," 58: "Außerhalb der engeren Gelehrtenrepublik aber kennt den bescheidenen Mönch beinah kein Mensch, einige

Hesse and Medieval Literature

stille, weltliche Verehrer etwa ausgenommen. Als solcher möchte ich von ihm reden" (outside the inner circles of the republic of intellectuals nobody knows the humble monk, apart from a few worldly admirers. I want to talk about him in that role). On Hesse's criticism of the universities, see *Gesammelte Werke* 12:238.

47. Quoted in *Geschichten aus dem Mittelalter*, 10.
48. For a bibliographical survey, see Grosse and Rautenberg.

Jeschute, or, How to Arrange the Taming of a Hero: The Myth of Parzival from Chrétien to Adolf Muschg

Otfrid Ehrismann

The encounter between Parzival and Jeschute represents one of the most remarkable junctions between Nature and Civilization in medieval literature. It reflects the hero's departure from the *status naturalis* and his accession to the *status curialis* and *civilis*, the transition from the world of the mother to the world of Arthur encoded by the confrontation of two ways of living in Nature: the boy who grew up in the wilderness meets a noblewoman in a *locus amoenus*, asleep in a pavilion. This single scene may be read as a multifaceted allegory of society, civilization, and finally of the feminine in general: it also opens a vista to the afterlife of the hero who ultimately becomes a mythological figure.[1]

A survey focused on the Jeschute episode in particular and on the *Arbeit am Mythos* in general,[2] that is, on successive constructions of the myth of Parzival between the milestones of Chrétien in the twelfth century and Adolf Muschg in the twentieth, is therefore called upon to analyze the texts with regard to their variant presentations of *Nature, Civilization, Society,* and *Heroism.*[3]

Chrétien de Troyes

In Chrétien's treatment of the scene, Perceval is hungry and enters a magnificent tent on the riverside, taking it for a church, in order to ask God for something to eat.[4] Inside, however, he becomes aware of a young woman asleep, *une pucelete endormie* (671), who now is awaking, frightened by the snorting of the shabby little pony on which our hero rode here. He immediately applies his mother's instructions: he greets the *damoisele*, and demands a kiss. She, however, trembles in fear, believing him to be mad. She advises him to leave, because her *amis* is nearby.

Perceval went too far, we are to assume, because he did not understand the idea of *honor* by which his mother had set great store:

> *Qui as dames honor ne porte,*
> *La soe honor doit estre morte.* (539f.)

One who does not honor the ladies possesses no honor himself.

It is not only this idea, representing the courtly, chivalrous world, which remains closed to him, however, it is also that he is unable to observe the fear of the young woman and to take to heart the advice to do nothing against a woman's will (544). Perceval in fact is not only unable to understand his mother, he explicitly ignores her teaching: she had said to ask for no more than one kiss (547f.). One could accept a ring, a belt, or a small purse, but only as a gift, it must not be taken by force: *se par amor ou par proiere* ("may be by love or by request," 552). The boy, however, robs with violence: he takes the ring and kisses the woman seven times. Her resistance, her tears and lamentations, do not move him.

Hunger then once again gains the upper hand, and he stuffs and pours into himself whatever is available. The woman's tears and the words she shrieks as he leaves he cannot grasp. He is the fool without any consciousness of wrongdoing, the child of nature at the dawn of civilization, into which he is just now entering and in which his life will end. Then there follow the adventure of the Red Knight and the teachings of Gornemanz.

Wolfram von Eschenbach

Wolfram makes the scene less crude, toning down Chrétien's emphasis on the hero's blunders.[5] Wolfram's Parzival follows his mother's teaching much more strictly than Chrétien's Perceval, and by this means the theme of misunderstanding is carried through more stringently. The audience comes to be more strongly aware of the problem of misunderstanding than in Chrétien, in whose narrative fun is more important than facts. Nevertheless, this adherence to the word does not serve to make Parzival into an Eulenspiegel, as is sometimes maintained, because Eulenspiegel knows that he is doing wrong, always aiming to unmask his opponents.[6] Compared with Chrétien, Wolfram achieves a higher intellectual level by a consistent play on various levels of meaning on the one hand—i. e., by a persistent shift from the literal to the symbolic level and back again—and by reducing the mother's educational theory to its foolish potential on the other hand, directing it towards Parzival's future more precisely than did Chrétien.

By such an adjustment Wolfram invites his audience to pay close heed to language, awarding at the same time greater emphasis to the woman. He intensifies the transition to courtly civilization, and thereby to society generally, which is represented by the court. As he always does with Chrétien's nameless figures, he gives the *damoisele* a name. Furthermore, he praises her chastity and her incomparable beauty. As was the case with the literal world, he thereby undermines the world of fact with the world of symbols.

Chrétien reports nothing of Jeschute's *hemede*, her shift. In Wolfram, she is not partly stripped as some would insist.[7] She had lain down. However, her first cover, that is, her courtly cover, had slipped and she therefore presents an erotic visual feast. Chrétien says nothing of her sable blanket, folded back to her hips because of the heat in the tent. He, Frenchman though he is, avoids any association with an erotic atmosphere and *wünne*, which means the delight representing the carefree courtly life, life as a party. Let us hear in contrast Wolfram (and afterward one will never maintain that a German is incapable of speaking about charm):

> *si truoc der minne wâfen,*
> *einen munt durchliuhtic rôt,*
> *und gerndes ritters herzen nôt.*
> *innen des diu frouwe slief,*
> *der munt ir von einander lief:*
> *der truoc der minne hitze fiur.*
> *sus lac des wunsches âventiur.* (130/4-10)

She bore the weapons of love: a brilliant red mouth, the very yearning of a knight's loving heart. Asleep, her lips had opened and showed the burning heat of love. There lay the most wonderful adventure.

The narrator's glance follows the topos of the *descriptio corporis*. Yet he immediately concentrates on the zone of highest erotic attraction, the red lips, which have unconsciously parted for a kiss. One can see snow-white teeth, long arms, and white hands—the ideal of a nonlaboring courtly woman and an anti-model of all countrywomen, the only women the boy has met hitherto. However, Wolfram does not suggest that the woman's charms are seductive. She therefore remains an image of pure and chaste beauty:

> *an ir was künste niht vermiten:*
> *got selbe worht ir süezen lîp.* (130/22f.)

She was a masterpiece of art: God himself had formed her lovely body.

Why does Wolfram evoke an erotic atmosphere in contrast to his source? He makes the signifiers of the courtly society visible, partly in order to underline the boy's *tumpheit* (simplicity, innocence), but also in order to foreground that society. He elevates Jeschute to a representative courtly figure and in this way marks the enormous difference between a life in Nature and a life in Civilization. In fact, it is only the woman's ring which attracts the boy, forcing him to jump on her bed. She wakes up, is frightened, and laments:

> *"wer hât mich entêret?*
> *junchêrre, es ist iu gar ze vil:*
> *ir möht iu nemen ander zil."* (131/8-10)

"Who took my honor? Master, you overshoot your mark; you should aim elsewhere."

In Chrétien, it was Perceval's mother who spoke about honor with great urgency: Herzeloyde, Parzival's mother, did not. Jeschute's woeful words recall the saying *Qui as dames honor ne porte, / La soe honor doit estre morte* (539f.). This was general courtly knowledge. The robbing of honor therefore carries no sexual connotation, but signifies a gauche insensitivity to women. The young boy cannot grasp the depth of this idea of honor, and when he says goodbye at the end of the scene with the words

> *wan schadet ez iu an êren,*
> *sô wil ich hinnen kêren* (132/17f.)

But if it is prejudicial to your honor, then I'll leave

he shows indeed that he has not forgotten his mother's words, but also that he did not grasp their meaning.

Now Parzival lies by the side of Jeschute, who feels dishonored. He embraces her (131/5). This is the *vaste umbefahen* ("the firm embrace," 127/30) that his mother recommended when he would meet a lady. The narrator uses the formula *wart dâ ringens vil getân* ("there was great wrestling," 131/21), and the courtly audience can decode it as a cipher for sexual intercourse. Robbing Jeschute of the ring now takes on the symbolism that we know for example from Brunhild's second bridal night. In addition, Parzival tears off the brooch which fastens Jeschute's *hemede*. These increments, not mentioned in Chrétien, fan the erotic atmosphere, so that the knowledge of the civilized audience differs from the primitive *tumpheit* of the hero.

The sexual symbolism comes to nothing.[8] The narrator, of course, breaks through the literal level and lays open the symbolic one, yet ironically always returns to the literal level. Wolfram does not work with the superiority of symbolism, in fact his technique is to join both levels, thus undermining the possibilities of a single interpretation.

The problem of a potential rape and consequent guilt is presented not to the audience but to Jeschute's husband Orilus, who cruelly punishes his wife.[9] He does so because he exchanges the literal meaning of facts—the trodden down grass, the missing ring, etc.—for their symbolic meaning. In this regard he represents the courtly society, who resemble Wolfram's audience in their handling of symbols. Wolfram plays with facts and symbols, and there is no justification for preferring the symbolic level to the literal one, or to reflect on a criminal rape.[10]

Wolfram's Herzeloyde had given a different advice to her son from what we find in Chrétien, because she had spoken specifically about a "good" woman, and not about women in general. She had made great demands on her child:

> *swa du guotes wîbes vingerlîn*
> *mügest erwerben unt ir gruoz,*
> *daz nim: ez tuot dir kumbers buoz.* (127/26-28)

Wherever you can get the ring of a good woman and her greeting: take it, it will make you free from sorrow.

And later on she repeated: *op si kiusche ist unde guot* ("if she is chaste and good," 128/2). The instruction to take the ring rather than asking for it neither excludes nor includes robbery as a method. To understand his mother, Parzival must know the courtly code of ethics.[11] The child of nature ignores what he does not grasp. He does not think about it. In the

The Myth of Parzival   51

same way he ignores the symbolism of the *vingerlîn*, which in the context of *gruoz*, *gelücke* and *hôher muot* applies to marriage. (This is the case in the later romance *Sir Perceval*, where an exchange of rings takes place.)[12] Wolfram's Jeschute plays the literal versus symbolic game. Psychologically this is not very convincing, because she is still frightened and not in the mood to play. She must play the part of the narrator to demonstrate the simplicity of the hero once more:

> *si sprach "ir solt mîn ezzen nieht.*
> *wært ir ze frumen wise,*
> *ir næmt iu ander spîse."* (131/24-26)

She said: "You should not eat me. If you would be a man of honor, you would eat something else."

It is not until his visit to Gurnemanz that Parzival's eyes are opened by shame and fear as he recalls the Jeschute episode. When Gurnemanz presents his daughter Lîâze, whose burning red mouth (176/10) and high chastity (176/12) portray a second Jeschute, he shows him his blunder, and shame wells up in Parzival's mind:[13]

> *"ouch solt an iuch* [i. e., Parzival] *gedinget sîn*
> *daz ir der meide* [i. e., Lîâze] *ir vingerlîn*
> *liezet, op siz möhte hân.*
> *nune hât sis niht, noch fürspan:*
> *wer gæbe ir solhen volleist*
> *so der frouwen in dem fôreist?*
> *. . .*
> *ir muget Lîâzen niht genemn."*
> *der gast begunde sich des schemn . . .* (175/29-176/8)

"I ask you to leave the girl's ring alone if she had one. Now she has none and no brooch either. Who would give her such precious things as the lady in the forest had? . . . You cannot take anything from Lîâze." The guest was ashamed . . . .

As he looks back, the meeting with Jeschute causes Parzival to be ashamed. The new civilization is a civilization of shame. Wolfram underscores Jeschute's shame repeatedly (131/6, 132/8), and it was he who sketched in Parzival's memory of Jeschute.[14] The Jeschute episode demonstrates the deficiency of shame, shown by the incapacity to distinguish between the literal and the symbolic meaning of words and facts.[15]

Parzival learns through experience. He bears the image of Jeschute in his heart, the virtue of shame, which his chivalrous teacher brings home to him. In this way the act of taming, i. e., the act of socialization, is closely associated with the internalization of shame. Shame is the basis on which the new courtly society, civilization, and culture respectively, are founded.

Between Wolfram and Tankred Dorst

It was not until Johann Jakob Bodmer's time that poets and scholars returned to the Parzival myth, and it was to take nearly a century until the myth was established.[16] During this process, and of course later on as well, the Jeschute episode played a small part only, but a typical one in mirroring the *Zeitgeist*.

In 1765 and 1767 Bodmer published a free version of some Parzival scenes reduced to the main action, and fourteen years later he devoted a rather long ballad to Jeschute, Parzival, and Orilus, which he called *Jestute*. Here is a sample:

> *Der Mund ihr von einander lief,*
> *Lang war der Arm und blank die Hand,*
> *Einen Ring von rothem Gold*
> *Der Knapp an dem kleinen Finger fand.*[17]

Her lips had opened, long was the arm and bright the hand; a ring of red gold found the page on her little finger.

In his portrayal of the encounter with Jeschute, Bodmer attempted to imitate Wolfram's style, but not at all his eroticism. For example, there was no mention of the *hemede* or the *vaste umbefahen*. He presented Parzival as an *unwissender Jüngling* ("ignorant young man") and he wanted to depict a cross-section of medieval life and customs. Above all, he condemned the cruel treatment of Jeschute by Orilus. In the age of Jean Jacques Rousseau, the idea of Nature acquired positive connotations "as the natural status of world and men became the principle of all moral values."[18] Therefore the medieval hero, treated with a certain critical irony by Wolfram, could advance to the *bon sauvage*, who was to be shaped by a civilized society. Thus, the difference between the century of Enlightenment and the Middle Ages concerning the assessment of Nature is a fundamental

The Myth of Parzival 53

one—unlike, however, the difference concerning Civilization as the only desirable state for mankind. The idea of civilization now had a powerful rival in the idea of Nature, which to some extent replaced the medieval idea of God.

Bodmer was not successful with the revitalization of the Parzival myth, and the same applies to its treatment by early Romanticism. Arthurian poetry could not be recycled as *Volkspoesie* like the *Nibelungenlied*, which began its great German career in those years. Nevertheless, something like a silent change took place which was to have an enormous influence in the future. This begins with August Wilhelm Schlegel, who was fascinated by the *geheimnisvollen mystischen Zauber* ("mystical magic, shrouded in secrecy") in the stories about Arthur. Interested above all in the Holy Grail, he established the future image of Parzival: the seeker of Grail and God, the chosen one, the mystic:

> *Äußerst kühn ist es, den jungen Helden, welcher von den Sternen ausersehen ist, das heiligste Abenteuer zu vollbringen, zuerst als einen fast blödsinnigen Toren seinen Eintritt in die Welt machen zu lassen: es liegt eine tiefe Wahrheit darin, daß die höchste Reinheit und Unschuld des Gemüts der Einfalt so nahe verwandt ist.*[19]

It is extremely bold, to make the young hero, elected by the stars, undertake the most holy adventure, his entrance into the world as an almost total fool: therein lies a deep truth, that the highest purity and innocence of mind is thus closely related to simplicity.

In fact, Schlegel did not mention the Jeschute episode, but it is this scene which represents entrance into the world and therefore the close relationship he proposed between the pure and innocent *Gemüt* and *Einfalt*. It is important to realize that the positive idea of Nature is linked with the idea of individuation. The Jeschute episode is not merely an entrance into society, but an entrance into the world. Society has become a secondary phenomenon. The romantic writer postpones his interest in the process of civilization and woos *Einfalt*, an idea, which expresses the identity between subject and object. Thus anti-intellectualism began to develop, which was possible as soon as the connection with the Romantic philosophy of Nature, which saw the world as generated from ideas, had been severed. The classical idea of *Bildung*, which viewed culture as the real, the higher nature, was shelved as well.

The philosophy of Idealism was trivialized in the later nineteenth century, and the hero himself became God. He began to lose any connection with society and civilization. The Parsifal created by Richard Wagner is a redeeming second Christ.[20] He is praised as the pure fool (*reiner Tor*) and the foolish pure man (*tör'ger Reiner*). No greater irony can be found and no more exalted idea of *Bildung*: it is a farewell to the spirit and a sincere welcome to mystical emotions. The values of civilization and intellectuality are done for, and the autonomous individual takes their place.

Wagner represents what could be called the noisy change of the Parzival myth, generating a considerable booming echo. The trivialization of his and of Nietzsche's aesthetics, connected with Darwin's ideas on evolution and natural selection and with a collective need for myths and mysticism in—to cite Hans Blumenberg—"a time of high-speed change," as the so-called *Gründerzeit* in Germany may be characterized, led to a simplified *Arbeit am Mythos*.[21] How could it be otherwise? Parzival grew into a charismatic, racially pure leader, transcending the mass. Wagner, understood or not, celebrated or rejected, marks the central junction where the myths of Romanticism and the Second German Empire meet. Between both, it is true, there lies a great difference in attitudes. Whereas the cosmopolitan Germans in the first half of the nineteenth century had tried what till this date they had been unable to achieve, namely to unify people and nation, they now joined the world-wide imperialism led by England and France. In addition, the social conflict between the working and the middle classes demanded integrated ideologies. Thus the stories of the Nibelungen, Parzival, or Faust could be used not only as national German myths, but as imperial ones, representing Germans as superior to all others and saving a decadent world. This was nothing but the notion of some political ideologists. Nevertheless, they had great influence on education, on academics and schoolmasters who compensated for their trifling political power with crude nationalistic ideologies. (Nowadays—you should pardon it—there is no need for compensation, and there is therefore no danger, because all our parliaments are crowded with teachers and academics.)

But the return to Nature stopped short of sexuality.[22] Parsifal's falling in love with Kundry in Wagner's opera reveals no physical aspects; it is akin to loving a mother (861), and functions as a medium of cognition, awakening the ability to save (852). The celebration of Nature does not refer to real nature but to the imagined *entsündigte Natur* ("nature cleansed of sin," 861).

The Myth of Parzival 55

While our Arthurian hero climbed to the top of national ideology on the one hand, he fell into the pits on the other, in children's books, where he shares the fate of other famous German fellow-sufferers like Siegfried, Dietrich, Roland, and Eulenspiegel. This signified the pretense of an intact world without natural wildness, a wildness now probably perceived as a threat to the *status civilis*. A prudish educational theory tabooed not only the physical side of love, but also the inner life. The outward, real world of the fairy-tale predominates in the Parzival for children; e. g., in Richard von Kralik's epic *Die Gralsage* (1907), in which we meet Jeschute again after a long absence:

> *Er* [i. e., Parzival] *kam zu einem Zelt und traf*
> *Jeschuten dort in süßem Schlaf,*
> *Orilus Gattin, Ereks Schwester.*
> *Was tut nun aller Ritter bester?*
> *Weil Herzeleid* [i. e., Herzeloyde] *mit treuem Sinne*
> *Ihm riet zu guter Frauen Minne,*
> *Küßt er Jeschuten, die erwacht*
> *Und laut sich wehrt, nimmt ihr mit Macht*
> *Den Ring und auch die Spange fort.*
> *Nicht hört er auf ihr flehend Wort.*
> *Nachdem er sich noch sattgegessen,*
> *Reitet er fröhlich fort.*[23]

He came to a tent and met Jeschute there in a sweet sleep, Orilus's wife, sister of Erek. What is the best of all knights doing now? Because Heartgrief had advised him in loyalty to obtain the love of good women, he kisses Jeschute who awakes and loudly offers resistance, and he takes her ring and brooch too by force. He does not hear her imploring words. After having eaten his fill he gaily rides away.

One can see little Jack going out into the world without falling into the clutches of socialization or sexuality. Only six verses are devoted to the teaching of Gurnemanz, another proof that both themes are intentionally suppressed:

> *Dieser* [i. e., Gurnemanz] *lehrte ganz*
> *Von Grund aus Zucht und gute Sitte*
> *Den Knaben, der mit keckem Schritte*
> *zum Ritter ward durch kühne Tat.*

Er gab ihm auch den weisen Rat,
Es sei nicht sittig, viel zu fragen. (193)

This one taught discipline and good behavior to the boy who became a knight with a bold step by a wise deed. He gave him the courageous advice, that it would not be modest to ask too many questions.

The presentation which in Wolfram's work laid bare a soul asleep, yet soon to wake, now remains mute. A stream of verses covers the events, without either shocking the audience or making it think about the hero's actions. Even the killing of Ither does not bring any irregular movement into this description. Of course, Jeschute and Lîâze are deprived of all erotic attributes, and Jeschute's sweetness is transformed into a sweet sleep.

Will Vesper, to mention another modern author, works with similar transformations in *Parzival, Ein Abenteurroman* (1911):[24] the heat of desire becomes the heat of noon, the *vingerlîn* a valuable ring (116), which it really is, a literal, tangible ring and no more. The son remembers his mother's words incorrectly: as in Chrétien's work she had spoken of a gift that ring or kiss could be (114), but not of the possibility of a robbery. The French poet must help to deflect any potentially erotic atmosphere, and naturally there is no place for a mention of the *hemede*.

In his "German heroic tale" *Parzival der Gralsucher* (1922), Hans von Wolzogen invents some maids to deactivate the embarrassing scene, which ends in a charming laughter:

> *Die Frau erwacht, erschreckt, erstaunt—wer ist dieser Fremde, der freche Dieb? Ein lieblicher Knabe! . . . sie ringt mit ihm, sie reißt sich los—sie ruft, sie schreit, es kommen die Mägde gelaufen und stehen verwundert: da steht auch der kindliche Fant lachend an der Herrin Lager . . .* (35f.)[25]

The woman awakes, frightened, being astonished—who is this stranger, this saucy thief? A lovely boy! . . . she wrestles with him, she breaks way—she calls, she cries, the maidens come running, wondering themselves: there stands the childish coxcomb, too, laughing beside the bed of the lady.

This deletion of sexuality and excitement is quite systematic: the affluent middle class of the Second German Empire rejects what could threaten order. It closes its mind to a world which makes ideas transparent by

The Myth of Parzival 57

making them relative. It does not want the fundamental values of society, above all the moral ones, to be rendered dubious, by subjecting them to critical examination. The taboo is no longer bypassed with effortless ease, as in Wolfram's narrative, it is kept secret.

Parzival was not one of the preferred heroes of Fascism, but certainly not a forgotten one either. The Nazis could take pleasure in the mysticism of the Grail and in the *Ordensburg* of its knights, transforming the medieval idea of *ordo* into the idea of a racial uniformity. However, a Parzival formed by doubt, faith, and courtly taming was alien to an ideology which saw the human as programmed by blood. The Nazi heroes were imaginary prehistoric figures or contemporaries of the *Bewegung*, but not genuine medieval ones. Jeschute, the model of a civilized courtly woman: how could she ever be a model for a Nazi *Mädel*?

In the literary scene of the Federal Republic of Germany the medieval myths had no chance until the later seventies, and even today they play a relatively small part. The literary Parzival revival begins in books for children, and here the principles of education had not changed. The Austrian writer Auguste Lechner, in *Parzival. Für die Jugend erzählt* (1977), puts Jeschute alongside Herzeloyde, following the same strategy as Wagner with Kundry:

> *Sie schien ihm* [i.e., Parzival] *sehr schön und sie sah auch fast so lieb und freundlich aus wie seine Mutter.* (84)[26]

She seemed very pretty to him and she looked nearly as lovely and friendly as his mother.

And a little later on:

> *"Sie wird schon aufwachen, wenn ich sie küsse," dachte er befriedigt, legte behutsam den Gabylot neben die Schläferin auf das Bett, schob den Arm unter ihre Schultern, hob sie ein wenig in die Höhe und küßte sie herzlich auf beide Wangen, genau wie er Frau Herzeloide zu küssen pflegte.* (84)

She will wake up when I kiss her, he thought contentedly; cautiously he laid the gabylot beside the sleeping woman on the bed, pushed his arm under her shoulders, lifted her a little and kissed her warmly on both cheeks, exactly as he had done with Herzeloyde.

58   Studies in Medievalism

The *bon sauvage* degenerates into a *braver Bub*, as an Austrian would say, into a good lad, treating his discovery very cautiously. The stouthearted leap onto the couch is lacking, as is the detailed *descriptio corporis*. The motif of the ring is defused, because Jeschute wears many rings on her hand, so that no sexual or matrimonial symbolism can develop. Parzival asks for one of them:

> *Starr vor Staunen ließ sie es geschehen, daß er den kostbarsten Ring mit dem Rubin von ihrer Hand zog und an seinen kleinen Finger steckte.*
> *Er lächelte. "Gott lohne es dir, Herrin. Ich habe dich auch genau angesehen, wie meine Mutter mir riet. Du gefällst mir und ihr würdest du gewiß auch gefallen." (86)*

Dumbfounded she allowed him to draw the precious ring with the ruby from her hand and put it on his little finger.
He smiled. "God may reward you, my Lady. I have carefully looked at you as my mother taught me. I take pleasure in you, and surely my mother would take pleasure in you too."

Let us return to our *leitmotif*, the taming of a young man. Lechner's young man does not need to be tamed, the taming is innate in him, and he is gentle by nature. Wild and disturbing nature has been eliminated, and with it the chance to think about Nature, and so education is given up. It is the family and not, as in the Middle Ages, society, which lays the foundation for a happy life. The story ends predictably with an idyllic family life, and the political task of the hero is as much as forgotten:

> *Parzival wagte den Blick nicht von der schönen Frau [i. e., Konduiramur] zu wenden, die dort an der Tür stand: er hatte Angst, sie könnte doch nur ein Traumbild sein und wieder entschwinden.*
> *Als sie ihn küßte, sah er, daß hinter ihr ein kleiner Knabe stand, der ihn mit ernsthaften Augen betrachtete.*
> *Konduiramur lächelte und schob den Knaben sanft vor ihn hin.*
> *"Dies ist dein Sohn Lohengrin," sagte sie. (257)*

Parzival did not risk turning his glance away from the beautiful woman who was standing there near the door: he feared she could only be a vision and disappear again.

The Myth of Parzival

> When she kissed him he saw a little boy standing behind
> her, looking at him with grave eyes.
> Konduiramur smiled and pushed the boy gently before him.
> "This is your son Lohengrin," she said.

Even this fleeting kiss has no meaning in itself, nor the woman who is dazzlingly beautiful, and who smiles. But behind her, and discovered only through the kiss, the secure future of the family appears in the shape of Lohengrin. It is just as well to avoid the political word dynasty. The myth of Parzival, apparently seen as threatening because of its social image, has been transformed into a middle class family idyll. In fact, it is the family which is here shown to ensure the structures of state and society. The Austrian government which gave an award for this book knew what it was doing.

Lechner's *Parzival* mirrors a typical facet of western society, whereas Werner Heiduczek's *Die seltsamen Abenteuer des Parzival* (1974) reflects a typical facet of the Communist East.[27] There it is precisely the theme of socializing which makes the biography of the hero attractive. Heiduczek therefore is not forced to manipulate the Jeschute episode. Nevertheless, his version is different from Wolfram's scene, because its social connection is different. The Marxist is fascinated by what he calls the inner contradictions of feudal society, and he can thus gloat over its ugliness with delight. He does not need to hide the symptoms of decadence, or sexuality. On the other hand, he does not understand Jeschute's chastity, and thus the phrase "in her lips still was the heat of received love" (36f.) creeps in in a telltale way.

The middle class idyll and the Christian courtly world are oriented towards eternal values. Marxism, however, always looks for change and history, and Heiduczek stresses the relativity of action:

> *Und selbst Parzival, der gegen manche Ritterregel lebte, unterwarf sich hier [i. e., in der Gralsburg] der vorgegebenen Norm, sei's aus Ehrfurcht vor dem, was ihm beschieden war, oder weil zuletzt doch jeder, selbst der Größte, in seiner Zeit befangen ist und manches fromm tut, was später Lebende belächeln.* (185)

And even Parzival who lived against many a chivalric rule, did submit here to the given norm, whether in respect of what was destined for him, or because after all everybody is embarrassed at some stage, even the greatest, and does various things piously at which those who live later, will smile.

60   Studies in Medievalism

It goes without saying that such a phrase, spoken in the society of the German Democratic Republic, hides an enormous subversive power. The narrator is actualizing history—always a well proven method for unmasking despotic regimes and yet avoiding their censorship.

In the eighties the myth of Arthur was imported into Germany for a second time, so to say, and this time not from France but from the USA, through the medium of fantasy and fantastic literature. The traditional pseudo-Germanic mysticism was finished, and intellectuals clung to it no longer. What came across the ocean, however, was a great mass of mythological kitsch that mirrors the need for myths in an epoch which is comparable to the *Gründerzeit* in its enormous social and emotional changes. Authors like Marion Zimmer Bradley, who tried to link the old myth with feminist ideas, had a considerable success in Germany as well as in the United States. Psychologists perhaps would condemn this kind of fiction as a flight from reality, but this would be only half the truth. Feminist circles seek their idols in the fairy past, taking it to be the Golden Age of matriarchy, and hoping this will be the reality to come. However, it is a literature which lulls to sleep critical intelligence, and is thus a move against the hypercritical seventies.

How it is possible to resist the anaesthetizing of the spirit by myths can be demonstrated by Tankred Dorst and Adolf Muschg.

Tankred Dorst

Tankred Dorst makes short work of the former Parzival-myth revival, and in his work one would also seek in vain both the soft-porn erotics of a Zimmer Bradley and the positive moralization of Nature by the picture of the *bon sauvage*.[28] His Jeschute remains a passive, foolish, giggling object:

> *Jeschute hat sich aufgerichtet, sie kichert, Parzival fängt an, die Knöpfe an ihrem Seidennegligé aufzunesteln, ihr nackter Körper ist weiß wie eine Feder. Sie kichert. Er tastet mit seinen dicken Händen über diesen Körper hin, drückt Dellen hinein mit dem Finger, sie kichert, er schüttelt sie an der Schulter, sie kichert, sie läßt sich nach hinten in die Kissen fallen, und Parzival steht erschrocken vor dem Bett und betrachtet sie.* (29)

Jeschute sat up, she giggles, Parzival begins to fiddle with the buttons on her silk négligée, her nude body is white like a feather. She giggles. He fumbles about on this body with his fat

The Myth of Parzival

hands, presses dents into it, she giggles, he shakes her shoulders, she giggles, she lets herself fall into the pillows and Parzival stands frightened before the bed and looks at her.

The encounter with Jeschute becomes an abstraction, it becomes an encounter with the element of strangeness, represented by the woman. She, as an object of study, does not offer any resistance, so that imagining a rape would be as wrong as male sarcasm, and it is Parzival who is afraid, not Jeschute.

The enquiry continues:

Er tritt zu Jeschute an das Bett, sie bewegt sich immer noch nicht. Er fängt an, sie zu betasten, vorsichtig, sehr behutsam—sie kichert. Er zupft an ihrem Kleid, an ihrem Haar, er zieht an ihren Fingern —sie kichert. (28)

He comes up to Jeschute's bed, she still does not move. He begins to touch her carefully, very gently—she giggles. He pulls at her clothes her hair, he pulls her fingers—she giggles.

The author calls his hero a wild man, a man of the woods, who has lost every form of relationship with his mother.[29] The difference between Dorst and Parzival-books for children is striking. Parzival here thinks logically in the categories of his experience of reality, and takes Jeschute for a strange animal, not because of her appearance, but because of the strange sounds she utters:

Oder war es ein Vogel? Er denkt, es müßte ein fremdartiger Vogel oder ein anderes Tier gewesen sein, das diese girrenden, glucksenden, kieksenden kleinen Töne hervorsprudelte, solche Töne hat er noch nie gehört. (28)

Or was it a bird? He thinks, it must be a strange bird or a different beast which was spluttering these cooing, gurgling, tittering little sounds. He had never heard such sounds.

By introducing this giggling, the author succeeds in evoking a pre-social atmosphere and action. If Parzival had known her to be a woman, he would have taken a considerable step on the way towards socialization. He would have been able to tell the difference between animals and human beings. Dorst, however, always wants to show the first meeting in his dramatic scenes. His perspective is that of an astonished child:

> *Der Täter, der aus der Wildnis kommt, der Wilde; alles, was ihm begegnet, begegnet ihm zum erstenmal, er weiß nicht, was Leben und Tod, was der Andere ist, er kennt die Regeln der Zivilisation, des menschlichen Zusammenlebens nicht, er macht Erfahrungen, wie sie der Mensch in seinem Anfang macht.*[30]

The doer coming from the wilderness, the wild man; all that happens to him, happens to him for the first time, he does not know, what life, and death, and the other means, he does not know the rules of civilization, of human living together, he gains experiences, which a human being gains at the beginning.

It seems that the Parzival of Tankred Dorst would be similar to the "naked man" of whom Richard Wagner spoke more than a hundred years before:

> *Aus dem entehrenden Sklavenjoche des allgemeinen Handwerkertums mit seiner bleichen Geldseele wollen wir uns zum freien künstlerischen Menschentume mit seiner strahlenden Weltseele aufschwingen; aus mühselig beladenen Tagelöhnern der Industrie wollen wir alle zu schönen, starken Menschen werden, denen die Welt gehört als ein ewig unversiegbarer Quell höchsten künstlerischen Genusses.*[31]

Out of the degrading yoke of slavery general daily work with its pale monetary soul we want to raise ourselves up to a free artistic humanity with a radiant world-soul; from industrial labourers, heavily loaded, we want to become beautiful, strong people to whom the world belongs as an eternal, inexhaustible source of the highest artistic enjoyment.

The modern hero, however, is not a celebrated one, is no idol, no saviour, and no bearer of a Utopia, or a new myth, as the earlier revival of Parzival wanted him to be.

Dorst's drama *Merlin*, which is to be seen as closely connected with his *Parzival*, unfolds the destruction of a civilizing myth, i. e., the myth of the Round Table which rises from an existence near Nature and drops

The Myth of Parzival   63

in the end back into Nature again.[32] Demythologizing, scepticism vis-à-vis Utopia and any teleological views of life, lost faith in the *bon sauvage* and presentation of the pure being: all this belongs to the postmodern imprint of modern drama.

Why does Parzival become frightened and jump out of the bed? Is it because of Orilus, who suddenly comes in, flinging open the tent?

> *Dann ist plötzlich grelles Tageslicht in dem Raum, die Zeltwand ist aufgerissen: der riesige Sir Orilus steht da und glotzt.* (29)

> Then suddenly the glaring light of day is in the room, the tent has been flung open: the gigantic Sir Orilus stands there and goggles.

The pure, unselfconscious being can be seen again in Parzival jumping up, as much as in the staring Orilus. It is left to the audience to think about the reasons of the thoughts and emotions of the characters. Light has fallen on the scene, the hero sees according to the traditional symbolism of light: he *knows*. What does he know, however? When pulling on her finger he had not taken Jeschute's ring, but bitten the finger off. He is still in the bestial state:[33]

> *MERLIN DER GROSSE HAHN: Ein schönes Andenken! Eine hübsche Trophäe von einer Dame!*

> *PARZIVAL besieht den Finger Jeschutes, den er in der Hand hält.*

> *MERLIN DER GROSSE HAHN: Ein Würmchen für den Hahn! Ein Köder für den Fisch! Ein Keimling, aus dem eine fleischige Blume wachsen soll! Was hast du denn da?* (29)

> MERLIN THE GREAT COCKEREL: A nice souvenir! A pretty trophy from a lady!

> PARZIVAL looks at the finger of Jeschute which he holds in his hand.

> MERLIN THE GREAT COCKEREL: A little worm for the cock! A bait for the fish! A sprout out of which should grow a fat flower! What have you got there?

Modernizing the Middle High German word *vingerlîn* only phonetically, not semantically, the author makes his postmodern joke. He, so to say, breaks up the female erotic-mythical symbol and transfers it to a male symbol, indicating the unity of death and life. When interpreting the finger symbolically as the threat of death (29), Parzival has taken an enormous step out of his animal being. The meeting with the element of strangeness has made him aware that life is finite.

More, however. Merlin compares him to a wolf:

MERLIN DER GROSSE HAHN: Ein Wolf hat der Dame den Finger abgebissen!

PARZIVAL: Ich war es! (29)

MERLIN THE GREAT COCKEREL: It was a wolf which has bitten off the finger of the lady!

PARZIVAL: It was me!

Parzival is frightened of himself, and he comes to know himself vis-à-vis the animal as different, as a human being, who now no longer wants to be a wild beast, and who is on the way to being tamed, civilized, and socialized. The medieval epic had led the hero to his divine and social destiny: the modern drama, however, remains open-ended. It no longer reflects the security of a closed *Weltbild*. Parzival does not obtain the Holy Grail. He can only see Sir Galahad on the other side of the glacier (110), stretching out his hands towards the floating chalice. Parzival's nearness to God remains without a final answer:

Ich [i. e., Parzival] *werfe mich in den Abgrund! Gott fängt mich auf mit einem Ginsterzweig.* (110)

I throw myself into the abyss! God will catch me with a branch from a broom-bush.

These words are indefinite in that the degree of certainty or hope they express cannot be known.

The end of the Jeschute scene and the following *Protokoll*, which could have the title "Male Fantasies," documents the fragility and sublimi-

The Myth of Parzival

65

nal brutality of our patriarchal civilization, so that the wild man Parzival is shown as its mirror, and not as its antithesis.[34]

Adolf Muschg

The Swiss novelist Adolf Muschg, in *Der Rote Ritter* (1993), puts the episode of the tent by the river under the title *Wie Parzivâl einer Frau Gewalt tut, um seiner Mutter Wort zu halten* ("How Parzivâl does violence to a woman to keep his word with his mother").[35] Unlike the earlier Parzival revival and the books for children, and unlike the drama of Tankred Dorst, this contemporary novelist expands the physical scene. He follows the imitator's principle of exaggeration, and he especially wants to intensify the theme of rape—now, however, no longer on the symbolic level like Wolfram, but in a fictional reality. The rape takes place as a matter of course, and the theme of chastity is lost. The myth of *Minne* has no chance today, because it can no longer be understood as a courtly game and because the strict separation between the courtly and real worlds can no longer be realized.

More narrative space is given to the sleeping Jeschute by Muschg, who devotes considerable space to the *hemede*:

> *So gut wie entblößt war auch der Frauenleib, nur ein zartes Hemd verkleidete ihn noch. Am Hals gerafft, teilte es sich über den Brüsten und ließ einen runden Nabel sehen, den der Atem hob und senkte. Die Decke, die über den Hüften lag, konnte nicht weiter sinken. Denn ein weißer Arm schmiegte sie an sich, mit schlafgelockerter Hand.* (317)

> The woman's body was almost naked, only a delicate shift was still disguising it. Gathered at the neck it was parted over the breasts and made visible a round navel, which breath raised and lowered. The coverlet which lay across the hips could not slip further. Because a white arm held it close with a hand opened in sleep.

What had been discreetly hidden by the medieval *descriptio corporis* is now fully verbalized, and so quite logically is the erection of the *viselîn*:

> *Warum hatte sich sein Fisel erhoben und stramm gemacht?* (318)

> Why had his *Fisel* erected itself and stiffened?

The innocence of this indirect question mediates between the naivety and the animal-like state of the hero who is reaching "new shores" (318), as it is called metaphorically. Bodily contact he had previously known only with his mother and with animals.

Jeschute's resistance decreases when she hears the name of Parzival's mother and they begin to talk. She defends herself with the vocabulary of the courtly world, misunderstood by Parzival, who is unable to grasp its real sense. The phrase "I am a noble lady" (319) would have meant "do not touch me," according to courtly convention:

> *Hört! ich bin eine edle Frau—*
> *Das paßt! sagte er.—So eine müßte ihr auch sein. Sonst darf*
> *ich Euch gar nicht küssen. Wißt Ihr was? Helft mir über den Fluß.*
> (319)

> Listen! I am a noble lady—
> All right! said he.—You have to be such a one. Otherwise
> I am not allowed to kiss you. Do you know what? Help me
> across the river.

In this way a new and cruel misunderstanding develops, because in the word-world of the child of nature the formula *to help across the river* means to sleep with, which, of course, cannot be grasped by Jeschute. Full of hope, but in vain, she therefore looks at the river in order to help him. He, however, seizes her roughly and takes her from the back as he used to do with his goats:

> *Ihr habt einen schönen Arsch! verkündete Parzival, denn die*
> *Sprache der Bauern war nicht ganz an ihm vorübergegangen; und*
> *die waren um Namen nicht verlegen, wo die Mutter sprachlos blieb.*
> *Bitte! Ich will Euch ja über den Fluß helfen! bitte! wimmerte*
> *die Frau.*
> *Ist ja gut! tröstete er, nur bitten darf ich mich nicht lassen, sagt*
> *meine Mutter! Ich muß Euch noch fester packen, pardon, Frau.*
> (320)

> You have a nice arse! announced Parzivâl, because the speech of
> the farmers had not passed him by totally; and these were not at
> a loss for names where his mother had remained silent.
> Please! I will help you across the river! please! whimpered
> the woman.

The Myth of Parzival

> Never mind! he consoled, but my mother said, I must not
> be asked! I must grip you more tightly, pardon me, woman.

The collision of the two worlds becomes grotesque, and the resistance
of the woman is understood as asking for love. As with Wolfram, the
intellectual enjoyment of recognition which the audience experiences tones
down the brutal act, here intensified to a consummated rape. The brutality, however, is reined in, because the young boy has no feeling of wrongdoing: he is an animal, as Jeschute calls him, a "perfect fool" (321-322) for
whose life she fears:

> *Du-bist-ein-vollkommener-Narr, flüsterte sie. Dann fuhr sie sich*
> *über den Mund.—Mein Leben! sagte sie.—Lauf! zischte sie durch die*
> *Finger.—Sitz auf, reite, so schnell du kannst!* (322)

> You-are-a-perfect-fool, she whispered. Then she passed her hand
> over her mouth.—My life! she said.—Run away! she hissed
> through her fingers.— Mount, ride as quickly as you can!

Farce mingles with seriousness, and as with Wolfram's *Parzival* today, the
amusement which the audience derives is ambivalent. We do not know
whether Wolfram's audience laughed at the scene, nor what they really
felt. The staging of Muschg, however, transcends the obscenity for one
reason only, because it transcends the literal level, and thereby forces us to
think about the relation between letter and sense, which is the theme of
the Jeschute episode. However, if both levels accomplish the same thing,
it is not the same after all. Wolfram played off the literal against the symbolic level, as the theory of medieval allegory had taught him. Muschg, in
contrast, operates with language itself, with its instability, and with the
problem of understanding in general.

When he performs the sex act for the first time with a woman and no
longer with goats, Parzival's socialization begins. The narrative does not
turn into a lament about the loss of Nature and of innocence, because the
question of guilt is here not connected with sexuality and the body. Both
are affirmed. This acceptance of Nature and the simultaneous acceptance
of socialization, which could take place only in the solid world of a Swiss
citizen, differs from the taming in the earlier Parzival-revival. Such an epic
and civic calmness vis-à-vis the world, which manifests itself in an ironical
distance from the events, makes the Jeschute episode representative for the
whole novel.

When elevating the hero to the representative of his class, Adolf Muschg writes a historical novel in a special sense. While Wolfram had understood the chivalry of the Holy Grail as the crown of the *civitas terrena*, and history as the history of salvation, Muschg takes history as the history of classes succeeding one another. The irony therefore logically mirrors the epoch, a possibility which was not available to the Middle Ages. Parzivâl is ruined by Lähelîn, the representative of the trading middle class and of democracy. A revolution in a typical postmodern German way takes place: an institution disappears, namely, chivalry. Its time is at an end. Perhaps this is a little melancholy, but there is no terror and no massacre. Chivalry hardly defends itself, and the hero accepts the new era of Lähelîn. He leaves the Grail and returns to his homeland. Muschg avoids any emotional comment on ruin, or surrender, as well as any triumph of victory. He says "yes" to the new commonwealth. Nevertheless, there is always a distinct, ironical scepticism to be felt in the novel. Therefore the work must be seen as written in resistance to the anti-intellectual and anti-civilizing trends of the earlier Arthurian revival in Germany. As the hero withdraws, the author cancels the heroic myth in general, and the myth of the Holy Grail in particular, which he invalidates. The taming of the hero leads to the perception that he has become superfluous. The mythic circle of Dorst's drama does not exist here, because there is no return to Nature. There is merely the sketch of a utopia of men living peacefully together.

What emerges from these successive revisions of the Jeschute episode? The history of the idea of taming is the history of the idea of Nature, which has undergone two fundamental revaluations. The negative view of the Middle Ages has been changed by two returns to Nature, in the era of Rousseau and in modern times. First it was *the Nature in man* which fascinated philosophers and poets, later it was *man in Nature*, and *as Nature*. First man was given a god-like status, which led him to a supra-social position, later he was awarded an animalistic status. The *bon sauvage* became the *wild sauvage*, because the ideas of Civilization and *Bildung*, preserved in the first return, came to be under suspicion. The loss of both was first compensated by hybrid egotism and heroism respectively; later, after heroism had become suspect, man had been accused of being an animal. This bleak picture is undermined by Adolf Muschg, who affirms bourgeois society.

All this may not be new. What is new, however, is that it can all be shown by the Jeschute episode of the Parzival myth. And this is what the historian of the great medieval myths can do: to show them as mirrors of their times, to show their eternal vitality as an eternal reinvention.

The Myth of Parzival

NOTES

This paper was originally presented in a plenary session at the Eighth International Conference on Medievalism, University of Leeds, September-October 1993.

1. The present study does not deal with the structure of the hero's path, the meeting with the knights as his first experience of alterity cannot be taken as a stage of change, because Parzival is not yet "on the way." This does not occur before the farewell to his mother; besides, it does not make sense to me to let "the way" begin before its movement, in Soltane, or later, i. e., from his first stay at Arthur's court. On this problem, see Alexandra Stein, "Wort unde werc. Studien zum narrativen Diskurs im 'Parzival' Wolframs von Eschenbach," *Mikrokosmos* 31 (1993), 56-59; also Marion E. Gibbs, *Wîplîchez wibes reht: A Study of the Women Characters in the Works of Wolfram von Eschenbach* (Pittsburgh: Duquesne University, 1972), 104: "She [Jeschute] marks the point of his departure form the closed circle of his boyhood into the world outside."

2. On this notion see Hans Blumenberg, *Arbeit am Mythos* (Frankfurt, 1981); on my idea of myth see Otfrid Ehrismann, *Germanistik und Mythologie. Überlegungen zur Rekonvaleszens der Altgermanistik*, Gießener Universitätsblätter 19 (1986): 53-63.

3. On the history of this idea see Heinrich Schipperes, *Natur*, in *Geschichtliche Grundbegriffe*, ed. Otto Brunner, Werner Conze, Reinhart Koselleck (Stuttgart, 1978), 215-44; also *Zivilisation, Kultur* (Stuttgart, 1992), 679-774.

4. Chrétien de Troyes, *Le Roman de Perceval ou Le Conte du Graal. Der Percevalroman oder Die Erzählung vom Gral*, ed. and trans. Felicitas Olef-Krafft (Stuttgart, 1991), 635-781.

5. *Parzival* 129/16-132/24, in *Wolfram von Eschenbach*, 6th ed., ed. Karl Lachmann (1926; rpt. Berlin, 1965). Cf. also the extensive commentary of David N. Yeandle, *Commentary on the Soltane and Jeschute Episodes in Book III of Wolfram von Eschenbach's Parzival (116,5-138,8)* (Heidelberg, 1984). For textual criticism, see Jürgen Kühnel, "Wolframs von Eschenbach 'Parzival' in der Überlieferung der Handschriften D (Cod. Sangall. 857) und G (CGM. 19). Zur Textgestalt des 'Dritten Buches,'" *Festschrift for Kurt Herbert Halbach* (Göppingen, 1972), 145-213. Bayard Quincy Morgan, in "Some Women in Parzival," *JEGP* 12 (1913): 175-98 (esp. 178-81), comments on Jeschute's servile attitude toward Orilus. Alois M. Haas, *Parzivals tumpheit bei Wolfram von Eschenbach*, Philologische Studien und Quellen 21 (Berlin, 1964), sees the idea of Nature in a modern Rousseauistic manner when speaking of the *naturhaften Herrlichkeit des Leibes* (73); furthermore he sees the scene as a manifestation of the *Erwähltsein* of the hero. A very sensible study of Jeschute's personality is given by Gibbs, 104-113.

6. Cf., for example, Haas, 72.

7. See Stein, 85 (*halbentblößt*).

8. To speak of a *verunglückten Liebesabenteuer*, as does Helmut Brall in *Gralsuche und Adelsheil. Studien zu Wolframs Parzival*, Germanische Bibliothek, 3rd series (207), however, would be overshooting the mark.

9. Stein (86-89) does not regard the Jeschute episode in respect to its function, and therefore sees Parzival as a defective person here.

10. Cf. also David Blamires, *Characterization and Individuality in Wolfram's "Parzival"* (Cambridge, 1966), 146.

11. Thus Wolfram does not demonstrate an exact "taking word for word"; see, however, for example Siegfried Richard Christoph, *Wolfram von Eschenbach's Couples*, Amsterdamer Publikationen zur Sprache und Literatur 44 (Amsterdam, 1981), 65f.

12. *Sir Perceval of Gales*, ed. J. Campion and F. Holthausen, Alt- und Mittelenglische Texte 5 (Heidelberg, 1913), Ch. 28-30. In this little romance, Parzival first reaches a hall in which he finds food for himself and his horse and meets a sleeping lady in another room. He takes her ring and puts the ring which his mother had given him as a sign of identification (*takynnynge*) on her finger.

13. See M. Huby, "Réflexions sur 'Parzival' et le 'Conte del Graal' II," *Etudes Germaniques* 35 (1980): 1-17, esp. 9f.

14. See, for a different view, Dietmar Peil, *Die Gebärde bei Chrétien, Hartmann und Wolfram. Erec-Iwein-Parzival*, Medium Aevum 28 (München, 1975), 221.

15. On the idea of *schame*, see Martina Gemeling, "*Schame* im Parzival Wolframs von Eschenbach," Diss. Universität Gießen, in progress.

16. Claudia Wasielewski-Knecht, *Studien zur deutschen Parzival-Rezeption in Epos und Drama des 18.-20. Jahrhunderts* (Frankfurt am Main, 1993); Ursula Schulze, "Stationen der Parzival-Rezeption. Strukturveränderung und ihre Folgen," *Mittelalter-Rezeption. Ein Symposion*, ed. Peter Wapnewski, Germanische Symposien Berichtsbände 6 (Stuttgart, 1986), 555-80.

17. Johann Jakob Bodmer, "Jestute," *Altenglische und altschwäbische Balladen*, in *Eschilbachs Versart*, vol. 2 (Zürich, 1781), 178-93.

18. See Schipperes, 234-35, regarding eighteenth-century constructions of the philosophy of life.

19. August Wilhelm Schlegel, *Geschichte der romantischen Literatur*, ed. Edgar Lohner, vol. 4 of *Kritische Schriften und Briefe* (Stuttgart, 1965), 123-25f.

20. Richard Wagner, *Die Musikdramen* (München, 1978), 821-72.

21. "Das macht Zeiten mit hohen Veränderungsgeschwindigkeiten ihrer Systemzustände begierig auf neue Mythen, auf Remythisierungen, aber auch ungeeignet, ihnen zu geben, was sie begehren. Denn nichts gestattet ihnen zu glauben, was sie gern glauben möchten, die Welt sei schon immer so oder schon einmal so gewesen, wie sie jetzt zu werden verspricht oder droht" (Blumenberg, 41).

22. See Wasielewski-Knecht, 103.

23. Richard von Kralik, *Die Gralsage. Gesammelt, erneuert und erläutert* (Ravensburg, 1907), 186f.

24. Will Vesper, *Parzival. Ein Abenteuerroman*, in *Tristan und Isolde, ein Liebesroman. Parzival, ein Abenteuerroman* (München, [1911]), 102-92.

25. Hans von Wolzogen, *Parzival der Gralsucher. Eine deutsche Heldenge-schichte von Wolfram von Eschenbach, neu erzählt* (Berlin, [1922]).

26. Auguste Lechner, *Parzival. Für die Jugend erzählt* (Innsbruck/ Wien/ München, 1977). Madame Lechner is an Austrian citizen, but her writings are widespread in Germany.

27. Werner Heiduczek, *Die seltsamen Abenteuer des Parzival. Nach Wolfram von Eschenbach neu erzählt* (Berlin/GDR, 1974; Frankfurt, 1989).

28. Tankred Dorst, *Parzival. Ein Szenarium*, with Ursula Ehler (Frankfurt, 1990), 28-34; Tankred Dorst, *Merlin oder das wüste Land*, with Ursula Ehler (Frankfurt, 1981), 101f; see Wasielewski-Knecht, 262-71, and Rüdiger Krohn, "Parzival und die Vergeblichkeit des Friedens. Über die Funktion einiger ausge-schiedener Materialien zu Tankred Dorsts 'Merlin,'" in *Tankred Dorst*, ed. Günther Erken (Frankfurt, 1989), 204.

29. Dorst planned a film on Parzival entitled *Der Wilde* just before his *Merlin* was published; see Erken, 204; also Ehler's *Vorbemerkung zu Parzival* in Dorst, *Parzival. Ein Szenarium*.

30. Ehler, *Vorbemerkung zu Parzival*, in Dorst, *Parzival. Ein Szenarium*.

31. Richard Wagner, *Die Kunst und die Revolution, Das Judentum in der Musik, Was ist deutsch?*, ed. Tibor Kneif (München, 1975), 36f. On the naked man, see Wagner, *Drei Operndichtungen nebst einer Mitteilung an seine Freunde also Vorwort* (Leipzig, 1852), 136.

32. See Wasielewski-Knecht, 236-62; Otfrid Ehrismann, "Von Geoffrey zu Handke. Der Artusmythos und seine deutsche Rezeption," in *Phantastische Welten. Märchen, Mythen, Fantasy*, ed. Thomas Le Blanc and Wilhelm Solms (Regensburg, 1994), 85-114.

33. The reader will not be aware of this before the following scene; see "Parzival. Auf er anderen Seite des Sees. Szenenbeschreibung," in Dorst, *Parzival. Ein Szenarium*, 138.

34. See "Erster Entwurf für des Hamburger Parzival Projekt," in Dorst, *Parzival. Ein Szenarium*, 114-16, esp. 114.

35. Adolf Muschg, *Der Rote Ritter. Eine Geschichte von Parzivâl* (Frankfurt, 1993), 316-23.

King and Marshal:
Ballad and Liturgy in
a Danish Music Drama

Nils Holger Petersen

One of the most fascinating events in Danish medieval history has proved to be the unsolved murder of King Erik V (also known by the mysterious surname *Klipping* or *Glipping*) in 1286. The king's Lord Marshal, Stig, was accused of the murder. In addition to traditional historical documents, a number of old popular Danish ballads convey their own accounts of the incident, generally letting Marshal Stig revenge the king's seduction of his wife. The marked nineteenth-century interest in the Middle Ages brought with it a creative preoccupation with this murder, resulting in, to mention only the best known works, *The Childhood of Erik Menved* (*Erik Menveds Barndom*; Erik Menved was the son of Erik V), a novel by B. S. Ingemann (1789-1862), 1827; *Erik Glipping*, a tragedy by Adam Oehlenschläger (1779-1850), 1844; *Marshal Stig* (*Marsk Stig*), a tragedy by Carsten Hauch (1790-1872), 1850; and a painting, *The Conspirators Ride Away from the Barn at Finnerup after the Murder of Erik Glipping* (*De Sammensvorne ride fra Finnerup Lade efter Mordet paa Erik Glipping*), by Otto Bache (1839-1927), now in the National History Museum. In the twentieth century as well, writers like Karen Blixen (Isak Dinesen) (1885-1962), Jens August Schade (1903-78), and Ebbe Kløvedal Reich (b. 1940) have occupied themselves with Erik's murder. The subject of this study is the opera *King and Marshal* (*Drot og marsk*), composed by Peter Heise (1830-79) to a libretto by the poet and Lutheran vicar Christian Richardt (1831-92).

Inspired by Hauch's tragedy, Heise wrote his *Marsk Stig Overture* in 1856, performed in Copenhagen in 1858 as his first orchestral work. The opera itself was written between 1875-77, with the 1856 piece incorporated

Studies in Medievalism VIII, 1996

as its overture (though since the opera's second performance only the slow introduction has been included). The first performance of *King and Marshal* took place at the Royal Theatre in Copenhagen on September 25, 1878. In spite of a fairly cool initial reception, the opera has since held an unrivaled position as the most significant Danish operatic work of the nineteenth century, though it has yet to enjoy a breakthrough in the international musical scene.[1]

Sources, traditions, and history

Nineteenth-century representations of King Erik's murder were based to a large extent on the old popular Danish ballads, generally considered medieval in origin. In 1853 Svend Grundtvig initiated the academic publication of these ballads with his authoritative collection the *Danmarks gamle folkeviser*. Based on surviving manuscripts from the period of the Renaissance, Grundtvig's editions and classifications are now classic, still used by scholars. The songs relating to the murder of King Erik appeared in the first part of the third volume, published in 1858. The dating of these ballads, however, has been an object of debate for years. Furthermore, their melodies do not seem to have been as well preserved as the texts, and in any case scholarly research on the extant melodies did not occur until this century.[2]

Recent research employing new methodological approaches to the ballads concerned with Erik's murder distinguish between a ballad prototype, composed very soon after the murder and before charges were raised concerning it, and much later ballads, which gradually mythologized explanations of the event in light of the conviction of Stig, the king's Lord Marshal. Changing legal and moral issues in subsequent centuries also influenced the variant versions.[3]

Besides these ballads in the Danish language, the melodies as well as the texts of some German songs extant at the time of the murder have been preserved. They were written by the German court poet and singer Meister Rumslant, who seems to have been brought to the Danish court by Margrave Otto V of Brandenburg, brother of Queen Agnes, Erik's wife.[4] Apparently Rumslant was hired by the Danish court after the murder to influence the opinion of the nobility, presumably in order to prepare the ground for the trial at the *Danehof*, the Danish moot or national assembly, in Nyborg in May of 1287, which convicted eight men (primarily noblemen) for plotting the murder and, in addition, the Esquire Arvid Bentsen for actually perpetrating it. It is not known whether these men were present at the moot which turned them into outlaws. Marshal

74   Studies in Medievalism

Stig (and most of the convicted men) afterwards managed to enter the service of the Norwegian king (who was at war with King Erik). In addition to the Danish and German songs, only a few early sources of information exist, mainly short notices in various annals, notably from the Cistercian Ryd Abbey in south Jutland, which reports that Erik was killed in bed, with fifty-six wounds inflicted by trusted men.[5]

Up to the present day historians have oscillated inconclusively between the view that at least part of the verdict of 1287 (concerning the planning of the murder) was a political act—the prevailing opinion for a long time in this century—and more recent, though hesitant, acceptance of the possibility that conviction of Lord Marshal Stig may in fact have been justified. This new view is based primarily on the probable independence of the *Danehof* from the royal court.[6] In any case, much seems to point toward a political motive, taking into consideration the turbulence of the period: quarrels between the king and the nobility had in 1282 resulted in a charter limiting royal rights and clarifying certain legal procedures, and in addition the Danish crown suffered conflicts with Sweden and Norway connected to a certain extent with hereditary claims on crown property and even to the Danish throne. King Erik had attempted to resolve some of these conflicts in 1284 by joining a league of German princes founded the previous year, which among other things obliged its members to certain common procedures in cases of *crimina maiestatis*.

Erik V was born in 1249 and became king-elect at the *Danehof* in 1254, but because of resistance from Jacob Erlandsen, the Archbishop of Lund, was not crowned until 1259, after the death of his father Kristoffer and the imprisonment of the Archbishop by the crown. History to some extent repeated itself as Erik managed to pronounce his then two-year-old son, Erik Menved, king-elect at the *Danehof* in 1276 when all the magnates present paid homage to the boy except Marshal Stig (who nevertheless remained the king's Lord Marshal in spite of this openly hostile action). There can be no doubt that King Erik and his marshal were not on the friendliest of terms, although Stig is recorded among the supporters of the main tenets of royal foreign policy.[7]

The medieval ballad tradition

Not all the recorded Danish ballads normally thought of as popular medieval compositions can be credited with a medieval origin: some in fact seem to be courtly compositions of the sixteenth century.[8] Of the fifteen recorded ballads relating to the murder of Erik V, only two seem traceable to the time immediately following the event. The common refrain of

Heise's *King and Marshal* 75

these two ballads (to which I will return shortly), probably originating from a single ballad sung at the markets in the winter of 1286-87, is also preserved (as is rare among the so-called popular ballads in Denmark) in a medieval fragment from the latter half of the fifteenth century.[9]

Richardt's libretto for *King and Marshal*, like most of the nineteenth-century artistic works based on the murder, tells the story as it is related in the longest of the ballads (no. 145 A in Grundtvig's edition), which is generally considered by recent scholarship to be a sixteenth-century composition.[10] This describes how Marshal Stig is sent to wage war in Sweden, during which time the king seduces Ingeborg, the marshal's wife, a story in some ways resembling the biblical narrative of King David, Uriah, and Bathsheba (II Sam. 11). However, when the marshal returns, Ingeborg tells him what has happened and begs him for revenge against the king, both for the sake of her honor and his. At a moot, Stig throws down the gauntlet to the king. With the help of the son of Ingeborg's sister, the Royal Chamberlain Rane, the king is led away from his retinue during a hunt. King Erik and Rane seek shelter in a barn near the small village of Finderup in northern Jutland after a short episode in which the king tries to seduce a young woman who turns out to be an elf-maid. Betrayed by Rane, the king is killed in Finderup by Stig and his accomplices. At the end of the ballad, attention is turned towards the fate of the outlawed marshal, who with his wife builds a castle on the island of Hjelm, which the new king is unable to wrest from him. Though the ballad confers a tone of tragedy on the murder of Erik, the prevailing attitude, as in most of the extant ballads on the theme, is one of contempt for the king and praise for the courage and perseverance of the marshal.

Richardt's libretto in its general outline follows this ballad in particular and is permeated with expressions more or less derived from it, but to some extent makes use of other ballads as well. The only ballads that deviate significantly from the model of 145 A are the aforementioned two which seem to antedate the trial of the accused nobles in 1287. They present a very different picture, one seemingly much more in line with the contemporary circumstances. Whereas the later ballads are all concerned with the role of Marshal Stig, these two, 145 F and 145 G in Grundtvig's edition, do not identify the murderers at all and do not even mention Stig. They do, however, refer to the turbulence of the Danish political situation in such a way that blame for the murder is not laid on one particular individual. Nor is the event seen as caused by one particular act on the part of the king. The opening lines merely state:

Ther saa mannge y Dannemarck

> *som alle wiill herrer werre . . .*
>
> There are so many in Denmark
> Who all want to become masters . . .[11]

There is no mention in these two ballads of the king's seduction of Ingeborg or of any other immoral conduct on his part. The songs appear faithful to the king—though not in a polemical way, like the courtly German songs of Rumslant mentioned above.[12]

This fact is one of the important points for dating the ballads, but as I see it it is also of signficance for interpreting the medievalism of Heise and Richardt's opera. The difference between the early ballad(s) and the later ones do not only concern historicity or changing attitudes toward the king and his murderers, but also emotional proximity to the event. The late ballads all bear the stamp of a generally narrative posture toward the matter: the murder constitutes a good story with a hero, a villain, and some excitement. The early ballad, on the other hand, reflects shock, clearly stated in the refrain:

> *Nu stander landen i wode.*
>
> Now the land is plunged in sorrow![13]

The text is however quite matter of fact with regard to the murder itself. There are no heroes and no villains except for the initial, and in a sense laconic, statement quoted earlier about the power struggle behind the murder. The song does not take sides, but at the same time it sees the regicide as tragic, very likely from the perspective of those with little or no political power.[14] In contrast to the later ballads, which are more dependent on narrative excitement, the early ballad seems to record a sense of impotence in relation to the nobility and their power struggles.

The ballad tradition in King and Marshal

King and Marshal expands the balladic sources narratively and psychologically, as would be expected in a large-scale music drama of the nineteenth century. With regard to its medievalism, I will limit myself to commenting on two important points: the role of Åse and the role of the king.

Heise and Richardt included an important fictional character drawn from the episode of the elf-maid which appeared in some of the ballads. The character, called Åse in the opera, had taken human form already in the works of Ingemann and Hauch, but in many respects the treatment of

Heise's *King and Marshal*

this figure in *King and Marshal* was quite independent. Heise and Richardt changed her into an innocent country girl to whom the king is attracted at the outset of the action, so that he brings her to his castle in Skander-borg. There Ingeborg arrives with the marshal, and the king loses all interest in Åse, who flees back to the woods. At the end of the opera the king meets her again, as, led by his chamberlain Rane, he is lost in the forest during a hunt on St. Cecilia's day.

Through the first two-thirds of the opera, the king is viewed basically as in the late ballad tradition, a careless scoundrel who cares neither about Åse and Ingeborg nor about the marshal or anything else. At the end of the third act, before the fatal hunt starts, however, the description is deepened—not least musically—to portray a recognizably modern man with a profoundly divided personality, trying to fill up his inner emptiness with lust and action, though not succeeding in the end. He is no Don Giovanni, but on the contrary a depressed man desperately searching for meaning and fulfillment in life. Now, toward the end of the opera and toward the end of his short life, he is realizing this himself.

In the wood he comes upon Åse's cottage. She has just sung her evening prayer. They recognize each other; Åse wants nothing to do with him, while he tries to seduce her again, but in a dreamlike, distracted way: half unconscious, half conscious of the futility of his desires. Rane, claiming to have found the way, calls for the king to mount his horse and leads him to Finderup. Åse stays and takes up her evening prayer again, now transforming it into a more sorrowful expression (in the minor key), praying for the king—for whom, it becomes clear, she still harbors warm feelings in spite of his betrayal.

In the barn at Finderup the weary king becomes increasingly desperate as he realizes both his precarious situation and the fact that it is the day of St. Cecilia, to which Ingeborg had summoned him in a dream. Obviously the king is not characterized as a hero: quite the contrary. It is interesting, however, that what in the ballad tradition and in earlier romantic reception of the story was deprecated becomes here a sympathetic representation of modern man: fearful, empty, and helpless to change his fate. Some of these implications are present in Carsten Hauch's tragedy as well, but they are not brought emotionally to the same level as in the opera.

The marshal arrives and demands that the king come forth. While the latter hides in the hay, Rane points to the hiding place, at the same time protesting aloud that the king is not there. The marshal states revenge as his purpose and together with his followers stabs the king. Already marked for death, the king—claiming his position as the Lord's anointed—thereupon condemns the marshal to be an outlaw and dies with Ingeborg's name on his lips. The marshal, though not particularly heroic at this point, can only state that even if he is to become an outlaw his deed will never be forgotten.

All leave—and the stage is gradually filled with a chorus of peasants, huntsmen, and monks from the nearby abbey. Dismay pervades the atmosphere, and all exclaim in woeful cries,

> *Vee! Dankongen i sit Blod!*
>
> Alas! Alas! Alas!
> The king lies in his blood![15]

Finally, Åse enters. She had found the sword the king had left in her cottage and wanted to bring it to him, aware of the dangers by which he was surrounded (especially since she heard the horses riding by). She now sings the following words to a melody only slightly transformed from that accompanying her first meeting with the king in the woods prior to their brief and unfulfilled love affair:

> I wanted to bring you your sword, King Erik! I was too late!
> But the sword-hilt is a cross and I place it now upon your blood-stained bier, bedewed with Aase's bitter, bitter tears.[16]

The melody, with the Danish text, is as follows:

Figure 1. Piano score for *Drot og marsk*, 270-71.

Rhythmically as well as melodically this softens the tense atmosphere of cries and orchestral chords. Furthermore, on the very last of Åse's notes, the chorus of people take up the rhythm of her brief song to the refrain of the early ballad text, already quoted above: *Now the land is plunged in sorrow!* At the same time monks chant *Requiem aeternam dona eis, Domine*, the text of the Introit of the medieval requiem mass, as a counterpoint to the ballad text. Åse and the people supplement this with the prayer *God in his mercy keep us all!*[17]

Heise's *King and Marshal*

Figure 2. Piano score for *Drot og marsk*, 271.

There can be no doubt that Åse's short lines, musically even more directly than textually, transform the scene from one of petrified shock into an expression of grief and prayer for the dead king. In a sense her singing permits the reinstatement of the medieval liturgy with which nineteenth-century man no longer preserved a spontaneous and direct contact: her sincere and tenderly innocent singing ushers in the song of mourning for Denmark as well as the requiem for the king. What is interesting is that for this final transition from the interpretation found in the late ballads—with the king as villain and the marshal as hero—to a nineteenth-century, almost *fin-de-siècle* interpretation of the tragic event, Heise and his librettist (who could have had no knowledge of the dating of the ballads) chose to use the text of the early ballad as well as the requiem mass, thus to some extent (inadvertently) approaching recorded reactions contemporary with the murder in the thirteenth century.

There is no appropriation of medieval music in the opera aside from what a Danish musicologist describes convincingly as "the gloss of musical popular ballad pastiche."[18] Instead, what we have is a musical underlining of the textual medievalism. The idea of a redemption through Åse is of course a romantic commonplace, and it is found in precisely the equivalent situation in Hauch's play, where the corresponding figure is called Sigrid, a noblewoman making her dwelling near an abbey in the woods, much as Åse does. She also brings the king his sword at his deathbed and, thereby concluding the tragedy, says,

> Alas! We came too late, it is in vain. The wild revenge has already found its victim.
>
> Oh, if only my soul could expire at your breast and if only life could end in this stream of tears as it has in the bloody spring pouring out of your heart.
>
> Nay, if only the love of another person can redeem a spirit then this shall happen to yours. For now my whole life will be transformed into an eternal requiem for your salvation.[19]

On the premises of secular music drama, *King and Marshal* assimilates a traditional romantic religious idea constituting an internal redemption from the despair accumulated over the course of the opera's action. The conclusion, in a fragmented requiem for King Erik interwoven with the lament refrain, *Nu stander landen i wode*, from the early ballad, shows how the music drama—in contrast to the tragedy it builds on—intuitively returned to the liturgy and the purest medieval ballad tradition: not only in order to present the theme of redemption, but also to express that theme by means of its musical and textual correlatives.

Heise's *King and Marshal*

NOTES

An earlier version of this paper was presented at the Twenty-Ninth International Congress on Medieval Studies, Western Michigan University, May 1994. My thanks to Fran Hopenwasser and Leif Stubbe Teglberg for a number of corrections, and for helping me express my thoughts in understandable English.

1. Details of Heise's life are from the only existing biography, Gustav Hetsch, *Peter Heise* (Copenhagen, 1926). On *King and Marshal*, see, in addition to Hetsch, Dan Fog, *Verzeichnis der gedruckten Kompositionen von Peter Heise* (Copenhagen, 1991), 78; Niels Martin Jensen, Introduction, liner notes for the Chandos recording of *King and Marshal*, conductor M. Schønwandt (Colchester, 1993), 7-10. Niels Schiørring, *Musikkens Historie i Danmark* (Copenhagen, 1977-78), gives 1854 as the date of the *Marsk Stig Overture*'s first performance (44).

Heise, who died only a year after the premiere of *King and Marshal*, did little to promote his works, either in Denmark or elsewhere. Even in Denmark, only a few of his works have been performed regularly, and mainly it is his songs that are still in print. At the turn of the century his opera was recommended, especially to the German stage, by Danish artists. The only result, however, was a production at the Court Opera in Stuttgart in 1906, with a rather cool reception and only three performances (Hetsch, 185-86). It is probably suggestive of the lack of notice Heise's opera received that it is not even mentioned in Jens Malte Fischer, "Singende Recken und blitzende Schwerter. Die Mittelalteroper neben und nach Wagner: Ein Überblick," in *Mittelalter-Rezeption*, ed. Peter Wapnewski (Stuttgart, 1986), 511-30; see especially Appendix A, 525-28, chronologically listing operas on medieval subjects from 1860-1927, thus covering a period including the first performance of *King and Marshal* as well as the Stuttgart performance.

A German-language piano score was printed in 1905 for the Stuttgart performance, containing some changes and abbreviations from the original edition of 1878-79 (Fog, 83-84). Even today the piano scores (in Danish and in German) are the only existing printed versions of the opera, not even reprinted in recent years. I refer to the Danish (original) and unabbreviated piano score by Axel Grandjean (Copenhagen: Wilhelm Hansen, n. d. [but first published 1878-79]); also the German-language score (Copenhagen and Leipzig: Wilhelm Hansen, n. d.), according to Fog (84) published in 1905.

2. Svend Grundtvig, ed., *Danmarks gamle folkeviser*, vol. 3 (Copenhagen, 1862); see especially 348-85, where fifteen different songs about the murder of King Erik V are classified (each with some variants), 145 A-145 O, with an introduction by Grundtvig, 338-49.

I refer also to the following more recent treatments of the transmitted ballads connected with the murder of King Erik: Ellen Jørgensen, ed., *Erik Klipping og hans sønner. Rigets opløsing. Udvalg af kilder til tidsrummet 1275-1340* (Copenhagen, 1927), 132-53; Ernst von der Recke, ed., *Danmarks Fornviser* (Copenhagen, 1928), 95-129; H. Grüner Nielsen and Karl-Ivar Hildeman, ed., *Danmarks gamle folkeviser*,

84   Studies in Medievalism

10. 1. *Teksttillæg* (Copenhagen, 1933-58), 318-31; Helge Toldberg, *Marsk Stig-viserne*, Studier fra Sprog-og oldtidsforskning 252 (Copenhagen, 1963); Leif Søndergaard, "Meningsdannelse og mytedannelse i marsk Stig-viserne," and Iørn Piø, "Hvem skrev den lange Marsk Stig-vise?" both in Jens E. Olesen, Reinhold Schröder, Leif Søndergaard, and Iørn Piø, ed., *Marsken rider igen. Om mordet på Erik Klipping, Rumelands sange og marsk Stig-viserne* (Odense, 1990), 59-85, especially 87-92.

For a more general approach to the medieval ballad I refer in particular to Iørn Piø, *Nye veje til folkevisen* (Copenhagen, 1985), with an English summary 327-34, and Nils Schiørring, "Transmission and Study of the Melodies," in Thorkild Knudsen, Svend Nielsen, and Nils Schiørring, ed., *Danmarks gamle folkeviser* (Copenhagen, 1976), 10 (*Tunes*): *9-*39.

3.   See particularly Søndergaard, 60-69, and Piø, *Nye veje*, 19-22, 246-52.

4.   Joachim Bumke, *Mäzene im Mittelalter. Die Gönner und Auftrager der höfischen Literatur in Deutschland 1150-1300* (Munich, 1979), 228, 614-16; Piø, *Nye veje*, 271; and Reinhold Schröder, "Dâvon sing ich ü diz liet. Rumelands strofer i anledning af Erik Klippings død," in Olesen et al., especially 47-50.

5.   See Jørgensen, 1-49. For recent discussions by Danish historians, I refer to Kai Hørby, "Velstands krise og tusind baghold, 1250-1400," *Gyldendals og Politikens Danmarkshistorie* (Copenhagen, 1989), 5: 135-54, and Jens E. Olesen, "Kongemord og fredløshedsdom," in Olesen et al., 10-34.

6.   Thus Hørby, 150-51; Olesen et al., especially 30-31.

7.   Hørby concludes, commenting on this fact, that this is symtomatic of the weak position of the crown at this time (135-36); see also 150.

8.   See Piø, *Nye veje*, 21, and Piø, "Hvem skrev."

9.   Ballads 145 F and G in Grundtvig's edition of 1858 are clearly interrelated and very different from all other transmitted ballads both in detail and overall composition. See Søndergaard, 59-60, compared with Piø, *Nye veje*, 246-52; see also Hørby, 146-47. Of these two ballads, Søndergaard has argued for the priority of 145 G as the more original (145 F preserves a number of its characteristics, however).

10.   See Piø, *Nye veje*, 246; Søndergaard, 61; and mainly Piø, "Hvem skrev."

11.   Piø, *Nye veje*, 248 (translation mine).

12.   Søndergaard, 71.

13.   Piø, *Nye veje*, 246; the translation is by Jonathan Sydenham from the liner notes to the Chandos recording, 65.

14.   Cf. Søndergaard, 71.

15.   Sydenham translation, 64; Danish piano score, 269-70.

16.   Sydenham translation, 65; Danish piano score, 271-73.

17.   Sydenham translation, 65; Danish piano score, 271-73.

18.   Jensen, 9. There are no medieval melodies preserved for the transmitted ballads except for a melody used in the Faroe Islands, most likely belonging to a different ballad, but in one instance, however, transmitted for the previously mentioned *Der er så mange* . . . See Hjalmar Thuren and H. Grüner-Nielsen, ed., *Færøske melodier til danske kæmpeviser* (Copenhagen, 1923), 42, no. 314, reprinted

Heise's *King and Marshal*

as addendum A, "Editions of Tunes in Faroese Tradition," in Knudsen, Nielsen, and Schiørring.

19. My (prose) translation of the following passage from Carsten Hauch, *Marsk Stig: Tragødie i fem Akter* (Copenhagen, 1850), 140-41:

Vee mig! Vi kom for seent, det er forgjeves;
Den vilde Hevn har alt sit Offer fundet.
O, kunde jeg min Sjæl udaande ved
Dit Bryst, og kunde Livet rinde bort
I denne Taarestrøm som i den Kilde,
Der blodig springer af dit Hjerte frem!
—Ja, hvis en Andens Kjærlighed en Aand
Forløse kan, da skal det skee med din;
Thi nu mit hele Liv skal sig forvandle
Til en bestandig Sjælemesse for din Frelse.

Medievalism in the Service of the Swedish Proletariat: Jan Fridegård's Viking Trilogy

Robert E. Bjork

Oppressed laborers and the Viking era were two subjects of passionate interest for Jan Fridegård (1897-1968), a prominent, influential, and still widely read Swedish novelist. Given his personal background, the first interest was inescapable. Fridegård was born into a poor working-class family of seven in Enköpings-Näs, an area in central Sweden just north of Lake Mälar. His father was a *statare*, a farm worker tied to a large estate and earning his wages partly in cash but mostly in kind (*stat*). The brutal estate-worker system, which arose in the eighteenth century to support the aristocratic estates and survived until 1945, almost guaranteed illiteracy and social immobility in its victims and has a pervasive role in Fridegård's work. Of his close to thirty novels and his numerous short stories and essays, most are autobiographical, depicting the wretched lives of lower-class working people.[1]

Given Fridegård's nationality, the second interest was inescapable as well. In Scandinavian literature the Viking world appears in a relatively unbroken line in works from such authors as Esaias Tegnér (1782-1846), Erik Gustaf Geijer (1783-1847), Adam Oehlenschläger (1779-1850), and Johan Ludwig Runeberg (1804-1877) to Henrik Ibsen (1828-1906), Frans G. Bengtsson (1894-1954), Vilhelm Moberg (1898-1973), Halldor Laxness (b. 1902), and Villy Sørensen (b. 1929).[2] The early writers naturally engage in romanticizing and idealizing the Viking warrior, turning him into a symbol of Scandinavian purity and strength, while later writers tend to take a much more sceptical, sometimes ironic, view. For Tegnér, the

Studies in Medievalism VIII, 1996

Fridegård's Viking Trilogy

Viking was a civilized, noble seafarer, but for Laxness, he was a grotesque parody of a true hero.[3]

When Fridegård, then, combined these two particular interests—the oppressed and the Vikings—into a compelling, powerful, tendentious trilogy of novels, he was working within an established tradition, even as he intended not to praise the Vikings but to use them as a medium for social criticism. His novels also fit within a subgroup of that critical tradition, the group focused on Viking thralls. Three Nobel Prize winners writing before Fridegård, for instance, the Dane Karl Gjellerup (1857-1919), the Swede Selma Lagerlöf (1858-1940), and the Norwegian Sigrid Undset (1882-1949), treat thralls sympathetically, and strictly within Swedish literature Fredrika Bremer (1801-65), Viktor Rydberg (1828-95), Verner von Heidenstam (1859-1940), and Gustaf Fröding (1860-1911) all show varying degrees of compassion for the Viking slave. Bremer does so in her play about oppression and hatred, *The Slave Girl* (*Trälinnan*, 1840); Rydberg in his attack on industrialism in his poem "The New Song of Grotti" ("Den nya Grottesången," 1891), a reworking of the Old Norse *Grottasongr*; Heidenstam in his mildly critical depiction of slavery in his novel about eleventh-century Sweden, *The Tree of the Folkungs* (*Folkungaträdet*, 1905, 1907); and Fröding in his radical reinterpretation of the Old Norse legend of Weyland in his poem "The Smith" ("Smeden," 1892), which I will discuss below.[4] No one before Fridegård, however, concentrated so much interest in the Viking thralls and what he felt had to be their inevitable fight for freedom.

His trilogy centers on a ninth-century thrall named Holme, Holme's wife Ausi, and their daughter Tora. The first of the novels, *Land of Wooden Gods* (*Trägudars land*, 1940), chronicles Holme's struggle against his enemies, initially as a relatively helpless blacksmith slave who witnesses his chieftain order Holme's newborn baby put out in the forest to die. The ruthless act moves Holme to his initial revolt: he rescues the child, returns to the settlement for Ausi, and then all three take refuge in a cave deep in the forest before leaving the area altogether. Holme eventually establishes himself as a respected blacksmith in a flourishing Viking trade center, probably based on the historical town Birka, on Lake Mälar.[5] The novel also begins the story of the clash between paganism and Christianity in Sweden. A missionary arrives at Birka simultaneously with Holme and his family, tries valiantly but gradually fails miserably in his efforts to convert the Swedes, and is finally sacrificed to the gods and hung in a sacred tree after attempting to burn down a heathen temple in Uppsala. The novel ends with the threat of renewed incursions of Christian missionaries, modelled on Ansgar, the archbishop of Hamburg, and his companion Witmar, who conducted the first recorded mission to Sweden in c. 830 A. D.

The second volume of the trilogy, *People of the Dawn* (*Gryningsfolket*, 1944), finds Holme struggling against his oppressors once more, primarily his former owner's wife and her brother Geire—a powerful Viking warrior who rapes Ausi with his sister's help—but also the Christians, who consider Holme their most awesome foe. By the end of the book, Holme has led an uprising of starving slaves against their masters and the merciless Christians, has killed Geire with his bare hands, and has again had to flee to the forest to save himself and his family. Sixteen years after escaping their owner in *Land of Wooden Gods*, Holme and Ausi return to exile and the safety of the cave once more.

The last volume of the trilogy, *Sacrificial Smoke* (*Offerrök*, 1949), develops the account of the increasingly bloody strife between the pagan darkness and the Christian light and between freemen, both Christian and pagan, and thralls. The Christians are more malevolent in the conflict than the heathens—"blood was always running wherever they went, despite their saying that they didn't offer human sacrifices" (60)—and Holme's blood finally does flow because of their malevolence. The Christian priests feel in their hearts that "it was they who should dispose of God's enemy. How they did it didn't matter" (111). The four warriors they send to ambush Holme at the novel's close die violently, and Holme makes his way arduously to the cave before succumbing to his own wounds. Ausi then commits suicide by her husband's side, and Fridegård concludes the trilogy as follows:

> A late summer cloud passed over the town on the island; the warring parties dispersed again without resolving the conflict, and the grinning wooden gods looked across at the Christian church. The Christian priests would flee this rugged land yet again, and what they called the heathen darkness would hover over it for a hundred years more.
> Like two trails of blood, Christendom and the fight for freedom would proceed through the centuries side by side. The town would be destroyed, and for centuries, no one would know where it had been. But the two trails that originated there have still not, a thousand years later, reached their destination. (186-87)[6]

Fridegård had little evidence for substantiating his portrayal of Viking slavery, just a brief study or two, and so most of the story and much of

Fridegård's Viking Trilogy

the milieu in the Holme trilogy Fridegård created himself.[7] The backdrop for Fridegård's anti-ideal saga basically develops out of three different kinds of sources: archaeological descriptions of the Viking period, such as a Norwegian museum catalogue and reports about excavation sites; cultural studies, such as a 1938 work on Nordic religion and Christianity; and a ninth-century life of St. Ansgar.[8] The first kind of source allows Fridegård to create a believable atmosphere, for which he has often been praised.[9] From descriptions of buildings to those of agricultural techniques, burial practices, and beer-brewing methods, Fridegård has been fairly precise, making only occasional and understandable errors, as when he refers to horned helmets, which Vikings never actually wore. To insure the right historical flavor, Fridegård even takes the names of his characters from rune stones in the Uppland area of Sweden and limits both dialogue and the use of archaisms to a minimum, since either device could easily make the novels sound false.[10]

The second kind of source material, cultural studies, enables Fridegård to establish a primitivistic or naturalistic atmosphere that he felt was so important for a period not as yet fully restricted by the Christian antipathy to sexuality. For example, he draws heavily on Helge Ljungberg's *Nordic Religion and Christianity: Studies in the Nordic Religious Shift during the Viking Period*, which provides a thorough analysis of the pagan temple at Uppsala and the nine-day festival of sacrifice that used to take place there.[11] In *Land of Wooden Gods*, Fridegård devotes over thirty pages (115-49) to that festival, detailing such matters as some of the seventy-two animal and human sacrifices to Odin and Thor, as well as the orgiastic tributes to Freyr, the fertility god. On the first day of offering to the latter, the following takes place:

> The singers gathered around the god, and the crowd fell completely silent. A man's loud, clear voice began singing, and Ausi listened, half-dazed. But what she heard couldn't be possible! What male thralls talked of only when they didn't think there was a woman around the man was singing about in front of everyone. You just didn't sing about such things! Everyone joined in; then the voice was alone again, still describing all that could happen between a man and a woman in private
> . . . .
> The singing continued, but something else was in the air. . . . Two people, a man and a woman, emerged from the temple. Both wore only light skirts and were the stateliest figures Ausi had ever seen . . . . The man and the woman performed a dance,

90 Studies in Medievalism

> revealing enough of what the skirts hid to drive the crowd wild. Ausi was burning with a flame that had to be quenched. . . . The dance of tribute to the fertility god ended with the beautiful couple partially blocked from view behind his effigy. There they enacted, actually or symbolically, something that made the crowd boil and surge like a forest in storm. The crowd could catch only rapid glimpses of one or the other's movements and then finally the woman's head on one side, cast back, flower-adorned hair hanging down. The god's body concealed the rest, and he grinned as if in mute empathy with the spectators. (141-42)

In creating a primitivistic atmosphere, Fridegård aligns himself with authors such as Sherwood Anderson (1876-1941), whose *Dark Laughter* (1925) he greatly admired, and D. H. Lawrence (1885-1930), whose *The Plumed Serpent* (1926) may have influenced his erotic descriptions in *Land of Wooden Gods* and *Sacrificial Smoke*.[12] Fridegård's "primitivism" in these novels further augments their sense of historical accuracy and verisimilitude.

The third source that Fridegård used in writing his trilogy, chiefly for *People of the Dawn* and *Sacrificial Smoke*, is Bishop Rimbert's *Vita Anskarii* (*The Life of Ansgar*), and this source, unlike the other two, he modifies for his own purposes.[13] While he frequently follows Rimbert quite closely, he just as frequently deviates severely from the *Vita*. Some of his inaccuracies may be inadvertent, such as his anachronistic depiction of Christ as a frail, effeminate god, an image that is the product of the late, not early, Middle Ages.[14] But others clearly are not. Ansgar, for example, did not neglect the poor, as Fridegård implies throughout *People of the Dawn* and *Sacrificial Smoke*, but instead founded a hospital for them in Bremen and "gave away for the support of the poor a tenth of the animals and of all his revenues and a tenth of the tithes which belonged to him, and whatever money or property of any kind came to him he gave a tenth for the benefit of the poor." Neither would Ansgar have countenanced the lust for money that Fridegård's priests display, especially in *Sacrificial Smoke*. Rimbert tells us that Ansgar gave strict orders to missionaries "that they should not desire nor seek to obtain the property of anyone" but rather "be content with food and raiment."[15] And finally, Fridegård's implication that Christianity exacerbated the problem of slavery instead of solving it does not bear scrutiny. Modern historians, in fact, tell us precisely the opposite.[16] Fridegård has obviously made deliberate changes in Rimbert's account of the period for a political agenda that is anarchist in origin and

Fridegård's Viking Trilogy   91

demands a rereading of history. Since little history actually exists for slaves, and none for the rebellions they raise in the trilogy, Fridegård creates a story fabricated in many particulars, but based on a socialist understanding of the processes of history and, from his point of view, therefore true in its essential outline: oppressed people necessarily rebel against their oppressors. As an anti-ideal designed to undermine a political and literary image of Sweden's past which venerates the Viking and ignores the thrall, the Holme trilogy remakes Nordic history to create a new ethos. In Fridegård's new myth, Holme functions centrally as a representative of the rising proletariat in Sweden, and the interconnections Fridegård establishes between him and the other characters in the novels becomes of paramount importance.[17] They are the focus of Fridegård's higher purpose of reinterpreting history through anarchist ideology, and they are what make the trilogy a serious work of social and philosophical criticism.

To understand how Fridegård uses Holme to advance his cause, we must look closely at Gustaf Fröding's "The Smith," a poem that greatly impressed Fridegård.[18] In forty-eight lines, Fröding recreates the Old Norse legend of Weyland (Völundr), the king of the elves and a skillful smith, who, along with his prize sword, is captured by the Swedish king Nithuthr. Nithuthr, wanting to take advantage of Weyland's skills, has Weyland's hamstrings cut so he cannot escape and then isolates him on an island where he has to make treasures for Nithuthr. When Nithuthr's two sons come to see Weyland work, he cuts off their heads and makes their skulls into silver vessels for Nithuthr, their eyes into jewels for Nithuthr's wife, and their teeth into a necklace for Nithuthr's daughter. Through artifice, a laughing Weyland then raises himself aloft and out of reach.[19]

In his rendition, Fröding dispenses with the specifics of the Weyland story, focusing instead on the idea of the smith's rebellion against his oppressors. The poem opens with the poet dreaming he is walking through a coal-black forest with treetops like iron and a wind that causes the surroundings to quake, not whisper. The path he walks on is strewn with soot, not covered with grass, and there he hears one noise that sounds like people tramping heavily and another that resembles the muffled sound of a sword clashing against a dagger. As he dreams, the poet discovers that he is near Weyland's valley and that the sound he hears carries the warning of impending storm "and the feud of the mighty powers" ("och de väldiga makternas fejd"). When he hears the clanging of a hammer and sees sparks rising, he moves forward to investigate, but all he finds is a scraggly, hunched, dishevelled smith, with low forehead and crooked back, a mere slave laborer, "one of the thralls who in cellars dwell / beneath the masters' trampling heels" ("en av trälarnes folk, som i källrar bo / under herrarnes trampande häl"). The poet thinks the man is a modern, harmless smith. But then the smith rises, becoming tall, noble, and straight. His mighty arm strikes with its tool at the smithy's iron roof, "and heavy as a mountain the hammer fell / and like thunder was the roar of the blow" ("och tungt som ett fjäll föll hammarens slag / och som åskan var slagets dån"). Weyland has been a thrall smith for a thousand years, says the poet, but now he fashions the sword of revenge that will destroy the dwelling of the gods. The dreamer then realizes that the forest is actually a modern factory that will one day feel the force of Weyland's revolt. It, like the forest, is filled with a noise like the clashing of sword against dagger, and soot covers its walls and roof as well.[20]

Now Fröding transforms the thrall smith in the course of the poem in three specific ways, all of which have importance for Fridegård's Holme trilogy: first, he changes the bent and scraggly thrall smith into a massive, noble figure; second, he turns the nameless, insignificant, unattractive slave into the legendary Weyland, who is capable of leading a revolution; and third, after changing the smith into Weyland, he also conflates Weyland with the Nordic god Thor, whose hammer makes thunder and protects gods and men from their enemies. Fridegård uses the same pattern of transformation in depicting Holme.

Holme's transformations into a noble figure and into a figure capable of leading a revolution are easy to apprehend. Although Holme is never bent and scraggly, he does crouch in *Land of Wooden Gods* as an animal would and is even likened there to various animals (e. g., he flew through the woods, "silent as an owl"; slept outside the cave "and snorted like a dog"; resembled "a wild animal ready to spring" [9, 30, 154]), as well as to a shadow and ghost. He also has "broader cheekbones than the others" (6), reminiscent of Fröding's smith's low forehead, and a primitive, "bent-kneed walk" (70). After he has established himself as a respected smith in Birka, however, such imagery rarely occurs, and his cheekbones make him "look like a wooden god" (171).[21] A change in Holme's relationship to his antagonists coincides with the disappearance of animal imagery. His stature, strength, and capabilities become magnified as the trilogy progresses, and he, like Weyland, becomes larger than life.

The outcome of his first major, life-threatening confrontation in *Land of Wooden Gods* seems doubtful from the start. After taking refuge in the cave with Ausi and their baby, Holme is discovered by the most powerful and feared warrior from the settlement, Stenulf, who orders all of them to come back with him. Holme refuses, a fight ensues, and Ausi, expecting to see Holme fall at any moment, takes action.

Fridegård's Viking Trilogy 93

Ausi crept out and grabbed the spear leaning against the cave entrance. Holme had been moving in a half-circle, and Stenulf, following him, had his back to her. Ausi took the spear in both hands, rushed forward, and thrust it into Stenulf from behind.

A severe jolt almost knocked her off her feet, and the spear shattered in two. Stenulf had swung violently behind his back with his sword, catching the spear in the middle. As he did so, he lost balance, reeled, and was unable to parry Holme's blow fully. The ax grazed his neck.

Inexplicably, the fight stopped. Stenulf sheathed his sword and, with a look of arrogance at the thralls, walked up the ridge toward the settlement. Blood pulsed from his neck . . . . (41)

Stenulf bleeds to death, clearly not the result of Holme's superior might. Holme never will know if he could have defeated Stenulf and will never feel proud of his dubious victory.

In the rest of the trilogy, however, neither Holme nor we have any doubts about his abilities and superiority to all his foes. His strength is manifest and feared throughout, and Geire's demise in *People of the Dawn* is swift because of it. Unable to draw his sword to fend off Holme's attack, he feels himself in Holme's grip and "could feel death in [its] incredible power. He felt himself rise into the air, saw the sky and the stone walls flash before his eyes, and then everything was dark and quiet" (187). And in *Sacrificial Smoke*, a band of invading Vikings scatters before Holme's charge: "The invaders began leaping out of the way of this raging giant. His reach exceeded theirs, and the power of his blows made their weapons fly from their hands" (170).

A change in Holme's relationship to other human beings also takes place as the trilogy progresses; Holme moves from committing selfish, brutal acts, to being moved by mercy and understanding. In *Land of Wooden Gods* we are told that Holme, like Stenulf before him and Geire after him, had raped Ausi. During Holme's fight with Stenulf, Ausi remembers the incident. "She hadn't been able to do anything to defend herself. She thought [Stenulf] was going to do it again once, but it turned out to be Holme instead. Though she feared and hated Holme, she had been glad it was him instead of Stenulf" (40). Holme also commits three other acts of brutality in the first volume that shock the reader and that Holme will come to regret later in the trilogy. On one occasion, in retribution for the chieftain's trying to kill Holme's baby, Holme hurls a rock at the chieftain's own child, hitting him at the base of the neck and permanently maiming him (32). On another, wanting a house that once was his, Holme confronts the current and rightful inhabitant, ordering him out, then killing him when the man objects. "There was no sound except the ax blow and the soft thud when the man hit the floor. Immediately Holme grabbed him and dragged him out into the woods" (191). And, most disturbingly, on the third occasion Holme puts Ausi's child by another man out in the forest to die. The child is the result of the orgies in honor of Freyr in Uppsala, and Holme wants no part of it. "But deep in the woods a tiny blue face shone rigidly and questioningly back at the moon, which sank gradually among the dense branches of the spruce trees. The baby's new mother—cold—had not taken long to lull it to sleep" (188).

In *People of the Dawn*, however, Holme would commit no such act. He has the chance, for example, to kill the two men responsible for carrying his baby into the woods to meet certain death, but he foregoes it because "they were alone and old now and had a right to stay and fend for themselves" (67). In the same novel, he leads starving thralls to the Christian storehouses and doles all the grain out to them, totally neglecting himself (57). This selflessness and concern for others develops into a full-fledged vision of freedom, without violence, for all humankind in *Sacrificial Smoke*. The transformation that begins within Holme eventually has ramifications for all around him as he becomes a revolutionary leader.

The third transformation of Holme, into a kind of Thor figure, is by far the most complex. It develops simultaneously with the other two, beginning, curiously enough, with the pre-Ansgarian missionary, "the Stranger," in *Land of Wooden Gods* and ending with the conflation of Holme, the Stranger, Christ, and Thor by the end of the trilogy. The Stranger, first of all, represents a primitive, "socialist" kind of Christianity that is egalitarian, non-materialistic, and dedicated to converting society from the bottom up.[22] In the Stranger's case, he begins with the thralls, going "down among the workers and the overburdened" as Christ once did (76). This socialist ideal has an obvious affinity with what Holme later develops in the trilogy, for he too works for an egalitarian society beginning with the thralls. Never forgetting the time he spent in servitude, he divides the smithy's earnings equally among all who work there (*Dawn*, 25), "associated with thralls as equals" even though he was free (37), and makes sure in handing out grain during the famine that every one, baptized or not, gets an equal share of food (56).

Other aspects of the Stranger's character and description, however, tie him still more closely to Holme. Both he and Holme, for example, come from distant lands, which makes them somewhat mysterious (*Wooden Gods*, 19, 67); both seem to some to be sorcerers (*Wooden Gods*, 19, 60, 68);

Fridegård's Viking Trilogy   95

both have striking eyes (*Wooden Gods*, 24, 30, 68, 74); and both have a powerful effect on Ausi, who perceives another similarity. The Stranger "must have been closer to Christ than those who came after him," and Holme too "was a lot like Christ" (*Dawn*, 152) in helping the poor (*Dawn*, 173) and defending the weak (*Smoke*, 46). Holme probably would not have appreciated the comparison, but Ausi makes it nonetheless and solidifies Holme's identification with Christ and the Stranger as the trilogy develops. The Stranger, for instance, actually becomes Christ. As Ausi walks through the market town in *People of the Dawn*, she has a revelation:

> Suddenly she stopped. Something was lighting up and expanding inside her, and she was breathing heavily. She saw everything now. The Stranger had been Christ Himself, come to earth once more. He was as gentle and good as the sun; He tolerated everything without complaint; and He wanted nothing for Himself. He endured death without fear. He was Christ, and He had come back for her sake. (76)

Ausi also feels that Christ and Holme live inside her ("With Christ and Holme living peacefully together within her, who could do her harm?" [*Dawn*, 83]), and she knows too that "for a long time she had belonged only to Holme and Christ" (*Dawn*, 99). In addition, Ausi observes, all three men are tormented and eventually die for their revolutionary faiths. The Stranger and Christ had both been tortured to death (*Dawn*, 76), and both Holme and Christ "had been beaten and persecuted; that was why He was on the side of Holme and the thralls" (*Dawn*, 198). Holme, more like Christ than His priests, was willing to offer his own life "if it meant saving his thrall companions" (*Smoke*, 183, 151).

Holme's faith and substance partakes of more than the primitive Christianity represented by the Stranger. It partakes as well of the Nordic religion represented by Thor. Here again, I believe, Fridegård takes liberties with his sources in order to advance his view of history as he transposes his paradigm for Christianity's development—from egalitarian to elitist—onto Nordic paganism. We have no evidence, after all, that the Norse gods were undemocratic in bestowing their favors on their subjects, as Fridegård says they were (e. g., *Wooden Gods*, 86, 137). Instead we have considerable proof that Thor was the god of common men and peasants, perhaps even thralls.[23] He was, in fact, more like the Weyland/Thor figure in Fröding's poem than the battle god in the trilogy, and Fridegård fashions Holme in the Fröding mold in distinct, though subtle, ways.

In *Land of Wooden Gods* Fridegård first creates a broad and loose association between the god and Holme by making the latter a smith as well as a thrall. Holme is not just any smith, but one who, like Weyland, "could do anything with his hands, coming as he probably did from across the sea where people had magic powers" (19). In addition, Thor was the patron of smiths, a fact that may account for the otherwise curious transformation that Weyland undergoes in Fröding's poem. And the thralls' weapon and tool, the ax, was considered "a bolt from the thunder god" (*Smoke*, 24) and was as strongly associated with Thor as his hammer was. That Holme actually uses both the hammer and ax in battle brings an even closer association between him and Thor. The silver amulets representing Thor's hammer may have been made in conscious opposition to symbols of the Cross, and Holme uses his hammer several times against Christian symbols.

In *People of the Dawn* "Holme ran without a sword toward the Christians; before anyone knew what had happened, he had smashed the baptismal font to bits with his sledgehammer" (56). He later topples the bell tower, caves in the church door, and finally demolishes the Christian altar with it: "the holy relics bounced high into the air and landed in the hands of thralls" (*Dawn*, 102-103). Holme's hammer, it seems, becomes Thor's, and his acts also reflect those of the god, to whom men turned for protection from Christ. Furthermore, consciously or not, Fridegård draws the parallel between Holme and Thor still tighter by alluding to Holme's intimidating power. In legend, Thor challenges Christ to battle, but Christ backs down before Thor's superior might.[24] In *People of the Dawn* Ausi knows that "Christ was powerful, but who could stand up against Holme?" (24). Holme renders all gods, "both the old ones and the new one," powerless (*Dawn*, 34). Finally, Fridegård likens Holme to a wooden god twice (*Wooden Gods*, 171; *Dawn*, 135), portrays him as the leader for "everyone who still believed in the ancient wooden gods" (*Smoke*, 136), and later places him in Thor's traditional spot in the middle of the heathen temple during the final confrontation with the Christians (*Smoke*, 148).

Holme, of course, never fully becomes Thor, just as he never fully becomes Christ. His life is far too rooted in a socio-economic, rather than a religious or spiritual, reality for him to be either. Instead, he rises up a noble, straight-backed, and clear-sighted man, with his thoughts fixed on the welfare of his fellows. His ultimate vision, then, fleetingly realized through Ausi's eyes in her dying moments, is not that of the destruction coming with a Ragnarök or Armageddon but of the creation of a just and different world. That vision gives him strength and stature, and the new myth that Fridegård creates through Holme thus proceeds not from a

Fridegård's Viking Trilogy 97

godhead, Christian or pagan, but from an idea—that to all humankind belong freedom and equality. Fridegård has rewritten myth in his Holme trilogy to give the proletariat a history and a hope. In the distant past, in the beginnings of Scandinavian society, lie the beginnings of a better future.

NOTES

This essay is a revised and expanded version of the afterword to my translation of Jan Fridegård's *Land of Wooden Gods* (*Trägudars land*, 1940; Lincoln: University of Nebraska Press, 1989), 195-207. The other two volumes, which I have also translated, are *People of the Dawn* (*Gryningsfolket*, 1940) and *Sacrificial Smoke* (*Offerrök*, 1949), also published by the University of Nebraska Press (1990, 1991).

1. See, for example, my translation of the Lars Hård trilogy: *I, Lars Hård* (*Jag Lard Hård*, 1935; Lincoln: University of Nebraska Press, 1983) and *Jacob's Ladder* and *Mercy* (*Tack för himlastegen* and *Barmhärtighet*, 1936; Lincoln: University of Nebraska Press, 1985).

2. On the use of Viking motifs in European and North and South American literature, see Jöran Mjöberg, "Romanticism and Revival," in David M. Wilson, ed., *The Northern World: The History and Heritage of Northern Europe A. D. 400-1000* (New York: Harry N. Abrams, 1980), 207-38. Mjöberg's *Drömmen om sagatiden*, 2 vols. (Stockholm: Natur och kultur, 1967-68), is the definitive work on the subject.

3. See Tegnér's *Frithiof's Saga*, trans. Ida Mauch (New York: Exposition Press, 1960), and Laxness's novel *The Happy Warriors* (*Gerpla*, 1952), trans. Katherine John (London: Methuen, 1958). See also Runeberg's epic poem *King Fialar: A Poem in Five Songs* (*King Fialar*, 1844), trans. Eirikr Magnussun (London: J. M. Dent, 1912). And for a classic Viking novel, see Bengtsson's justly famous *The Long Ships. A Saga of the Viking Age* (*Röde Orm*, 1941, 1945), trans. Michael Meyer (1954; rpt. New York: Collins, 1986).

4. Karl Gjellerup, *Brynhild* (1884) and *Kong Hjarne Skald* (1893); Selma Lagerlöf, "The Legend of Reor" ("Reors saga," 1893), in *Invisible Links*, trans. Pauline Bancroft Flach (Garden City, New York: Doubleday, 1899), and "Astrid" (1899), in *The Queens of Kungahälla and Other Sketches* (*Drottningar i Kungahälla*, 1899), trans. C. Field (London: T. Werner Laurie, 1917); Fredrika Bremer, *The H-Family: Trälinnan: Axel and Anna and Other Tales*, trans. Mary Howitt, 2 vols. (London: Longman, Brown, Green, and Långmans, 1844); Verner von Heidenstam, *The Tree of the Folkungs*, trans. A. Chater (New York: Gyldendal, 1925). For a discussion of these writers, see Mjöberg, "Romanticism and Revival," 234, and *Drömmen om sagatiden*, 2:285-86, 452ff.; Mjöberg discusses the Viking slave motif in Scandinavian literature in *Drömmen om sagatiden*, 285-90.

5. Fridegård never mentions the name of the market town, but it is unmistakably Birka, which was established around 800 A. D. and flourished for about two hundred years. Its ruins lie about twenty miles west of present-day Stockholm. Fridegård uses the town as the setting for most of his Holme trilogy.

6. The mission efforts of Ansgar and his successors are considered a mere episode, having little impact on Swedish history. Archbishop Unni of Hamburg renewed the mission in about 936, but likewise met with brief and questionable success. Unni died in Birka, perhaps by stoning, on 17 September 936, "the first precise date we know for domestic Swedish history" (Franklin D. Scott, *Sweden: The Nation's History* [Minneapolis: University of Minnesota Press, 1977], 35). Birka essentially vanished at the end of the tenth century and was not rediscovered until the end of the seventeenth. See Birgit Arrhenius, ed., *Ansgars Birka* (Stockholm: Norstedts, 1965).

7. Ebbe Schön, *Jan Fridegård och forntiden. En studie i diktverk och källor* (Uppsala: Almqvist & Wiksell, 1973), 61ff., discusses some of the popular works on Viking slavery that Fridegård may have read. For a discussion of thralls in the Viking period, see Peter G. Foote and David M. Wilson, *The Viking Achievement: A Survey of the Society and Culture of Early Medieval Scandinavia* (New York: Praeger, 1970), 65-78, and Ruth Mazo Karras, *Slavery and Society in Medieval Scandinavia* (New Haven: Yale University Press, 1988).

8. Schön, 23-153, offers a thorough analysis of Fridegård's sources.

9. See, for example, Erik Hjalmar Linder, *Fem decennier av nittonhundratalet*, 4th ed., vol. 2 of *Ny illustrerad svensk litteraturhistoria* (Stockholm: Natur och kultur, 1966), 589-90.

10. Schön, 152-53; 30, 52.

11. Helge Ljungberg, *Den nordiska religionen och kristendomen. Studier över det nordiska religionsskiftet under vikingatiden* (Stockholm: Hugo Gebers, 1938).

12. Schön, 95, 113.

13. Fridegård's account begins with Chapter 10 of Rimbert's. For an English translation, see Charles H. Robinson, *Anskar: Apostle of the North, 801-865* (London: Society for the Propagation of the Gospel in Foreign Parts, 1921).

14. On Christ as Germanic hero, see Ljungberg, *Den nordiska religionen och kristendomen*, 95; Axel Olrik, *Viking Civilization* (1930; rpt. New York: Norton, 1971), 141 ff.; Chapter 8 ("Christ as Poetic Hero") in Stanley B. Greenfield and Daniel G. Calder, *A New Critical History of Old English Literature* (New York: New York University Press, 1986); and G. Ronald Murphy, S. J., *The Saxon Savior: The Germanic Transformation of the Gospel in the Ninth-Century Heliand* (Oxford: Oxford University Press, 1989).

15. *Anskar: Apostle of the North*, Chapter XXXV, 112; XXXIII, 104-105.

16. See, for example, Foote and Wilson, 77ff.

17. See Schön, 61-79. Schön notes (51) that Fridegård sometimes wrote in conscious opposition to Tegnér's *Frithiof's Saga* and observes that the story about Holme "is to a certain extent to be regarded as a kind of social myth where Fridegård, with the help of his imagination, tries to explain the origin of the struggle of the proletariat" in Sweden (28).

Fridegård's Viking Trilogy

18. Schön, 50. Mjöberg, *Drömmen om sagatiden*, 2:291-92, asserts, but does not really show, the importance of Fröding's poem to Fridegård's trilogy.

19. For a translation of "The Lay of Völundr" or "Weyland," see D. G. Calder, R. E. Bjork, P. K. Ford, D. F. Melia, *Sources and Analogues of Old English Poetry II: The Major Germanic and Celtic Texts in Translation* (Cambridge: D. S. Brewer, 1985), 65-69.

20. Germund Michanek, ed., *Gustaf Frödings poesi* (Stockholm: Wahlström & Widstrand, 1993), 421-22.

21. Animal imagery recurs when Holme is back at the settlement or fleeing from his persecutors in *Sacrificial Smoke* (i. e., "pig," "night animal," "wolf," and "fox"). In the same novel, he is also compared to a troll on one occasion.

22. See Ljungberg, 77ff., and Schön, 124-25.

23. See E. O. G. Turville-Petre's chapter on Thor in *Myth and Religion of the North* (New York: Holt, Rinehart, and Winston, 1964), 75-105.

24. Turville-Petre, 90.

The Cradle and the Crucible: Envisioning the Middle Ages in French Romanticism

Michael Glencross

If the centrality of nature in French Romantic thought has always been acknowledged, the importance of what may be considered its opposing pole, history, has been recognized only more recently, thanks especially to the work of British and American scholars such as Stephen Bann, Ceri Crossley, and Lionel Gossman.[1] Though the impulse for the French Romantics' engagement with history was, as Crossley in particular has shown, the experience and the aftermath of the French Revolution, no period benefited more from this renewed interest in the national past than the Middle Ages. In this essay I wish to examine some of the fictional and "factual" representations of the medieval period in order to explore how French writers constructed and projected their vision of the Middle Ages in the early nineteenth century, especially the Restoration period (1815-1830). In so doing I will consider to what extent the Middle Ages were appropriated in contrasting ways and made to serve differing ideological interests, and I will also examine how far historians, scholars, and creative writers shared a similar imaginative vision of the Middle Ages. For this study I will survey a range of contemporary works of historiography, scholarship, and literature devoted to the French Middle Ages. All three types of writing are unquestionably manifestations of medievalism, the cultural construction of the Middle Ages in the post-medieval period. However, it is legitimate to consider whether it is possible or useful to draw up a typology of French Romantic medievalism, distinguishing between what could be termed respectively interpretative/analytical, preservative/replicative, and (re)creative medievalisms. To avoid this survey becoming little more than a set of discrete encyclopedia-like entries

Studies in Medievalism VIII, 1996

on obscure—or, less frequently—well known works, I shall select a number of key texts and representative writers in each of my three sections and make some comparative and contrastive links between them.

I

An obvious but still appropriate starting point for a survey of the ideological function of the Middle Ages in early nineteenth-century France is the work of that group by whom the term "idéologie" was invented, the Idéologues.[2] The two members of this group of philosophers, scientists, and historians with the strongest interest in the Middle Ages were Pierre-Louis Ginguené (1748-1816) and Pierre Daunou (1761-1840). Both made significant contributions to the *Histoire littéraire de la France*, a work which itself is an interesting indicator of the shift from the antiquarian, ecclesiastical tradition of medieval scholarship under the *ancien régime* to a state-sponsored secularized and "nationalized" interpretation of medieval culture in the First Empire. The *Histoire* was begun in 1733 by the Benedictine monks of Saint-Maur, and though by the time of the Revolution it consisted of twelve volumes, it had still only reached the twelfth century in its coverage of the literary history of France. By decreeing its continuation in 1808, Napoleon signaled his belief in the need to identify a specifically national literary tradition, a position later taken up in the Romantic debate of the Restoration and used against a classical tradition seen as lacking rootedness and "Frenchness."

Ginguené and Daunou are representative of the Idéologues' attitude to the Middle Ages in that although they devoted much of their energies to studying the period they were deeply critical of its values and its culture. Daunou's long essay in the *Histoire* entitled *Discours sur l'état des lettres en France au XIIIe siècle*[3] is a bitter attack on the religious fanaticism of the Middle Ages, worthy of the Enlightenment thinkers to whom the Idéologues were indebted for their political views on human freedom and for their materialist philosophy. Ginguené, who has been called the founder of literary history by a modern scholar,[4] was also unsparing in his criticism of medieval French literature, which he called "ces informes essais de notre poésie" ("these formless efforts of our poetry").[5] The official renewal of interest in the Middle Ages in the Napoleonic period should not then be seen as an aesthetic revival, as a recognition of the artistic values of medieval culture. It is part of the post-Revolutionary attempt to consecrate the consensual notion of a national tradition, to heal the historical wound inflicted by the Revolution itself.

102   Studies in Medievalism

For an alternative view of the Middle Ages we can turn to another focus of opposition to Napoleonic power and ideology, the so-called *groupe de Coppet* centered on Madame de Staël.[6] Though both groups came into conflict with Napoleon over the issue of human freedom, their aesthetic views differed significantly. The Idéologues were classical by virtue of their attachment to a belief in an essential human nature and permanent standards of taste, whereas the intellectuals and scholars who belonged to Madame de Staël's circle were much closer to a position of cultural relativism or, to use Karl Mannheim's term, relationism.[7] It is this group which was instrumental in fomenting the French literary debate on Romanticism from 1813, after the publication of Sismondi's *De la littérature du Midi de l'Europe* and Madame de Staël's own controversial study *De l'Allemagne*, banned and pulped by Napoleon in 1810 for being "un-French" but published in London in 1813.[8] In both works the terms medieval and Romantic as applied to literature are synonymous. Madame de Staël's definition of Romantic poetry as born of chivalry and Christianity is the better known, but Sismondi's discussion of the relations between medieval and Romantic literature provides a much more detailed treatment of the topic.[9] For him the term Romantic is associated not with the Germanic and Northern medieval tradition but with the Southern tradition of the troubadours, exponents of the *langue d'oc*, pre-eminent among the Romance languages. Consistent with this emphasis on the imagination of the South is the importance Sismondi gives to Arab influence on Old Provençal literature.

The relative importance of the North and South within the French medieval literary tradition, that is, between the *trouvères* and the *troubadours*, had given rise in the 1780s to a famous literary quarrel initiated by the medievalist Legrand d'Aussy which, as I have discussed elsewhere,[10] was reflected in the Romantic debate in the late Empire and early Restoration period because of a new scholarly interest in the works of the troubadours and because of the continuing success of the *genre troubadour*, a literary phenomenon I will discuss later. By coincidence Madame de Staël's circle also counted among its members two out of the four most important *provençalistes* of the period, Claude Fauriel and August-Wilhelm von Schlegel, the others being Raynouard and Rochegude. There remained, then, within this circle of medievalists a division between what we might call the *nordistes* and the *sudistes*, just as there were religious differences between, for example, the Protestant Sismondi and the Catholic Schlegel. However, what these writers held in common was a comparative approach to literature, informed by a cosmopolitan background and outlook. For them literature in general and French literature in particular was

Middle Ages in French Romanticism 103

not bound by unchanging rules of taste and form but subject to variable and particular historical conditions within which the freedom of the individual sought expression. The dominant intellectual assumptions of this group were individual freedom and historical change, and the often uneasy relations between the two. Medieval literature took a pivotal position in this tension because it constituted both historically and aesthetically a discrete entity and because its achievement was collective rather than individual. From this perception arises a contradiction frequent in later French Romantic medievalism, the celebration of the "poetic" nature and spirit of the Middle Ages themselves and the lament for the lack of writers of individual genius.

If the approaches to the Middle Ages present in the writings of the Idéologues and the *groupe de Coppet* were primarily secular, it is essential to remember the importance of Catholic ideology in Romantic medievalism, best seen in the early period in the works of Bonald and Chateaubriand. The latter's *Génie du christianisme* (1802) is, so to speak, the classic formulation of Catholic Romantic medievalism, a celebration of the ideals of the Christian Middle Ages realized in their highest form in the moral values of chivalry and the heroic self-sacrifice of the crusades. The extent of Chateaubriand's influence on contemporary representations of the Middle Ages can be seen in the now forgotten works of Louis-Antoine-François (de) Marchangy. Marchangy's two major works of medievalism are *La Gaule poétique* (1813-1817) and *Tristan le voyageur* (1825). The earlier work is a hybrid of historiographical and imaginative writing, an attempt to use as a literary resource the matter of French history from the early Middle Ages down to the reign of Louis XIV. This publication was a great success in the early Restoration and went through five editions between 1817 and 1834. Contemporary reviews of the work are a useful indicator of the changing ideological dominants within medievalism between the early and late Restoration, that is, the shift from a royalist to a liberal interpretation of the Middle Ages.[11] This change mirrors closely the general political evolution of French Romanticism in the 1820s, best exemplified by the young Victor Hugo. Unlike their English counterparts who, disenchanted with the French Revolution, took up an increasingly conservative position, French Romantic poets were radicalized by the reactionary policies pursued during the later Restoration.

While in most early reviews the author of *La Gaule poétique* was saluted as a worthy successor to Chateaubriand, the publication of *Tristan le voyageur* was greeted with much less acclaim.[12] This latter work, set in fourteenth-century France, is a cross between a historical novel, a genre popularized by the immense contemporary vogue in France for Sir Walter

104 Studies in Medievalism

Scott, and a travel romance, in the manner of the Abbé Barthélemy's *Voyage du jeune Anacharsis en Grèce*, first published in 1788. Barthélemy's work, which used classical Greece as its setting, remained successful into the 1820s, largely thanks to the current of philhellenism created by the Greeks' struggle for independence (1821-1830) from Turkish rule. Marchangy's work attempted but failed to do for Romantic medievalism what Barthélemy had succeeded in doing for neo-classical hellenism and then Romantic philhellenism. Marchangy's royalist version of medievalism with its apologia of feudalism could still find favor in the columns of an *ultra* periodical like the short-lived *L'Oriflamme* (1824-5), but by this time the political color of French Romanticism was changing and the prevailing opinion growing much closer to that expressed in the leading liberal and pro-Romantic journal of the period, *Le Globe*, which ridiculed Marchangy's literary style as overblown and denounced his politics as dangerously reactionary, views enthusiastically endorsed by famous contemporaries such as Stendhal and Hugo.[13]

Chateaubriand's impact on Romantic medievalism was not confined to his influence on Marchangy and was not due solely to the *Génie du christianisme*. In some ways a more influential work was, paradoxically, his prose epic *Les Martyrs* (1809), set in the time of the Roman persecution of the first Christians. I wish to deal with this work here rather than in the later section on literary representations of the Middle Ages because of its relation to the *Génie* and because of its overall impact on the historical imagination of French Romanticism. Chateaubriand's purpose in writing *Les Martyrs* was twofold. First and foremost he wished to demonstrate by example an idea put forward in *Le Génie du christianisme*, that the defining feature of epic in French neoclassical literary theory, the use of the *merveilleux*, the supernatural, could be realized just as successfully through the use of Christian as through pagan material. In this way the imaginative work grows out of the earlier apologia for Christianity. Secondly, he wished to demonstrate the appropriateness of prose as a vehicle for the epic. The success of *Les Martyrs* presents us, then, with a double paradox: the importance for Romanticism of a work written in but also against the neo-classical tradition and the significance for Romantic medievalism of a work set in late classical antiquity. The relevance of the work for Romantic medievalism lies in two of the best known sections of the work, the hero Eudore's account of his encounter with the Franks (Books 5-7) and his visit to Armorica, recounted in Book 9. The latter contains the most famous episode in the work, the impossible and tragic love between the Christian Eudore and the pagan Celtic druidess Velléda, which ends in

Velléda killing herself out of religious guilt and Eudore from the same motives returning to Christianity.

In both episodes Chateaubriand evokes a "barbarian" world sharply distinct from that of Greco-Roman civilization. Germanic and Celtic society are seen, however, not merely as primitive and barbaric but as endowed with a vitality and power which contrast with the enervated effeteness of a declining classical civilization. While they certainly constitute a threat to the stability of the present, they contain a promise of renewal. In the chronology of the discourse of *Les Martyrs* the Middle Ages belong to the future, not the past, but this only reinforces the way in which they connote energy and dynamism. This public world of violence and conflict is in sharp contrast to the private, domestic world of the medieval court and castle which was the privileged place in the imagined medieval world of the *genre troubadour*. Chateaubriand's portrayal of the early medieval world in *Les Martyrs* marks, then, an important shift in contemporary representations of the Middle Ages, through its incorporation of Celtic and Germanic elements. Germanic society is homologous to Celtic landscape: both represent the wild, the untamed, the free and the natural.

After 1830 attempts to identify Germanic and especially Celtic elements in the formation of French national identity and culture became an essential preoccupation of Romantic historians such as Michelet, Quinet, and, above all, Henri Martin. In the 1820s the historian who gave the greatest importance to national identity and to racial difference was Augustin Thierry, who is also the best witness to Chateaubriand's power as an *éveilleur de vocations*. Thierry attributed his decision to become an historian to reading the description in *Les Martyrs* of the Franks preparing for battle.[14] However, in his masterwork of this period, the *Histoire de la conquête de l'Angleterre par les Normands* (1825), it was not French but English medieval history which provided the subject matter.

Thierry's historical writings of the 1820s are seminal works of the new school of history and of French Romantic medievalism for a number of reasons. Indeed, Marcel Gauchet has argued that the publication in 1820 of his *Lettres sur l'histoire de France* was as significant an event for the development of French Romanticism as the appearance of Lamartine's collection *Les Méditations* in the same year.[15] Thierry's early essays illustrate the use of local color via defamiliarization techniques such as the Germanicizing of proper names. Above all they show how historiography is an essential manifestation of the Romantics' preoccupation with and evocation of the Middle Ages. At the same time that the novel turns towards history for its subject matter, history looks to the novel for its

106   Studies in Medievalism

textual paradigm, narrative discourse. In the introduction to the *Histoire de la conquête* Thierry explains his approach to the material thus:

> Enfin, j'ai toujours conservé la forme narrative, pour que le lecteur ne passât pas brusquement d'un récit antique à un commentaire moderne, et que l'ouvrage ne présentât point les dissonances qu'offriraient des fragments de chroniques entremêlés de dissertations. J'ai cru d'ailleurs que, si je m'attachais plutôt à raconter qu'à disserter, même dans l'exposition des faits et des résultats généraux, je pourrais donner une sorte de vie historique aux masses d'hommes comme aux personnages individuels, et que, de cette manière, la destinée politique des nations offrirait quelque chose de cet intérêt humain qu'inspire involontairement le détail naïf des changements de fortune et des aventures d'un seul homme.[16]

> (Finally, I have always kept to the narrative form, so that the reader did not move suddenly from an ancient tale to a modern commentary, and so that the work did not show the disharmony created by fragments of chronicles interspersed with dissertations. I considered, moreover, that if I sought to narrate rather than discourse upon events, even in the treatment of facts and general results, I might impart a sort of historical life to the mass of men as to individual characters, and that, in this way, the political destiny of nations would offer some of this human interest that is spontaneously inspired by the naïve detail of changes of fortune and adventures that befall an individual man.)

Thierry's clearly stated objective is the seamless narrative, the same ambition as that of another liberal Romantic historian, Prosper de Barante, who in his *Histoire des ducs de Bourgogne* (1824-6) took as his epigraph Quintilian's phrase *scribitur ad narrandum non ad probandum* ("it is written in order to narrate not to prove"). There is no need to demonstrate here the *aporia* to which the idea of a (his)tory telling itself leads, but it is important to note that Thierry sees the task of the historian as that of an artist and imaginative writer, as someone who has the gift to enable the reader to identify imaginatively with people who have been dead for centuries and to abolish thereby the distinction between the past and the present and even between the present and the future. Thierry's professed admiration for Scott, especially *Ivanhoe*, is further proof of the way in which he saw the historical and the literary imagination as inextricably linked.

It would be wrong, however, to see Thierry merely as a member of the narrative school of historiography. The latter is best illustrated, as I have already mentioned, by Barante's *Histoire des ducs de Bourgogne*, a work which Chateaubriand praised for its style and direct use of sources, though not for its implicit liberal ideology.[17] The significance of Thierry's contribution to the cultural construction of the Middle Ages in French Romanticism lies less in his use of narrative form than in his overarching historical idea, the notion of conquest and its consequences, racial and then social conflict. Thierry gives a dynamic, conflictual interpretation of medieval history which is intended to explain post-medieval history, the collapse of feudalism and the decline of the aristocracy, together with the rise of the bourgeoisie in alliance with the monarchy. Though the apparent—and real—subject-matter of the *Histoire de la conquête* is English history, the question of the relations between an exogenous conquering people and the indigenous population has an obvious application to French history. The Saxon/Norman conflict can be read as a displacement of the problematical relations between the Gauls—the third estate—and the Franks—the nobility—in French history. This issue had given rise to the historiographical quarrel between the Germanist and the Romanist theses in the eighteenth century, but its revival during this period shows again how the Middle Ages are central to differing political interpretations of French history and to conflicting attempts to legitimate contemporary ideological interests.[18]

At the heart of Thierry's narrative lies the story of a people, more than an account of the rise and fall of dynasties. This change of emphasis from the individual to the collective is another central tenet of Romantic liberal historiography in France. Its most emblematic expression is in the title of Sismondi's massive study of French history (1821-44), which he was careful to call *Histoire des Français* rather than the conventional *Histoire de France*, an anticipation of the change in appellation of Louis-Philippe from "roi de France" to "roi des Français."[19] In some of his concluding remarks to the *Histoire de la conquête*, Thierry, as well as restating his belief in the the power of the imagination to overcome the gap between past and present, describes his aim as having been to "raconter les aventures de la vie sociale et non celles de la vie individuelle" ("recount the adventures of the lives of social groups and not those of an individual").[20] The reader, he claims, can identify as much with the collective feelings and sufferings of a group as with those of an individual. This primacy given to the collective over the individual may appear to be at odds with traditional Romantic notions of the exaltation of the self, but the otherness of the Middle Ages which is an essential explanation of its attractiveness for the Romantics resides partly in the way in which the individual both socially and artistically merges with rather than stands out from the general background. It is the integration and wholeness of medieval culture and society which make it a recourse against the fragmentation of the present.

The importance of Thierry's contribution to French Romantic medievalism lies in the way in which he seeks to reduce the gap between historiography and imaginative writing in his historical representation of the Middle Ages. In this he is following the path opened up by Chateaubriand, but the two writers differ significantly in their ideological exploitation of the Middle Ages. Chateaubriand explains the interest in the medieval past as the cult of ruins, stimulated by what he calls "un sentiment de regret et de curiosité religieuse" ("a sense of loss and of curiosity for religion").[21] Medievalism is thus a search for reassurance, the reclaiming of a lost identity, a nostalgic cult of a distant and lost past. Thierry, on the other hand, looks back to the Middle Ages to seek for an active principle of change and finds it in racial/social conflict. In this view the Middle Ages contain the elements whose often violent interaction produces the present. This liberal vision foregrounds the principle of dynamic conflict in interpreting medieval history, whereas the conservative royalist alternative stresses hierarchical stability and a firmly fixed—and enforced—unity. However, while grounding social conflict in the (distant) past, liberal bourgeois ideology looks forward to a (near) consensual future. Inconveniently, 1830 did not prove to be the end of history, and the events of 1848 presented liberal historians and especially Thierry with a massive challenge to their earlier convictions.

The Middle Ages proved a focal point for alternative interpretations and appropriations of French history. The medieval period was for all parties what the French call *une auberge espagnole*, a place where you find only what you bring to it. In this discussion I hope also to have shown how historiography should be seen as part of, not distinct from, French Romantic medievalism. Before examining fictional rather than "factual" representations of the Middle Ages I wish to consider the state of scholarly medievalism during the period 1800-1830, in particular the extent to which it too was informed by the ideological and aesthetic correlates of Romanticism.

II

Medievalism understood as the modern discipline of medieval studies was a product of the specialization and professionalization of knowledge

Middle Ages in French Romanticism 109

which occurred especially in Germany in the latter part of the nineteenth century. The conditions of the founding of the discipline have recently been illuminated by a number of studies which constitute significant contributions to what Karl Mannheim called the sociology of knowledge.[22] This work has revealed in particular the nationalistic ideology underpinning the growth of medieval studies in France and Germany over this period, leading to what one modern scholar has called a philological arms race between the two countries.[23] The three decades I am primarily concerned with in this essay belong to the prehistory of institutionalized and professionalized scholarly medievalism in France. Only after 1830, thanks largely to the impact of the refounded Ecole des Chartes and the creation of university chairs of literary history, did there appear a cadre of professional medievalists in France. However, the years before 1830 were marked by the work of two outstanding French medieval scholars, François-Juste-Marie Raynouard (1761-1836), the founder of comparative Romance philology in France, and Claude Fauriel (1772-1844), the founder of comparative literary history. Coincidentally each of these scholars devoted much of their energies to the language and the literature of the troubadours. Largely because of their efforts it was the language and literature of the South of France which dominated medieval French studies in this period. I wish therefore to consider briefly the impact of the works of these two scholars in the period before 1830.

Though Raynouard's most lasting scholarly monument is his mainly posthumous *Lexique roman* (1836-1844), his most influential work in shaping French Romantic conceptions of the Middle Ages was the *Choix des poésies originales des troubadours* (1816-1821). The mere publication of original texts of the troubadours indicates, as John M. Graham has pointed out,[24] a significant shift in attitudes towards medieval vernacular poetry since the scholarship of the late eighteenth century exemplified by the work of La Curne de Sainte-Palaye. Besides extensive untranslated extracts from the works of the main troubadours, Raynouard's publication contains a description of the grammar of Old Provençal—*la langue romane* in his terminology—in which he mistakenly argues that this language in its original form was the common ancestor of all the other Romance languages. In addition, the second volume contains an account of the so-called courts of love based on Andreas Capellanus's treatise *De Amore*.

Raynouard's intention in publishing samples of the original poetry of the troubadours was certainly not to further the general cause of Romanticism. As a member (1807) and then secretary (1817-1826) of the Académie Française, in the early Restoration he was by necessity but also from personal conviction an upholder of the literary doctrines of classicism. As the earlier author of a successful play, *Les Templiers* (1805), his own creative work was clearly situated within the classical tradition, even though it used national history rather than Greek or Roman material. His assessment of troubadour poetry also gives little recognition to its sophisticated literary techniques, and even its originality is seen as a purely accidental benefit of ignorance, a lack of acquaintance with classical literary models. Despite all this, the *Choix des poésies originales* did have an impact on the development of Romanticism in France because it made available for the first time medieval texts which were part of the national literary tradition and which could be claimed as part of a non-classical canon. A review written by Charles Nodier in the *Journal des débats* (9 June 1817) shows how Raynouard's medieval philological scholarship could serve contemporary literary criticism. In the course of an enthusiastic account of the first volume of the work, Nodier accepts uncritically Raynouard's thesis about the origins of Old Provençal and its primacy over the other Romance languages but uses Raynouard to promote his own view of language, which has a strongly Romantic bias:

> Chose merveilleuse! Ces langues, le chef-d'oeuvre de la civilisation, ce ne sont pas les philosophes qui les ont faites! elles s'instituent, s'améliorent, se modifient par une force cachée qui ne provient point de l'homme, et dont les effets se coordonnent aux lieux et aux circonstances sans notre participation. Supposez dans une île sauvage au bout de l'univers, cinq ou six générations successives de créatures à visage humain, prises parmi les plus imparfaites de l'espèce; si elles ont d'ailleurs tous leurs sens, elles parleront; et cette langue qu'elles auront créée sans le savoir et qui aura sa grammaire, sa poésie et son génie, comme toutes les langues, jamais toutes les académies de la terre ne lui donneroient de cours chez un peuple, même de son consentement, parce que les langues ne se font pas ni ne se prescrivent: elles se perçoivent et se communiquent. Notre science ne va pas plus loin.

> (What a wonderful thing! These languages, civilization's masterpiece, are not the product of philosophers! They are created, improved and altered by a hidden force which does not proceed from man, and the effects of which are matched to places and circumstances without our involvement. Imagine on a desert island at the ends of the earth, five or six successive generations of creatures with a human appearance, chosen amongst the least perfect of the species; if, moreover, they have all their senses,

they will speak; and in the case of this language which they will have unknowingly created, and which will have its own grammar, poetry and unique spirit, like all other languages, never would all the academies on earth be able to give it currency among a people, even with the latter's consent, because languages are not constructed or prescribed: they are sensed and passed on. Our knowledge goes no further.)

Nodier here celebrates in language the same qualities that he values in literature; both are seen as the spontaneous, natural expression of the people. Poetry and grammar are coterminous, both being free from artificially and externally imposed constraints but still rule-governed.

Seeing the language of the troubadours as rule-governed rather than subject to random variation was, in fact, one of Raynouard's achievements in his grammatical description of Old Provençal. Although it may be argued that Raynouard's "discovery" of the case system—the distinction between nominative and accusative forms—reflected a classical desire for rules and order, this position did help to raise the status of the language and the literature of the Middle Ages by the very fact of showing that they obeyed certain rules. It was an answer to scholars critical of medieval culture such as Daunou, who saw variation in manuscript readings and spellings as the linguistic and literary equivalent of the general social anarchy of the Middle Ages realized in feudalism. It was not until 1828 that Daunou accepted the thesis of the existence of grammatical rules such as the case system, when Raynouard rather belatedly applied it to Old French and not just Old Provençal.[25]

Compared with Raynouard, Fauriel was much more directly involved with and influential upon the Romantic movement in France, despite the fact that his main scholarly studies of medieval literature and history were not published until after 1830, his *Histoire de la Gaule méridionale sous la domination des conquérants germains* in 1836 and his *Histoire de la poésie provençale* posthumously in 1846. Fauriel's main contribution to the emergent Romantic school of the 1820s was his *Chants populaires de la Grèce moderne* (1824-5), an edition of modern Greek folk poetry which enjoyed a great success thanks largely to the philhellenic current in French Romanticism during this time of the Greek war of independence. This collection reflects not just what might be considered a passing interest in modern Greece on Fauriel's part but a fundamental preoccupation in his literary scholarship, whether dealing with classical or modern literature, Greek or French: the importance of oral transmission of the literary tradition. It is Fauriel, then, who should be taken as the best French exemplar of the new interest in oral poetry and the folk tradition, rather than Raynouard as claimed by Foucault in his discussion of the rise of comparative philology in early nineteenth-century culture.[26] Ironically, the value of Fauriel's contribution to medieval scholarship was diminished and even dismissed by succeeding generations of scholars because of an error of appreciation similar to that committed by Raynouard. In the case of Fauriel it was the excessive role he gave to the place of the literature of the South of France in the development and transmission of epic poetry in the *langue d'oïl*, a parallel to Raynouard's theory of the *langue d'oc* being the original and common Romance vernacular.

To his contemporaries in literary circles Fauriel was seen as an influential figure despite the relative paucity of his published work. For Sainte-Beuve he was an essential channel for the circulation of new ideas, "l'*inoculateur* de la plupart des esprits distingués de ce temps-ci en histoire, en méthode littéraire, en critique" ("the *inoculator* of the majority of outstanding minds of that time in history, literary method and criticism").[27] It is then no surprise to discover that when Stendhal dealt with the subject of courtly love in Provence in his *De l'Amour* (1822) it was to the Romantically inclined Fauriel that he paid tribute rather than to the classically minded Raynouard. Fauriel is referred to as a man with the most brilliant mind but at the same time as erudite as ten German scholars put together. On the other hand, although Stendhal draws heavily on Raynouard's account of the courts of love and Andreas Capellanus he summarily dismisses in a footnote the author of the *Choix des poésies originales des troubadours* as someone who praised the troubadours too much and did not know them enough, a manifestly unfair judgement on both counts. Fauriel's influence is also clear in Stendhal's positive appreciation of the sophistication and complexity of the poetic language and style of the troubadour, especially the effects derived from the use of rhyme in what the latter calls "cette jolie langue provençale, si remplie de délicatesse et si tourmentée par la rime" ("this pretty Provençal language, so filled with delicacy and so tortured by rhyme").[28]

Fauriel's interpretation of medieval French culture is focused on but at the same time distorted by the centrality and superiority which he accords to the civilization of the South of France over that of the North. It is in the South of France that he sees realized in their fullest form the two essential constituents of his liberal vision of medieval French history, firstly municipal freedoms which symbolize the republican, secular ideal and show the continuity of Roman civilization in the South, and secondly the institution of chivalry which shows the progressive and civilizing principle in human history. As a literary historian Fauriel sees the creation of a new chivalric literature in the South of France as an illustration of another fundamental tenet of French Romanticism, literature as an expression of society. Again Fauriel's influence on the Stendhal of *De l'Amour* is easy to see.[29] The preference for southern over northern culture and the need to situate literature in its social context both inform Stendhal's account of love in Provence. However, such views extend also well beyond Stendhal and show how important and representative a figure Fauriel is for French Romanticism and how medievalism in its most scholarly form affected its literary avatar.

III

The visions of the Middle Ages I have identified so far in discussing French Romantic historiography and scholarship have been informed by more or less explicitly formulated conceptual distinctions or oppositions between order/stability and conflict/change, and between North and South or civilization and barbarism. In works of history, including literary and linguistic history, the Romantic imagination is primarily metonymic in its representation of a dynamic Middle Ages. It uses race (e.g., Saxons and Normans or Franks and Gauls) or class (the knight and the priest) or place (North and South) to figure and to embody its ideas. Even in the early historical essays of Edgar Quinet we find the same figurative but metonymic processes at work, realized in his case by the opposition between church and castle.[30] In the final part of this survey of French Romantic medievalism I wish to examine representations of the Middle Ages to be found in the imaginative literature of the early Romantic period and to consider whether this vision is metaphorical rather than metonymic.

The main difficulties in covering the representations of the Middle Ages in early nineteenth-century French literature[31] include not only the diversity but also the obscurity and inaccessibility of the works. Apart from *Les Martyrs*, which I have already discussed, the only medievalist texts published before Hugo's *Notre-Dame de Paris* (1831) which have entered the Romantic canon are individual poems such as Vigny's *Le Cor* (1826) and Hugo's collection *Odes et Ballades* (1826 and 1828). In fact, however, there is a large corpus of texts belonging to all the main genres which illustrate the widespread diffusion of medievalist themes in contemporary writing. Given the importance of genre in classical literary theory and given the attempts of the French Romantics to prove themselves in the literary forms most prized by classical precept and practice, the epic and the dramatic, it is appropriate to use genre as the organizing principle of this discussion and to consider whether there is any correlation between differences in genre and alternative ways of envisioning the Middle Ages.

To the French Romantics the epic poem was the ultimate literary goal and prize. It was also to prove the most elusive. The epic was in theory the ideal medium for Romanticism to lay claim to the classical inheritance and to forge its own identity by asserting both its spiritual and its humanitarian credo.[32] In place of the pagan hero could stand the Christian martyr or the crusading knight. There was no difficulty in identifying suitable medieval themes for treatment by the Romantic epic. Unfortunately Horace's warning issued in his *Ars Poetica* that *parturient montes, nascetur ridiculus mus* ("the mountains will go into labor but a silly little mouse will be born") proved only too prophetic and apposite. In practice, with the notable exception of Hugo's short epics in *La Légende des siècles* (1859), French Romantic medievalism produced no major works in the genre, unless we include in this category Quinet's late prose work *Merlin l'enchanteur* (1860). In the period 1800 to 1830 epic poems on medieval subjects were quite common, as H. J. Hunt's bibliography shows, but despite their use of figures or episodes from medieval French history or literature they remained feeble imitations of an exhausted classical tradition, the last gasp of an old culture rather than the first stirrings of the new. The most extended epic treatment of medieval material published between 1800 and 1830 was Creuzé de Lesser's trilogy, *Les Chevaliers de la Table Ronde* (1811), *Amadis de Gaule* (1813), and *Roland* (1815). Though they enjoyed considerable success in their day, especially the Arthurian poem, they are backward-looking works steeped in a sentimentalism occasionally leavened by a playful irony, the standard recipe for the aristocratic medievalism of late eighteenth-century pre-Revolutionary culture.

As the works of Marchangy have already shown, medieval French history provided plenty of scope for the play of royalist as well as liberal ideologies. For another example, but this time in the epic form, we can use a now justly forgotten epic poem, *Philippe-Auguste, poème heroïque en douze chants*, published in 1826 by Parseval de Grandmaison (1759-1834). Like many of his contemporaries Parseval negotiated for himself a successful transition from the authoritarianism of the Empire to that of the restored monarchy. As a member of the Académie Française and fervent supporter of classical literary doctrine, he asserts in his opening invocation to the Muse—which, fortunately or unfortunately, loses nothing in translation—the royalist reading of medieval history as the triumph of the monarchy over a rebellious, overpowerful aristocracy:

Muse, chante ce roi qui soumit au devoir

Middle Ages in French Romanticism   115

Les orgueilleux vassaux jaloux de son pouvoir,
Ce roi qui, toujours grand sans cesser d'être juste,
Par ses faits glorieux conquit le nom d'Auguste,
Aux rebelles barons sut imposer des lois,
Fut l'amour des Français et l'exemple des rois.

(Muse, sing of this king who subjected to duty
The proud barons jealous of his power,
This king who, always great without ever ceasing to be just,
By his glorious deeds achieved the title of Augustus,
Succeeded in imposing laws on the rebellious barons,
And was loved by the French people and was an example
        to kings.)

This glorification of a medieval monarch, which culminates in an account of his victory at Bouvines, can obviously be read as an attempt to flatter Charles X, whose accession to the throne in 1824 and coronation in 1825 with the pomp and splendour of the *ancien régime* produced an outpouring of *poésies de circonstances*. Just as Charlemagne had been a favorite subject for epic poetry under the emperor Napoleon, so the medieval kings of France, notably Philip-Augustus and Louis IX, could be used by literary propagandists of royalism to promote their cause. [33]

The extent to which the literary treatment of national and especially medieval history remained rooted in the neoclassical tradition is to be seen not only in the epic but also, and perhaps even more clearly, in tragedy. Raynouard's drama *Les Templiers*, though a work from an earlier period (1805), is a representative example of the way in which medieval material could be incorporated within the classical conventions. The central figure in Raynouard's play is not the king, Philippe-le-Bel, but Jacques de Molay, the Grand Master of the order of the Knights Templar. Raynouard's sympathies, as his historical introduction to the play clearly shows, lie firmly with the Templars. His purpose was no less than the historical rehabilitation of the order. Jacques de Molay thus becomes a Christian martyr, a theme given its most famous tragic treatment in Corneille's *Polyeucte*. The king, on the other hand, is presented unconvincingly. Whereas in his historical introduction Raynouard presents the king's motives for destroying the order as having been primarily financial, in the play Philippe-le-Bel's motives for accusing de Molay and his order of heresy are never very clear. As might be expected, Napoleon's interest in the play focused on the figure of the king and, according to Michèle Jones, [34] he criticized Raynouard for failing to make Philippe the tragic hero. For

Napoleon the modern tragic hero was the victim and accomplice not of the gods but of political force of circumstance. In this view the medieval historical material could, and indeed should, replace the classical subject matter, but the conception of the tragic hero and the literary conventions used remained neo-classical.

The only significant medievalist work in French Romantic drama before 1830 is an early work by Prosper Mérimée who later, as inspector of historic monuments (1834-1860), played a very prominent role in the preservation and restoration of France's medieval architectural heritage.[35] Though it was not intended for the stage and has been neglected in most studies of Romantic drama, *La Jacquerie* (1828) is a forceful illustration of the type of dramatic writing argued for by Stendhal in his *Racine et Shakespeare* (1823) and offers a typical liberal interpretation of medieval French history.[36] Taking as its subject the peasant revolts of the mid-fourteenth century, the play dramatizes the outbreak and ultimate failure of an uprising led by an outlaw and by a priest who is converted to the cause of the people (though the latter in the end turn against him and kill him). It is a drama of class conflict, between peasants and nobles with, in the middle, a rising bourgeoisie. Instead of a simple plot bringing together at a moment of crisis a small number of characters related by ties of family or love, the play involves large numbers of characters and consists of a loosely linked series of short scenes which justify its subtitle of *scènes féodales*. The unity of the action lies in the dramatic principle of social conflict. Whatever its failings as a play, *La Jacquerie* gives powerful evidence of how liberal French Romanticism constructs a dynamic view of the Middle Ages founded on social conflict and collective struggle.

One of the many paradoxes of French Romanticism is the gap and time-lag between literary theory and practice. The history of the movement in France shows the primacy in French literary culture of self-definition and the precedence of theory over practice. However, while a small group of writers sought to advance their cause by arguing for a new type of drama, the reading public were more concerned to consume another type of writing, the historical novel. The enormous vogue for Scott's novels was probably the most important single feature of French literary culture in the 1820s.[37] In *Illusions perdues*, Balzac's great novel about the ambitions and disillusions of an aspiring young provincial writer trying to make his mark in the Parisian literary world of the early 1820s, the hero, Lucien de Rubempré, is the author of a novel à la Scott entitled *L'Archer de Charles IX*. In the same work Balzac ridicules the most popular French novelist of the period, d'Arlincourt, nicknamed "l'inversif vicomte" because of his overuse of inversion as an archaizing stylistic device.[38] In a best-selling novel like d'Arlincourt's *L'Etrangère* (1825), set in Brittany during the reign of Philip-Augustus, we can see in a caricaturally crude form the devices used to fabricate a literary Middle Ages which combined features of the Gothic novel, based on surprise, shock, and horror, with those of the *genre troubadour*, sentimental romances which originated in the versions of the medieval courtly romances produced for a late eighteenth-century aristocratic public by writers like Tressan and other contributors to the *Bibliothèque universelle des romans*. The only successful narrative work which could be placed in this category is Chateaubriand's *Les Aventures du dernier Abencérage*, a sort of *roman troubadour* set in fifteenth-century Spain which recounts another *amour impossible*, like the Velléda episode in *Les Martyrs*, though this time the Christian figure is the lady and her lover is the exiled infidel. Though not published until 1826, this text was written in the Napoleonic era and is steeped in the nostalgia and sense of loss felt by the *émigré* aristocracy in the aftermath of the Revolution: it shows how the *genre troubadour* gives a nostalgic, static representation of the past.

The failure to integrate into an artistic and imaginative whole two constrasting visions of the Middle Ages, the Gothic and the troubadour, are typical of the medievalist writings of the Restoration, especially in narrative fiction. Nevertheless in the hands of a great writer these conflicting elements could be used to great effect. Though he does not use these terms, Hugo's vision of the Middle Ages can be seen as structured in the same way, but its artistic impact is incomparably more effective than that of contemporary novelists and finds its most complete expression in *Notre-Dame de Paris* (1831). However, even in his early reviews of Scott, Hugo's dramatic and epic vision of the Middle Ages is already formed. In these pieces Hugo sets out his own literary ideal and prefigures the theory of the sublime and the grotesque developed in the famous preface to his play *Cromwell* (1827). He describes the ideal novel as an imitation of life and for that reason "un drame bizarre où se mêlent le bon et le mauvais, le beau et le laid, le haut et le bas, loi dont le pouvoir n'expire que hors de la création" ("a strange drama in which are mixed together the good and the bad, the beautiful and the ugly, the high and the low, a law the power of which extends over the whole of creation").[39] However much he admired the author of *Ivanhoe* and *Quentin Durward*, the young Hugo still had the sublime confidence to state that a greater work was still to be written, the poetic novel which would unite drama and epic or, in his image, enshrine Walter Scott within Homer. Hugo here prefigures—and prejudges without false modesty—his own novel *Notre-Dame de Paris*, which is indisputably the crowning achievement of French Romantic medievalism, at once a product of its time and a work of individual genius.

It is in Hugo's imaginative vision and most powerfully in this text that the Romantic Middle Ages find their most metaphorical expression.[40] Transfer becomes transformation, even transfiguration. The transforming power of Hugo's medievalism can best be seen in the function of the cathedral in the text. Foregrounded in the French title but not in its English translation, the cathedral occupies the central symbolic space in the narrative and brings together the contradictions in Hugo's attitude towards the Middle Ages. It is a place of refuge and sanctuary for Quasimodo, but it is also the focus of the mob's destructive anger and the object of their mindless and violent assault at the end of the novel. It is the only book which the people can read but it represents a cultural and political system which is theocratic not democratic. Like Quasimodo who combines the physically ugly and the morally sublime, the cathedral connotes spiritual and material beauty but also, through the figure of Claude Frollo, is associated with and defiled by sexual lust and corruption. A similar ambiguity lies in the representation of the people in the text. On the overtly political level the book's message is optimistic: it announces and celebrates the movement from government by the Church and the nobility to government by the people, in alliance with the monarchy. However, Hugo's underlying ideological position is ambivalent. The people, as well embodying the rising force of democracy, are also a dangerous, unruly rabble. In *Notre-Dame de Paris* Hugo expresses in its richest and most poetic form the awareness of duality and contradiction which is the hallmark of the liberal French Romantics' view of the Middle Ages, but this poetic richness is also infused with a certain ideological ambiguity and uncertainty.

In the final literary genre I have to examine, lyric poetry, the evolution of the imaginative vision of Middle Ages in Restoration literature follows quite a clear pattern. The early writing of the period is dominated by the poetic tradition of the *genre troubadour*, illustrated particularly in the case of lyric poetry by the form known as *romance*. It should be noted here in passing that French, unlike English, lexicalizes the distinction between lyric poetry (*la romance*) and narrative fiction (*le roman*), though it has no simple equivalent of the English distinction between novel and romance. This type of poetry is again derived from *ancien régime* literary culture. In its early nineteenth-century medievalized version this poetry evokes a private world of love and loss, which can be interpreted, as I have already argued in the case of *Les Aventures du dernier Abencérage*, as a literary displacement of the *émigré* aristocrats' loss of power and identity after the Revolution. As Gérard Gengembre has shown, it is a literature of counter-revolution.[41] However, examples of this type of poetry continued to be published well after the re-establishment of the monarchy in 1815. Its continuing success can be seen in the poems collected in annual anthologies such as *Le Chansonnier des Grâces*, *Le Souvenir des ménestrels*, and, most notably, *L'Almanach des Muses*.

Whilst the romance survived throughout the period under consideration here, its private, intimate type of medievalism was increasingly challenged in the 1820s by a different lyric genre, the *ballade*, evocative of a darker, wilder, and more mysterious Middle Ages. The opposition between these two lyric forms corresponds, I would argue, to the difference between Gothic and troubadour elements in the novel. The best and most famous examples of this genre are to be found in Hugo's *Odes et ballades* (1826 and 1828). The success of this type of medievalism is also evidenced in the parodies of the genre published by the Toulouse poet Baour-Lormian (1770-1854) in his *Légendes, ballades et fabliaux* (1829). By the late 1820s the very success of Gothic medievalism, especially in lyric poetry, was becoming in "advanced" literary circles a subject for concern and mockery. It was this sense of surfeit and excess which found its most powerful expression in the scathing attack on the superficiality of contemporary medievalism launched by Gautier in his preface to *Mademoiselle de Maupin* (1835), in which Gautier's critic ridicules the fashionability of a mere cardboard cut-out version of the Middle Ages.[42]

As I hope to have shown from this discussion, medieval themes were commonplace in the literature of the French Restoration across the whole range of literary genres. Moreover, just as in historiography the Middle Ages could be used in the service of either royalist or liberal politics, so in literature they could be exploited either within a classical or a Romantic aesthetic. Nevertheless, in literature as in historiography a clear dominant emerged in the late Restoration, so that medievalism and Romanticism became congruent, even synonymous, just like Romanticism and liberalism. The consequences of this situation are with us even today in that medievalism is still typically seen as incompatible with classicism, an assumption which is open to question.

In the course of this survey of three realizations of French Romantic medievalism, in historiography, scholarship, and literature, I have tried to show the presence of competing and sometimes conflicting elements within evolving forms. As I argued earlier, works in the first two categories typically (con)figure the Middle Ages, either explicitly or implicitly, in terms of metonymy. Their approach is structured by the importance given

120 Studies in Medievalism

to race or class or place. In the literary texts the situation is more complex and, ironically, less clearly articulated. Beyond the considerable diversity of expression of literary medievalism there does, however, seem to be a deeper unity, one that can be realized in metaphor more appropriately than in metonymy. The Middle Ages, instead of being captured by a representative material attribute, are figured by a symbolic form. This new imaginative vision can best be reflected in the imagery of darkness and light. It progressively rejects the sentimental, nostalgic view of the Middle Ages cultivated in the *genre troubadour* in favour of the more sombre, mysterious world of the Gothic.

The three forms of French Romantic medievalism I have explored in this essay are not to be seen as discrete. They constitute three overlapping manifestations of the renewed interest in the Middle Ages which followed the destruction of the *ancien régime* and the re-establishment of the monarchy. For the conflicting ideologies of royalism and liberalism the Middle Ages provided a link between past and present. In the case of the former it was legitimation through a sense of continuity and permanence. For the latter the Middle Ages served the same function but by a different means, that of a search for the distant origins of newly gained powers and freedoms. The divisions within French Romantic medievalism, therefore, do not lie between historians, scholars, and writers but within each group. At the same time there is a discernible pattern of evolution: the royalist Catholic medievalism of the early Restoration gradually gives way to a liberal consensus in the late 1820s. In this process the Middle Ages come to be seen, by historians, philologists, and creative writers, less as a nostalgic search for reassurance by a return to the past than as a means of confronting the contradictions of the present. To unite all three visions in the metaphor I have embedded in the title of this essay, the cradle has been abandoned in favor of the crucible.

NOTES

1. See the following works by these three scholars: Stephen Bann, *The Clothing of Clio: A Study of the Representation of History in Nineteenth-Century Britain and France* (Cambridge: Cambridge University Press, 1984), and the same author's *Romanticism and the Rise of History* (New York: Twayne, 1995); Ceri Crossley, *French Historians and Romanticism* (London: Routledge, 1993); Lionel Gossman, *Between History and Literature* (Cambridge, Mass.: Harvard University Press, 1990). The pioneering studies in this field are Stanley Mellon's *The Political Uses of History: A Study of Historians in the French Restoration* (Stanford: University

Press, 1958) and Boris Reizov, *L'Historiographie romantique française, 1815-1830* (Moscow: Editions en langues étrangères [1962]).

2. For an outline of the thought of the Idéologues and especially their conception of the study of history see Crossley, 10-19. For a detailed study see Cheryl B. Welch, *Liberty and Utility: The French Idéologues and the Transformation of Liberalism* (New York: Columbia University Press, 1984).

3. *Histoire littéraire de la France*, XVI (1824): 1-254.

4. Ginguené was best known for his *Histoire littéraire de l'Italie* (1811-1819), but he published a number of important essays on twelfth-century French literature in volumes XIII and XIV of the *Histoire littéraire de la France*. On Ginguené's role in the development of literary history see Marc Régaldo, "Un breton (sic) méconnu: Ginguené, fondateur de l'histoire littéraire," in *Missions et démarches de la critique. Mélanges offerts au Professeur J. A. Vier* (Paris: Klincksieck, 1973), 77-90.

5. *Le Mercure de France* 35 (1809): 327.

6. On attitudes towards the Middle Ages in Madame de Staël's circle see Norman King's excellent essay "Le Moyen Age à Coppet" in Simone Balayé and Jean-Daniel Candaux, eds., *Le Groupe de Coppet. Actes et documents du deuxième Colloque de Coppet* (Geneva/Paris: Slatkine/Champion, 1977), 375-99. See also in the same volume H. Duranton, "L'interprétation du mythe troubadour par le Groupe de Coppet" (349-373).

7. Karl Mannheim, *Ideology and Utopia* (London: Routledge & Kegan Paul, 1936), 70-71.

8. For a detailed study of the impact of *De l'Allemagne* on Romanticism see John C. Isbell, *The Birth of European Romanticism: Truth and Propaganda in Staël's "De l'Allemagne"* (Cambridge: Cambridge University Press, 1994).

9. On Sismondi's attitude towards the Middle Ages see Norman King, "Chevalerie et liberté," in *Sismondi européen. Actes du colloque international tenu à Genève les 14 et 15 septembre 1973* (Geneva/Paris: Slatkine/Champion, 1976), 241-58.

10. See my article "Tradition nationale et clivages régionalistes: la querelle des trouvères et des troubadours dans le romantisme français (1815-1830)," *Les Lettres Romanes* 48 (1994): 175-188.

11. I have studied the contemporary reception of *La Gaule poétique* in my article "Deux interprètes romantiques de la littérature française du Moyen Age: Sismondi et Marchangy," *Studi Francesi* 37 (1993): 545-554.

12. For a useful study of *Tristan le voyageur* see Monique Streiff-Moretti, "*Tristan le voyageur ou la France au XIVe siècle* de L.-A.-F. de Marchangy," in Georges Cesbron, ed., *Ouest et romantismes* (Angers: Presses Universitaires, 1990), 1: 339-52.

13. See the review of a new edition of *La Gaule poétique* in *L'Oriflamme* 2 (1824): 254-61; 369-77; 501-8, and for the review of *Tristan le voyageur* see *Le Globe* 17 September 1825. For a comprehensive study of the importance of *Le Globe* in French Romanticism see Jean-Jacques Goblot, *La Jeune France libérale: 'Le Globe' et son groupe littéraire 1824-1830* (Paris: Plon, 1995).

14. See Thierry's preface to his *Récit des temps mérovingiens* (1840).

15. See Marcel Gauchet, "Les Lettres sur l'histoire de France d'Augustin Thierry," in Pierre Nora, ed., *Les Lieux de mémoire 2: La nation* (Paris: Gallimard, 1986), 1: 247-316.

16. *Histoire de la conquête*, 5th ed. (Paris, 1838), 3:13.

17. Chateaubriand's reviews of Barante's work are reprinted in his *Mélanges politiques et littéraires* (Paris: Firmin Didot, 1854), 533-550.

18. On the debate about the respective roles of the Gauls and the Franks in French historiography see Martin Thom, "Tribes within nations: the ancient Germans and the history of modern France," in Homi K. Bhabha, ed., *Nation and Narration* (London and New York: Routledge, 1991), 23-43; also, Krzysztof Pomian's important essay "Francs et Gaulois," in Nora, ed., *Les Lieux de mémoire 3: Les France* (Paris: Gallimard, 1992), 1: 40-105.

19. On Sismondi's *Histoire des Français* see Louis Trénard, "L'*Histoire des Français* devant l'opinion française" in *Sismondi européen*, 317-48.

20. *Histoire de la conquête*, 4: 128.

21. Chateaubriand, *Mélanges politiques et littéraires*, 534.

22. See in particular the essays in R. Howard Bloch and Stephen G. Nichols eds., *Medievalism and the Modernist Temper* (Baltimore: Johns Hopkins University Press, 1996). Also in France the work of Michel Espagne, such as his article "Claude Fauriel en quête d'une méthode, ou l'Idéologie à l'écoute de l'Allemagne," *Romantisme* 73 (1991): 7-18, and the same author's *Le Paradigme de l'étranger: les chaires de littérature étrangère au XIXe siècle* (Paris: Le Cerf, 1993).

23. John M. Graham, "National Identity and the Politics of Publishing the Troubadours," in Bloch and Nichols, 57-94 (75). See also the related essay by Laura Kendrick, "The Science of Imposture and the Professionalization of Medieval Occitan Studies," 95-126.

24. See his article in Bloch and Nichols, cited above.

25. Raynouard set out the theory of the case system of Old French in a review published in the *Journal des Savans* (*sic*) in 1828 and in more detail in his *Observations philologiques et grammaticales sur le roman de Rou et sur quelques règles dans la langue des trouvères au douzième siècle* (Rouen: Frère, 1829). For Daunou's review of this work see the *Journal des Savans*, March 1829: 677-82.

26. Michel Foucault, *Les Mots et les choses* (Paris: Gallimard, 1966), 298.

27. C.-A. Sainte-Beuve, *Portraits contemporains* (Paris: Calmann Lévy, 1889), 4: 127.

28. Stendhal, *De l'Amour*, ed. Michel Crouzet (Paris: Garnier-Flammarion, 1965), 189.

29. On Stendhal's actual debt to both Raynouard and Fauriel, see Ulrich Mölk, "Stendhal, die Liebe und das Mittelalter: Bemerkungen zu *De l'Amour*," *Stendhal Club* 24 (1981-2): 424-34.

30. See Quinet's essay "Essai sur l'histoire moderne considérée dans ses rapports avec l'imagination" in Willy Aeschimann, *La Pensée d'Edgar Quinet* (Paris and Geneva: Anthropos/Georg, 1986), 426-34.

31. For a useful bibliography on medievalism in French Romantic literature see Norris J. Lacy, "The French Romantics and Medieval Literature: A Bibliographical Essay," *Studies in Medievalism* 3.1 (1987): 87-97. For two recent studies dealing with some of this material see Barbara G. Keller, *The Middle Ages Reconsidered: Attitudes in France from the Eighteenth Century through the Romantic Movement* (New York: Peter Lang, 1994), and my own *Reconstructing Camelot: French Romantic Medievalism and the Arthurian Tradition* (Cambridge: D. S. Brewer, 1995). On medievalism in later nineteenth-century French literature the standard work is Janine R. Dakyns, *The Middle Ages in French Literature 1851-1900* (London: Oxford University Press, 1973).

32. The standard studies on the epic in French Romanticism are Herbert J. Hunt, *The Epic in Nineteenth-Century France* (Oxford: Blackwell, 1941), and Leon Cellier, *L'Epopée humanitaire et les grands mythes romantiques* (Paris: SEDES, 1971).

33. On nineteenth-century treatments of figures from medieval French history see Christian Amalvi, *De l'art et la manière d'accommoder les héros de l'histoire de France* (Paris: Albin Michel, 1988), and his recent *Le Goût du Moyen Age* (Paris: Plon, 1996); also Barbara T. Cooper, "Creating a Royal Stand-in: History, Politics, and Medievalism in a French Restoration Tragedy," *Medievalism and Romanticism*, ed. Leslie J. Workman, *Poetica* 39-40 (1994): 225-45.

34. Michèle H. Jones, *Le Théâtre national en France de 1800 à 1830* (Paris: Klincksieck, 1975), 47-8.

35. On Mérimée's role as "inspecteur général des Monuments historiques," see André Fermiguier, "Mérimée et l'inspection des monuments historiques," in Nora, *Les Lieux de mémoire 2: La nation* (Paris: Gallimard, 1986), 2: 593-611.

36. For a useful essay on *La Jacquerie*, see Roger Bellet, "Jacques Bonhomme, Loup-Garou et la lutte des classes dans la Jacquerie," *Europe* 53 no. 557 (1975): 8-30.

37. On the impact of Scott in France during the Romantic period see Klauss Massmann, *Die Rezeption der historischen Romane Sir Walter Scotts in Frankreich, 1816-1832* (Heidelberg: Carl Winter Universitätsverlag, 1972).

38. H. de Balzac, *Illusions perdues*, ed. Antoine Adam (Paris: Garnier, 1961), 255-6.

39. V. Hugo, *Oeuvres complètes: Critique*, ed. Jean-Pierre Reynaud (Paris: Lafont, 1985), 148.

40. The standard work on Hugo and the Middle Ages is Patricia A. Ward, *The Medievalism of Victor Hugo* (University Park: Pennsylvania State University Press, 1975). See also Paul Zumthor, "Le moyen âge de Victor Hugo," *Littérales*, 6 (1990): 117-24. For a detailed study of *Notre-Dame de Paris*, see Rachel Killick, *Hugo: Notre-Dame de Paris* (Glasgow: University of Glasgow French and German Publications, 1994); for another discussion of Hugo's medievalism see Mary Anne O'Neil, "Classic Terror/Gothic Terror: Victor Hugo's *Quatrevingt-treize*," in Workman: 259-273.

41. Gérard Gengembre, "Le genre troubadour: permanence ou mutation?" *Littérales* 6 (1990), 15-24. See also his *La Contre-révolution ou l'histoire désespérante*

(Paris: Imago, 1989): 234-8. On the equivalent fashion in painting see F. Pupil, *Le Style troubadour ou la nostalgie du bon vieux temps* (Nancy: Presses Universitaires, 1985).

42. T. Gautier, *Mademoiselle de Maupin*, ed. Adolphe Boschot (Paris: Garnier, 1966), 13-14.

Medievalism in the Midi: Inventing the Medieval House in Nineteenth-Century France

Martha L. MacFarlane

Since the early nineteenth century, travelers in France have been enchanted by the country's medieval cities, whether encircled by fortifications, as at Carcassonne, or surmounted by a picturesque castle or church, as at Mont-Saint-Michel. Although such sites have long been examined for their history and architecture, successive restorations and refabrications in the last two centuries have slowly severed these communities from their medieval identities. Today, well preserved medieval towns like Carcassonne and Mont-Saint-Michel more often convey nineteenth- or twentieth-century ideas and perceptions of the Middle Ages than they do their historic origins. The particular example of the extensively studied and highly restored late medieval town of Cordes, in France's Languedoc region, provides a special viewpoint from which to examine the architectural and historical reinvention of a medieval community.

Nestled upon a steep hill overlooking the Cérou River, Cordes captured the attention of nineteenth-century scholars and enthusiasts because of its picturesque site and the distinctive medieval stone houses which line its main street, the Grande Rue. Founded in 1222 by Count Raymond VII of Toulouse, Cordes is historically significant as the first of over five hundred *bastides* established on the French and Aquitanian frontier in southwestern France during the later Middle Ages.[1] The governmental freedoms and unique urban privileges which characterized the *bastides* allowed towns like Cordes to prosper until their decline during the Hundred Years War (1337-1453).

Studies in Medievalism VIII, 1996

Now a small rural community in the *département* of the Tarn just east of Toulouse, Cordes was subject to extensive visual and textual documentation following the Revolution. Numerous restorations, archaeological surveys, and historical studies have resulted in a town with a rich historiography and some of the finest surviving examples of thirteenth- and fourteenth-century French domestic architecture.[2] The nineteenth-century documents for the medieval houses of Cordes, which range from manuals of architectural history to tourist guides, popularized these curious monuments for a national audience, often by cementing long-standing community myths. In so doing, these sources helped to reshape Cordes into a well preserved and convincingly "medieval" community. Today, the gentrified charm of houses such as the Grand Ecuyer (Great Squire), now an elegant hotel and four-star restaurant, the Grand Fauconnier (Great Falconer), and the Grand Veneur (Great Hunter) sustain Cordes's economy. According to one popular American tourist guide, the Bastille Day celebration in Cordes, called the Fête du Grand Fauconnier after its famous house, "sends Cordes back 500 years. Townspeople wrap their homes in garlands and medieval bunting and cavort as queens, princes, knights and fair damsels, celebrating with a banquet and a torchlit procession in a festival unrelated to the French national holiday."[3] However, this celebration bears no relationship to the true historic past of Cordes, whose communal laws prevented queens, princes, and knights from populating the city. Clearly, the collective memory of Cordes's inhabitants and visitors is, as it was in the early nineteenth century, exceptionally selective. As I shall argue here, it has been equally inventive.

This essay considers how the earliest historiography of Cordes, which dates from the first third of the nineteenth century, strengthened communal mythologies and laid the foundation for the textual, visual, and, much later, architectural reinvention of the town's medieval houses. Since the entire historiography of Cordes is beyond the scope of the present study, I focus particularly upon the contributions of the antiquarian Alexandre du Mège (1780-1862) and the Baron Isidore-Justin-Séverin Taylor (1789-1879), editor of the well known book series *Voyages pittoresques et romantiques dans l'ancien France* (published between 1820 and 1878). Together, the works of these individuals constitute the most formative nineteenth-century studies of medieval Cordes. My examination of these sources explores the primary question, unanswered in any recent research on the French medieval house, of why medieval houses and communities were deemed important to the nineteenth century.[4] Furthermore, to understand the institutions and initiatives which informed early nineteenth-century perceptions of medieval secular architecture, I consider these

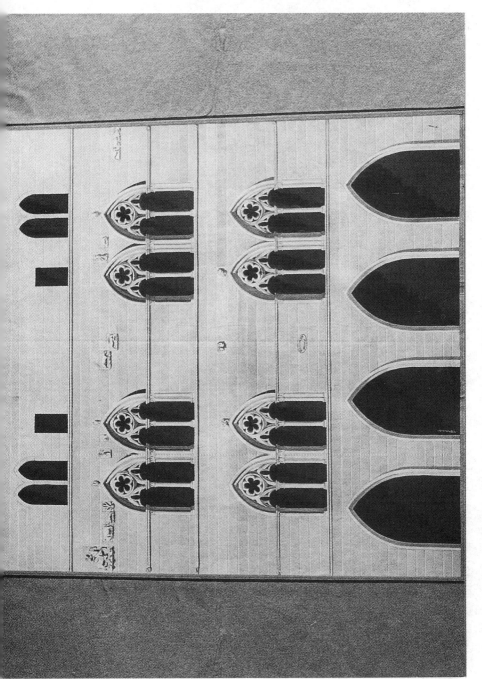

Figure 1. Alexandre du Mège, drawing of the façade of the Palais du Comte Raymond VII, from the *Mémoire sur les monuments antiques du Tarn* (1821). Paris: Bibliothèque Mazarine ms. 4178, part I, fol. 11.

Figure 2, detail. Third-story windows.

Figure 2. Maison du Grand Veneur, Cordes.
Late nineteenth- or early twentieth-century photograph.

Figure 4. T. Boys and A. Dauzats, lithograph from *Voyages pittoresques et romantiques dans l'ancien France*. Languedoc edition, vol. I (c. 1833). *See following page.*

Figure 3. The Maison du Grand Veneur today. Photo: author.

Figure 5. Adrien Dauzats, Hôtel du Comte Raymond, Cordes, lithograph from *Voyages pittoresques*. Languedoc edition, vol. I, part 2, book 35, plate 82 (1835).

Figure 4, detail.

Inventing the Medieval House

individuals and their products within their multiple historical, cultural, and popular contexts. This reassessment of the early historiography of a particular medieval site will contribute to a larger awareness of the way medieval houses and communities are currently studied and valued.

Alexandre du Mège and the archaeology of the medieval house

Medieval archaeology, first evident in England from the early eighteenth century, did not begin to develop across the Channel until over a century later.[5] Action was taken to record and preserve French historic monuments only after the country had experienced a revolution, the ensuing vandalism, and the confiscation of its artistic treasures by outsiders. Some of the better known early examples of French archaeology, such as Gerville's *Monuments de la Manche* (1810), naturally focused upon Normandy because of the region's proximity to the British Isles, a highly literate population, an impressive tax base, and well organized archaeological societies founded after the English model, as exemplified in the outstanding work of Arcisse de Caumont and the Société des Antiquaires de Normandie (founded in 1824).[6] In contrast to the Norman contribution, the southern *département* of the Tarn had never been the subject of archaeological attention before 1820. The Benedictine and Tarnais historians Vaissète and Devic examined the region in their vast *Histoire générale de Languedoc* (1730-45), but this work is of a purely historical nature and excludes monuments. Many early antiquarian travelers in the Midi, such as Louis-Aubin Millin (1804), avoided the sparsely populated and agricultural Tarnais region, favoring coastal sites in Provence and the Hérault. Those who did visit the Tarn, particularly the military captain and *savant* Lavallée (1798-99), expressed a primary interest in describing, from a distance, the department's citizens and principal cities.[7] In producing his never-published *Mémoire sur les monuments antiques du Tarn*, the Toulousain antiquarian Alexandre-Louis-Charles-André du Mège became the first not only to expose the archaeological and artistic richness of the region but to shape and reinvent its very character.[8]

Born in The Hague on 5 December 1780, Du Mège was the only child of Charles-Louis du Mège, a respected dramatic artist in the Comédie Française, an amateur historian and antiquarian, and a highly ranked Freemason.[9] The family moved to Toulouse in 1786, but little is known of Du Mège's childhood and education save that he attended the Ecole Centrale in Toulouse around the time of its opening in 1795.[10] However, Du Mège's biographer and contemporary Auguste d'Aldéguier suggests that Du Mège was destined from an early age to become an archaeologist and records that in order to fulfill his dream, he "locked himself in all the libraries to which he had access" and studied "literature and history . . . Latin, Greek and Hebrew."[11]

Du Mège was initially attracted to the Middle Ages by a circuitous route through Egyptology and *Celtomanie.* He followed his father into a Masonic order sometime after 1801, when Freemasonry was re-established in France; in 1804 he was a member of the Napoléomagne (likely a contraction of Napoléon-Charlemagne) lodge in Toulouse, contributing to the restoration of Freemasonry in the Toulousain. As he progressed to higher levels within the order, founding and designing the mother lodge of the Souveraine Pyramide des Amis du Désert (Auch, *département* of Gers) with Pierre Sentetz in 1806, he demonstrated an intense interest in Egypt. Since much of the contemporary Masonic rite was based on supposed Egyptian and Middle Eastern traditions, the proposed pyramid was to have an altar dedicated to *Dieu Humanité-Vérité* placed between figures of Isis and Osiris.[12] The entrance would be guarded by two sphinxes and the interior decorated by hieroglyphics, which ironically could not be translated until the advent of Champollion fifteen years later.[13] Du Mège also made provisions for the Masonic rites, indicating the "Egyptian" attire of the members, from the initiates to the officers.[14] But eighteenth- and early nineteenth-century Masonic practices were also often linked to Celtic Druids in the belief that the early Celts maintained ancient customs subsequently transmitted to the modern Masonic lodge.[15] Furthermore, just as westerners since the Renaissance have perceived Egypt as the homeland of wisdom and science, the early Celts came to be synonymous with the spiritual and cultural origins of France.[16] Du Mège was certainly sensitive to these viewpoints, since he became one of the first corresponding members of the newly-founded Académie Celtique in 1804.

As evident in his writings, Du Mège perceived the medieval culture and art of southwestern France as evolving out of the very early Celtic and Gallo-Roman history of the Midi. Du Mège understood the historical richness of southwestern France and focused particularly upon its Celtic and Gallo-Roman roots in the initial years of his career. His goal became to study southwestern France more deeply, to rediscover "the ancient megaliths (*menhirs*), the bethels of the Old Celts" and, more importantly, "the mythology of the Pyrénées."[17] In 1802, Richard, the Prefect of the Haute-Garonne, assigned Du Mège with the study of the antiquities of Saint-Bertrand-des-Comminges. This work became the foundation for his *Mémoire sur les antiquités de la Haute-Garonne* of 1803, proving him to be the first serious student of the artistic traditions of the Pyrénées and the surrounding region.[18] Recognizing his particular knowledge of the

Inventing the Medieval House 129

southwest, the Académie Celtique published a "Notice sur un voyage d'antiquités de M. Dumège dans le département de la Haute-Garonne et dans les départements voisins" in its *Mémoires* of 1807.[19]

In 1806 Du Mège began actively to salvage historic monuments after receiving a Christian (possibly Merovingian) sarcophagus from his Masonic colleague Sentetz. Struck by post-Revolutionary vandalism and ineffective legal measures which destined French artifacts to certain destruction, Du Mège told his fellow Masons,

> If these objects appear barbaric to you . . . and if you do not judge it appropriate to conserve them yourself, I will handle it. I will pay their value, their transport, etc. But above all, save them; the monuments of the Middle Ages are becoming, due to Revolutionary vandalism and to the ignorance of buyers for the national domaine, an extraordinary rarity.[20]

Du Mège was appointed Commissioner for Antiquities Research in the Haute-Garonne the following year and was ordered by Interior Minister Montalivet in 1810 to record extant monuments in southwestern France; the charge was renewed in 1820 by Montalivet's successor Lainé (who had also been responsible for Du Mège's assignment as Inspector of Antiquities in the Haute-Garonne in 1819). Although his exact remuneration is unknown, sometime in 1820 he received support from the departmental Prefect to undertake a study of the Tarn. In 1821 Du Mège presented the Prefect and General Council with what was intended as the first of many installments of his studies; since his post was unfortunately terminated in 1823, however, this manuscript remains the only record of his work.

Preserved in the Departmental Archives of the Tarn (Albi), Du Mège's *Mémoire sur les monuments antiques du Tarn* consists of three handwritten bound volumes which lack a clear internal order. Although Du Mège aimed to divide his monographs of individual monuments and communities into four periods—ancient Gaul, the Roman occupation, the Middle Ages (which he delimits from the seventh to fifteenth centuries), and finally the sixteenth to seventeenth centuries—these historical demarcations are vague, often mixed, in the completed work.[21] Following a lengthy introduction in which Du Mège notes that "no one has yet published, or even drawn attention to, any monument discovered in this part of the Kingdom," the *Mémoire* focuses primarily upon the history and archaeology of the northern portion of the department.[22] Moreover, having first devoted so much of his attention to Gallo-Roman culture, Du Mège rarely moved beyond medieval monuments. The incomplete state

130   Studies in Medievalism

of the manuscript reflects not only the premature termination of Du Mège's studies but also the antiquarian's pronounced preference for the early history of France.[23]

At a time when most French antiquarians and scholars viewed domestic architecture as a mere curiosity, Du Mège's interest in medieval buildings also extended to housing. Due to a sizable clerical presence in French historical writing, an academic preference for the architecture of churches and cathedrals was readily apparent from the seventeenth to the mid-nineteenth centuries. Such a preference arguably continues to exist. While ecclesiastical architecture was regularly elevated to the status of high art, houses, regardless of age, were considered too common and therefore expendable. In contrast, Du Mège's description of medieval domestic architecture in the *Mémoire* offers considerable insight into his perception of medieval habitations and his reasons for studying them.

Du Mège asserts that "the remains of private dwellings merit our attention almost more than palaces, temples and fortresses" since they are records of the habits and values of a distant past.[24] His description of two Albigensian houses nevertheless conveys his difficulty with such unfamiliar material.[25] For example, despite his lengthy descriptions of sculptural elements on the Albi houses, Du Mège was unsure of their secular iconography and routinely dismissed certain examples as unimportant while devoting many lines to the similarities between selected sculptural motifs and the design on Druidic megaliths.[26] Although his discussion of domestic construction is reduced to a brief stylistic analysis, Du Mège's description of the Albi houses is important to archaeological historiography in his acknowledgment of postmedieval changes to the houses and in his lament over the modernization and urban growth which had led to the destruction of so much medieval domestic architecture.

Du Mége's discussion of Cordes and its houses, the earliest recorded, occupies several pages of the first volume of his *Mémoire*. Here, as in the case of the Albi houses, Du Mège's description offers little sense of how domestic architecture was actually used, despite his insistence that housing reflects the customs and values of its inhabitants. Exteriors and interiors, for example, receive different treatment in the *Mémoire*. In order to dismiss domestic interior organization as irrelevant, Du Mège acknowledged the often extensive changes made by subsequent owners. The same case is not made for the façades, however. No mention is made in the text of the incongruous doors and windows which, as postmedieval additions, scarred the façades of the houses. In dismissing the importance of the medieval house as a whole entity and in focusing upon very specific elements, Du Mège strengthened his arguments for the noble past of the

Inventing the Medieval House

community and enriched the longstanding communal myths associated with the Cordes houses.

Although Du Mège appropriated historical information outlined in Jean-François Massol's *Description du département du Tarn suivi de l'histoire de l'ancien pays d'Albigeois* (1818), a work of questionable accuracy, much of the historical context which Du Mège provided in his description of Cordes follows local lore or was his own invention.[27] Perhaps unaware of the foundation charter of Cordes, Du Mège asserted that the town was founded by Raymond VI, Count of Toulouse, when in fact it was founded in 1222 by his son, Count Raymond VII. More significant and influential is Du Mège's belief that the town was founded to provide a hunting retreat for the younger count and his entourage. Misdating the fourteenth-century houses, Du Mège argued that the imposing stone structures were built to shelter members of the thirteenth-century court. Du Mège's description of Cordes thus recorded for the first time an association between the medieval houses of Cordes and important personages who were affiliated with the community from its foundation.

One house in particular attracted Du Mège's attention: the so-called Palais du Comte Raymond VII, known today as the Maison du Grand Veneur. For Du Mège, the façade of this house, particularly its sculpture, provided ample evidence of an illustrious past. Asserting that the house was once the hunting lodge of the young count and a gift from his deputy, Sicard d'Alaman (also a supposed resident of Cordes), Du Mège offered a highly detailed description of the façade sculpture, accompanied by numerous images.[28] As in the description of the medieval houses in Albi, certain sculptural elements were ignored as "mere decoration" while others, especially those which suggested a noble patronage, were discussed in depth. A sculptural frieze depicting a hunt on the second story of the façade was, for Du Mège, crucial proof of his theories: "The most remarkable figure represents a young man on a horse: a headband on his head, a distinctive sign of sovereignty," he stated, and repeated the same point on the following page.[29] To strengthen his argument, he observed that Raymond loved to hunt and "often traveled in the forests of the *Albigeois*, especially in those which adjoined the châteaux of Penne and Cordes."[30] In other words, Du Mège invented a uniquely noble patronage for Cordes, despite a lack of evidence, and sculpture plays a crucial role in upholding these myths.[31] Moreover, his last statement reveals how he tried to create a very localized mythology which would appeal to a regional audience.

Du Mège's turn towards medieval domestic architecture was sparked in part by the very recent and unprecedented discoveries at Pompeii.

132   Studies in Medievalism

Pompeian ruins and inscriptions were discovered as early as 1594-1600 by the architect Domenico Fontana as he constructed an underground aqueduct. Systematic excavations of Pompeii were not begun, however, until the middle of the eighteenth century and received even greater stimulus during the period of French domination in Italy (1806-14). The French were responsible for the site until 1861 when the project was returned to the Italian authorities. Du Mège, who was working in the Tarn during the French government's deepest involvement in the excavations, was excited by the continuing rediscovery of this ancient community in which over thirty relatively intact houses survive, spanning all types and socio-economic levels. Du Mège wrote in his *Mémoire*,

> If, soon tired of seeing nothing but temples, palaces and tombs, one . . . . directs his course towards Italy, an entire village torn away from oblivion, raised from the midst of ashes thrown up by Vesuvius, offers us the most stirring subjects for meditation. There one finds the houses of an entire people. The arts and manners of the unfortunate inhabitants of Pompeii appear all at once for our regards. One meets with each step the traces of a population which is no longer.[32]

The rediscovery of Pompeii provided fundamental resources for classical scholars and archaeologists and enriched a classical revival in architecture already well in place by the late eighteenth century.[33] For Du Mège, the findings translated into a greater respect for historic domestic architecture and the information it offers about the daily lives of its former inhabitants. Du Mège's specific reference to Pompeii in his *Mémoire* suggests that such impressive archaeological discoveries of domestic architecture were responsible for the interest in medieval domestic architecture which initially arises in the first quarter of the nineteenth century.

A second factor in the early nineteenth-century French discovery of medieval secular architecture was the importation of British social history. The English historian Henry Hallam (1777-1859) inspired a generation of French archaeologists and antiquarians with his three-volume work, *View of the State of Europe during the Middle Ages* (1818), published just two years before Du Mège commenced his endeavors in the Tarn.[34] The first two volumes of the *State of Europe* are devoted to the political, legal, and military history of France, Germany, England, Italy, and Spain. In the last chapter (Chapter IX) of the third volume, entitled "On The State of Society in Europe During the Middle Ages," Hallam discussed social and

Inventing the Medieval House

cultural issues. Although the subjects within his chapters have no recognizable organization (for example, the topics "Progress of Refinement in Manners" and "Domestic Architecture" are sandwiched between "Progress of Commercial Improvement" and "The Value of Money"), his discussion of ecclesiastical architecture is, uncommonly, *preceded* by a section on medieval domestic architecture, in which he states:

> No chapter in the history of national manners would illustrate so well, if duly executed, the progress of social life as that dedicated to domestic architecture. The fashions of dress and of amusements are generally capricious and irreducible to rule; but every change in the dwellings of mankind, from the rudest wooden cabin to the stately mansion, has been dictated by some principle of convenience, neatness, comfort, or magnificence. Yet this most interesting field of research has been less beaten by our antiquaries than others comparatively barren.[35]

Although he does not mention Pompeii, Hallam anticipates Du Mège in his belief that domestic architecture is the best resource for examining the history of daily life. Hallam commenced this section on domestic architecture with examples from England, citing the only sources available at the time, "Dr. Whitaker's *History of Whalley*" and "Mr. King's Essays on Ancient Castles in the *Archaeologia*."[36] However, the latter source brings him out of the realm of common domestic architecture to fortifications. On French domestic architecture, he briefly states that

> France by no means appears to have made a greater progress than our own country in domestic architecture. Except fortified castles, I do not find . . . any considerable dwellings mentioned before the reign of Charles VII, and very few of so early a date. . . . It is obvious that the long calamities which France endured before the expulsion of the English must have retarded this eminent branch of national improvement.[37]

Despite his general ignorance of surviving vestiges of medieval domestic architecture, Hallam nevertheless for the first time proposed a more inclusive history.[38] He argued from the outset of the *State of Europe* that

> There remains a large tract to be explored, if we would complete the circle of historical information, and give to our knowledge

134   Studies in Medievalism

that copiousness and clear perception which arise from comprehending a subject under numerous relations. The philosophy of history embraces far more than the wars and treaties, the factions and cabals of common political narration; it extends to whatever illustrates the character of the human species in a particular period, to their reasonings and sentiments, their arts and industry.[39]

His methodology brings to mind the socialist vision of later English writers and historical theorists, such as William Morris. Morris was in fact specifically indebted to Hallam for having drawn attention to the medieval house.[40]

Hallam's *State of Europe* was published in French as *L'Europe au Moyen Age* in 1820-21, offering a new perspective to French archaeologists and antiquarians. France of course had important writers of social history and theory during the first half of the nineteenth century, including Saint-Simon (1760-1825), Augustin Thierry (1795-1856), and François Guizot (1787-1874), but their work contributed mainly to the reassessment of politics, institutions, and historical methodologies and, unlike Hallam, did not demonstrate a call to study and preserve historic domestic architecture. Although Du Mège made no mention of Hallam, his contemporary Arcisse de Caumont proved the historian's influence abroad by quoting Hallam word for word in the preface to his *Abécédaire, ou rudiment de l'archéologie* of 1850.[41]

Hallam's work helped give rise to the belief that the Middle Ages marked a transitional point during which history gradually changed hands from the religious and ruling classes to the people. The dignity which socio-historical methodologies imposed upon the worker, denoting him a shaper of history, had significant implications for the burgeoning Industrial Age.[42] Furthermore, the opinion that medieval history was also a history of "daily life" became deeply embedded in the historical and art-historical research of the second half of the nineteenth century. John Henry Parker's *Some Account of Domestic Architecture in England from Edward I to Richard II* (1853), the first extensive study devoted exclusively to medieval domestic architecture, resulted from this new mentality.

Images of the medieval house: Du Mège and the Voyages pittoresques

The *Mémoire's* textual idealization and mystification of the medieval house is equally apparent in the accompanying images. Du Mège illustrated each *notice*, or monograph, with plans or drawings which he

Inventing the Medieval House   135

himself "made with care."[43]   According to his introduction, Du Mége included seventy folio-sized plates in his *Mémoire*, supplemented with smaller drawings of sculpture, paintings, stained glass windows, inscriptions, and tombs, having collected some of these objects for the Musée des Augustins in Toulouse which opened in 1817.[44] Du Mège also announced his intention to continue his work in the northern portion of the department and expected, when the work was complete, to include over two hundred folio-sized plates in the *Mémoire*.[45]   Some time prior to Emile Jolibois's publication of the introduction to the *Mémoire* in 1878-79, the Prefect of the Tarn forwarded the rich treasure of five folio-sized plates and thirty-two smaller illustrations to the Minister of the Interior in Paris, who subsequently deposited them in the Library of the Institut de France where they remain today.[46]

Du Mège's drawing of the façade of the Palais du Comte Raymond VII is the first known representation of this edifice (Figure 1) and demonstrates the singular attraction of the imposing stone house for artists and antiquarians of the nineteenth century.   This early image in fact foreshadows the great popularity this house would achieve, becoming the most frequently represented dwelling in Cordes.

Du Mège depicted the four-story stone structure frontally. The house is so tightly condensed within the dark frame of the image that it appears without a roof, let alone a surrounding environment.   The image represents only the square façade of the building, extracted from its urban and residential contexts. The drawing is highly refined, in the tradition of much architectural drawing from the Ecole des Beaux-Arts in Paris.[47] Except for the inclusion of sculptural elements on the façade, the thin lines which perfectly describe each stone of the building and the inky blackness of the open doors and windows suggest a building completely lacking any unique character.

Du Mège's drawing lacks character, however, because it draws so little from its model. For example, subsequent images of the house, as well as its restoration history, suggest that the two sets of twin bay windows of the first story existed in an altered state until the late twentieth century.[48] Photographs dating from around the turn of the century show that by that date all windows at the topmost level had been walled off or closed with shutters (Figure 2 and detail). The four large arches at ground level were little more than vestiges, having been altered to create storefronts. Indeed, Du Mège depicted the house in a highly restored state, copying the bays of the second level from those of the third while tidying and leveling the ground floor arches (the ground level actually slopes). His "restoration" furthermore omitted the *anneaux de fer*, or iron rings, which are such a

136   Studies in Medievalism

curious part of the façade. That Du Mège's drawing, which ironically resembles Yves Boiret's completed restoration of the 1970s (Figure 3), bears no relationship to the contemporary structure is strengthened by a comparison with Adrien Dauzats's interpretation of the same monument for the Languedoc edition of the *Voyages pittoresques et romantiques dans l'ancienne France* (Figures 4 and 5).[49]

The first version of the *Voyages pittoresques* was published by Benjamin de la Borde from 1784 until his execution during the Terror in 1794; the more familiar version appeared in 1820, with an edition devoted to the Haute-Normandie, at the instigation of Alphonse de Cailleux, Charles Nodier, and the Baron Isidore-Séverin-Justin Taylor. Nodier and De Cailleux contributed to this edition, but it was Taylor who brought the entire series to fruition. Born in Brussels in 1789 (d. 1879), Taylor had studied drawing under the painter Suvé, and by the age of eighteen he was living off his artistic talents.[50] Entering the military in his twenties to support the Bourbon cause, Taylor devoted himself upon his release to artistic and literary concerns and fought strongly against vandalism. Simultaneous with his work on the *Voyages pittoresques* were many other "voyages pittoresques" to Spain and North Africa (1826), and the Middle East (1837 and 1841), as well as to the European continent and the British Isles (1843). Taylor, like Du Mége, had a strong interest in Egypt and was commissioned to oversee the French acquisition of obelisks from Luxor.

Each of the ten parts of the new *Voyages pittoresques*, twenty-one oversized volumes in all, was published by Didot. According to the biographer Gustave Vapereau, the *Voyages pittoresques* was "the first publication which used lithography and which offered, in the ensemble of its vast series, the topography, the history, and the artistic souvenirs of all the French departments within the boundaries of our ancient [i. e., pre-Napoleonic] provinces."[51] The extent and variety of the visual material in the *Voyages pittoresques* easily reached a popular audience, with the added result of profoundly influencing the future course of French patrimony. Eight parts examine regions of northern or central France, but the Languedoc edition, published in four volumes between 1833 and 1838 under the sole responsibility of Taylor, is distinguished as having the greatest number of plates (760), volumes and sections (146) of any of the editions. The Languedoc edition coincided with Du Mège's 1831 foundation of the Société Archéologique du Midi de la France (SAMF), one of the most powerful learned societies in southwestern France and certainly a factor in Taylor's decision to focus on the region.[52]

Taylor enlisted the help of many great artists for his volumes, including the Romantic painter Théodore Géricault (1791-1824); Géricault's theoretical rival, the Montaubanois Jean-Auguste-Dominique Ingres (1780-1867); and the marine and landscape painter Eugène-Gabriel Isabey (1803-86). For his Languedoc edition, however, Taylor chose a young southwesterner who had accompanied him upon many of his voyages in Europe and the orient.[53] Adrien Dauzats was born in Bordeaux in 1808 and later studied painting in the Parisian *atelier* of Julien-Michel Gué. In 1828 Dauzats began to specialize in watercolors and lithography. Taylor stationed Dauzats, whose paternal lineage was Tarnais, in the departmental capital of Albi. From this center, Dauzats served as Taylor's right arm and created more than one hundred plates for the Languedoc edition, largely concerning the regions surrounding Albi, Toulouse, Moissac, and Perpignan.[54]

The Languedoc edition contains the earliest published images of the medieval houses of Cordes, Dauzats's two depictions of the Palais, or as it is termed here, the Hôtel du Comte Raymond. The date of Dauzats's visit to Cordes is uncertain, but the images were most likely made during his residence in nearby Albi. The earliest of the lithographs, appearing in a section entitled "Les Environs d'Albi" in part one of the first volume of the Languedoc edition, was made sometime before the volume was published in 1833.[55] The image accompanies a descriptive and historical text about Cordes, framed by a gothic architectural motif created by the artist T. Boys (Figure 4). The bottom center of this gothicizing frame contains a small image, also by Dauzats, of an unidentified fortified entry into Cordes. The later image of the Hôtel du Comte Raymond appears by itself in Volume I, Part 2 of the Languedoc edition (1835).[56]

In the later illustration, Dauzats's frontally-depicted Hôtel du Comte Raymond occupies virtually all of the frame, much like the Du Mège image (Figure 5). In contrast to Du Mège's work, however, here the level street forms a *repoussoir*, which works with the open space around the building to create distance between viewer and monument. Dauzats's image is also more specific than that by Du Mège, suggesting his greater interest in visual accuracy. In addition to representing the monument in an unrestored state, Dauzats has even included *anneaux de fer* on the third level of the house. Nevertheless, there are still significant and perplexing differences between Dauzats's image of the house and photographs of it prior to its restoration (Figure 2). Although Dauzats presented a more credible version when compared with that of Du Mège, his contributions were no less inventive. In addition to appropriating the noble mythology of the community, Dauzats subtly restyled the house, lending symmetry to an actually asymmetrical façade while representing deeply recessed third-level windows (these are actually flush with the façade) to increase the

138   Studies in Medievalism

suggestion of light and shadow upon the building. Furthermore, Dauzats's image does not offer any sense of the true materials of the façade, suggesting a deteriorating plaster or stucco rather than high-quality sandstone. These elements indicate the artist's sacrifice of visual accuracy for the sake of striking and picturesque effects.[57]

Reinventions of the medieval house: resources and motives

Charles Portal, the foremost historian of Cordes at the turn of the present century, wrote in 1902 of the section on Cordes in the *Voyages pittoresques* that

> these authors give an historical resumé without value and studded with errors such as this: "In 1274 Sicard d'Alaman . . . was seigneur of Cordes". The drawings by Boys and Dauzats represent the house called *Grand Veneur* in too fantastic a fashion and a fortified portal which it is impossible for me to identify. Elsewhere the said house is, according to the text [that is, the descriptive caption], that of "Count Raymond"; such an attribution cannot be serious.[58]

Portal spent his career combating the early nineteenth-century inventions of Cordes, but he never addressed why such falsifications were deemed necessary by antiquarians and artists such as Du Mège, Taylor, and Dauzats. Rather than arguing for the historical naïveté of their contributions, it is far more pertinent to understand their resources and motives.

A reason often claimed for the increased fascination with the Middle Ages during the first half of the nineteenth century was the strongly historicist tenor of France's July Monarchy (1830-1848). As the first representative of the *bourgeois*, the "Citizen King" Louis-Philippe (1773-1850) and his administration provided the means for unprecedented changes out of which French archaeology and historical studies eventually grew. Numerous publications reflected the growing interest in medieval French history and historic preservation. Jules Michelet's *Histoire de France*, published between 1833-43, ends at the Middle Ages. Victor Hugo's famous 1831 novel *Notre Dame de Paris* employs a famous medieval monument as its main character. The preservationist challenge which Hugo offers in this book and elsewhere popularized the need for a massive movement to save French antiquities in the face of continuing vandalism. The new historicist *mentalité* also sparked momentous institutional changes. In 1830, then Prime Minister Louis-Adolphe Thiers

Inventing the Medieval House

(1797-1877) and Minister of Public Instruction François-Pierre-Guillaume Guizot (1787-1874) established the position of General Inspector of Historical Monuments. Shortly thereafter, the role of General Inspector came under the jurisdiction of the Commission des Monuments Historiques, established in 1837 to preserve the artistic and architectural heritage of France.

While organizations such as the Commission des Monuments Historiques would arguably become the most important contributors to the nineteenth-century preservation and study of medieval architecture, Du Mège, Taylor, and Dauzats formed part of a small undercurrent of architects, antiquarians, and archaeologists who demonstrated a strong interest in medieval history and archaeology even prior to the July Monarchy. Their reinventions of the medieval houses of Cordes were affected by multiple and highly interconnected factors, including post-Revolutionary vandalism, a growing romantic movement, and, most importantly, the needs and expectations of their respective audiences.

In the case of Du Mège, the mentality which enabled and even encouraged him to interpret the Palais du Comte Raymond VII as a virtually unrecognizable and highly restored monument was familiar among French antiquarians of the early nineteenth century. Du Mège has been particularly compared with his older contemporary, Alexandre Lenoir. On 6 June 1791, Lenoir, then a twenty-eight year-old *élève* in the atelier of a former royal painter, was nominated to supervise the monument *dépôt* at the former convent of the Petits-Augustins on Paris's left bank. From a mass of objects displaced by Revolutionary decree on 2 November 1789, Lenoir formed the Musée des monuments français. By 1795, the museum had opened in its completed form; a chronological survey of French art, principally sculpture and funerary monuments, from the Middle Ages to the Renaissance. The Musée des monuments français was closed by royal decree on 24 April 1816, only one year before the public opening of Du Mège's Musée des Augustins, also on the site of a former Augustinian convent.[59]

Lenoir's motivation was educational and nationalistic. In the spirit of the Revolution, Lenoir freed displaced monuments from their former feudal and monarchical associations by incorporating them within the framework of a museum, simultaneously lending them a new identity as French historical monuments. Lenoir's historicist outlook was publicized through the open lectures on French art history which he gave at the Athénée Royal in Paris, and through the over twenty volumes and forty memoirs which he wrote on this subject in his lifetime.[60] Lenoir wanted to reaffirm France's post-Revolutionary national identity, even by the most unusual measures. In 1793, Lenoir legally exhumed the mortal remains of some of France's most illustrious historical figures, including Descartes, La Fontaine, Molière, Turenne, Heloïse and Abélard. He fabricated elaborate monuments for their remains, sometimes out of existing sculptural fragments, and placed them in the museum's large garden, aptly named the *Elysée*.[61] Lenoir fabricated other monuments, even falsely attributed some others, in his attempt to secure a seamless chronological sequence of rooms and to create a spectacular setting.[62]

Like Lenoir, Du Mège, who began to collect objects for his museum as early as 1808, fabricated monuments which until the late twentieth century were thought to be authentic. The case of the twelfth-century portal from the chapter house of Saint-Etienne in Toulouse, compiled from pieces salvaged from the cathedral's cloister, has received particular notoriety and aroused lively controversy among experts in Romanesque art. In 1964, Linda Seidel was the first to argue that although the portal was "praised as one of the artistic glories of the Middle Ages" beginning in the first half of the nineteenth century, it was nevertheless a completely novel creation by Du Mège.[63] Seidel bases her argument upon a stylistic analysis and careful documentary and historiographic research which reveal Du Mège's arrangement of the sculptural fragments to be derived from his own imagination. She proposes that no such portal existed in the Middle Ages. Rather, these figures stood separately in the cathedral's chapter house.[64] The Saint-Etienne portal, and such examples as a "Roman" relief of the Triumph of Tetricus and the tomb of Denys de Beauvoir, were little more than the inventions of Du Mège—inventions which he never acknowledged.[65]

Du Mège saw himself as both the successor and southern counterpart to Lenoir. For Du Mège, as for many of his contemporaries, the Musée des monuments français was a significant factor in his turn towards the art and architecture of the Middle Ages.[66] Du Mège was aware of Lenoir's work in Paris, often citing Lenoir in his museum catalogues, and closely followed his predecessor's plan in the design of his own museum.[67] Furthermore, the two were fellow members of the Académie Celtique. One questions, therefore, whether Du Mège's work, and above all his historical inventions, so closely linked with those of Lenoir, evolved from the same nationalist, or even regionalist sentiment as his Parisian colleague.

Through their "inventions," Du Mège and Lenoir certainly demonstrated a mutual desire to control history and to reshape it to their own designs. One senses that Du Mège, in the very image of antiquarian *machismo*, could not examine the disorganized sculptural remains of Saint Etienne and the dilapidated façade of the Palais du Comte Raymond

Inventing the Medieval House   141

without wanting to change them in some way, to perfect them according to his own vision.[68] Indeed, Du Mège's whole career was characterized by the reinvention of the past. Consider again, for example, his model for the "Egyptian" pyramid at Auch in which he attempted to reconcile his foggy historical knowledge with what Marcel Durliat has termed nineteenth-century "mystical revelation."[69] Moreover, the very notion of a museum, such as the Musée des Augustins or the Musée des monuments français, implies cultural ownership and historical manipulation.[70] Considering the period in which Du Mège and Lenoir were raised and educated, both may have chosen such careers and methodologies as a response to, and means of controlling, the multifaceted upheaval of the Revolution. Lenoir and Du Mège were deeply concerned with the historic roots of their country, whether manifested in its Celtic, Roman, or Frankish branches. Their fabrication of the past, particularly the nation's past, simultaneously reinvented the collective memory of France.

Du Mège's many archaeological activities in southwestern France, as exemplified in the *Mémoire* he presented to the Prefect of the Tarn in 1821, have characterized him as an intense regionalist.[71] However, a reconsideration of Du Mège's goals in writing and illustrating the *Mémoire* reveals that his textual and visual invention of the medieval houses of Cordes may have had more to do with his audience. Writing decades before the "Occitan Revival" which would engulf the Languedoc, Du Mège demonstrated his contempt for the customs and languages of the region. He referred to Occitan as the "vulgar language of the country" and little more than a "corrupt dialect of the [Latin] language."[72] In contrast, his professional reputation and livelihood are recurring themes in the introduction to his *Mémoire*. Subordinate to and financially dependent upon the departmental administration, Du Mège was aware that his sole audience was the Prefect of the Tarn and perhaps the General Council.[73] His letter to the Prefect in the *Mémoire* is a subtly crafted request for additional funds and the publication of his work. Appealing to the Prefect's local pride, Du Mège pointed out,

> In a great number of departments, the general councils have not only voted funds for the research of their antiquities, but they have also published particular studies on their venerable remaining objects. The reunion of those in the Tarn would offer a precious collection . . . one would find within it something which doesn't exist in the voluminous histories which we possess, particularly the true picture of the values, customs and arts of the Albigensian people. The expense would be, it is true,

142   Studies in Medievalism

> more considerable; but the general council would raise a monument, whereas still extant materials will be, perhaps, in a few years, dispersed or destroyed.[74]

This statement suggests that although Du Mège's regional interests were sincere, the unstable conditions of his employment, combined with a highly localized audience, were more likely the real reasons behind his glorification of local history and validation of regional mythology.

Like Du Mège, Dauzats and Taylor recognized that the mystification of historic architecture could potentially preserve a national or regional memory. To this end, the *Voyages pittoresques* appropriated the local myths first recorded by Du Mège. Through the careful organization of setting, moreover, Dauzats and the *Voyages pittoresques* conveyed a deceptively authentic view of Cordes. For example, despite its seemingly naturalistic qualities, Dauzats's earlier view of the Hôtel du Comte Raymond and its surroundings from the Place de l'Eglise Saint-Michel inaccurately depicts the setting (Figure 4 and detail). Since none of the buildings surrounding the central Hôtel du Comte Raymond ever existed, nor do they resemble any past or present building in Cordes, this image again raises the issue of architectural invention or fantasy. The building immediately to the left of the Hôtel is not recorded in any other image or photograph of the street. It appears to recede from the Grande Rue, but this is unclear given the angle at which it sits. Furthermore, the building to the immediate right of the Hôtel du Comte Raymond today comes to only half its height. Although it is possible but unlikely that the building was reduced in a later epoch, the sketchy details of the building's lower portion again point to the artist's deliberate lack of precision. When combined with the distinct *chiaroscuro* of the image as a whole, these elements produce an image which is at once mysterious, dramatic, and confounding. Paul Guinard echoes these perceptions in his characterization of Dauzats's *oeuvre* as employing an "element of contrast, of shock, which makes one sense the majesty of the whole."[75] These characteristics typify the body of images in Taylor's romantic and picturesque editions. Furthermore, the inherent flexibility of lithography is uniquely suited to the creation of these effects.[76]

The construction of this image demonstrates that Dauzats and Taylor understood the popular appeal of spectacular, perplexing, and, above all, theatrical imagery. The numerous figures in the foreground, whose necessity one doubts, are assembled in early nineteenth-century dress before the Hôtel du Comte Raymond as if the cast in an ongoing production. The steeply sloping Grand Rue has been leveled by Dauzats,

Inventing the Medieval House

reinforcing the stage-like setting. The architectural community thus becomes a backdrop for an imagined drama. Re-examination of the image within its larger visual context shows it to be a type of diorama, allowing the reader to enter the stage and become a part of the modest spectacle.

In comparison with the Dauzats lithograph shown in Figure 5, this 1833 representation of the Hôtel du Comte Raymond possesses a greater complexity as it is combined with text, an elaborate frame, and still another image (Figure 4). The text, which discusses the early history of Cordes, is extensively drawn from Vaissète and Devic's mid eighteenth-century *Histoire générale de Languedoc*.[77] Since the text makes no mention of a single architectural monument in Cordes nor to the community's character, it bears no apparent relationship to Dauzats' image.[78] The three components of text, image, and frame work together, however, when one perceives Taylor's work not as a guide to a voyage, but as the voyage itself. Through the cooperation of text and image, the reader pauses in the village, learns of its history, and views its streets and passageways. The small image of a fortified gate in the frame further emphasizes the suggestion of entry into an as yet unknown community. This notion of a diorama is reinforced by the extremely large size of the volumes, which could not have accompanied the reader on travels throughout France. Rather, each image-filled volume would have been studied in one's private library or parlor. As the reader turned each page, the voyage would unfold.

If Dauzats's image of the Hôtel du Comte Raymond seemingly depicts an act in a play, then it was the reader's responsibility to supply the story. The contemporary costumes indicate that the story took place in the original (i. e., early nineteenth-century) reader's present. Moreover, the Hôtel du Comte Raymond, as the visual center of the image and its most dominant and detailed subject, is the protagonist of the drama, surrounded by a supporting cast of townspeople and less significant buildings. The reader engaged with the current community of Cordes, while the book simultaneously recreated the town's past.

Taylor and Dauzats's strong theatrical backgrounds explain in part the character of the images for the Languedoc edition of the *Voyages pittoresques*. By 1822, Taylor had written five theater pieces (*Betram, ou le château de Saint-Aldobrand; le Délateur; Ismaïl et Marie; le Chevalier d'Assas;* and *Amour et étourderie*) which attest to his interest in romanticism, medievalism, and the exotic. In 1824 he was appointed Royal Commissioner to the Comédie Française. Dauzats was the son of a *machiniste* in the Grand Théâtre de Bordeaux and received his initial artistic training as a set decorator.[79] As a testament to these foundations in set design,

144   Studies in Medievalism

evident throughout Dauzats's work, Paul Guinard refers to him as "a marvelous *metteur en scène*."[80]

Portal, without a sufficient understanding of their popular or professional intent, expected the *Voyages pittoresques* and Du Mège's *Mémoire* to be visual and textual documents. Instead, Du Mège's drawing of the Palais du Comte Raymond VII points to the antiquarian's twofold fabrication of the medieval houses of Cordes: while mythologizing the city's past, the image itself is an idealized departure from the true state of this monument in 1820. In contrast to Du Mège, Dauzats dramatized the medieval houses of Cordes and made them part of a stage set. In so doing, he maintained much of the true character of the house while placing it within a subtly crafted environment. For the *Voyages pittoresques*, such "crafting" was intentional. While Du Mège's career was marked by the blatant invention or fabrication of historic objects in order to strengthen the identity of southwestern France and possibly guard his often tenuous position, Dauzats was legitimately dedicated to the present state of the monument, accepting its imperfect, dilapidated condition and respecting its limitations. Through his lithographs, Dauzats offered the *impression* of historical importance and credibility in order to provide the popular, generalized audience of the *Voyages pittoresques* with a convincing, if inaccurate, window upon the distant past.

As the visual and textual contributions of Du Mège and Taylor demonstrate, the earliest studies of French medieval domestic architecture were frequently inspired by real or invented historical associations. The Maison du Prince Noir (House of the Black Prince) in the *bastide* of Monflanquin as well as the celebrated Maison des Musiciens (House of Musicians) in Reims are among the numerous remaining French medieval houses named after esteemed founders or mysterious former inhabitants. Now destroyed, the thirteenth-century Maison des Musiciens was embellished with five almost life-size sculptures of seated musicians, again indicating the central role of sculptural decoration in creating the mythology of a given monument.[81]

The mythological and pseudo-historical identities attributed to the medieval house in the nineteenth century were further strengthened by the incessant visual and textual focus upon the façade of the monument, to the detriment of other significant elements. Separated from the larger architectural community, even from its own architectural context, the façade and the sculpture it supported were used as isolated evidence of an illustrious feudal history. Frequently, as in the early studies of Cordes, these mythologies were encouraged as a means of inciting popular interest

Inventing the Medieval House   145

in the community and in the region as a whole. The perpetual association of Cordes with Count Raymond VII, for example, carried significant implications for the community's autonomous historical identity and for its identity as part of the Languedoc.

As much as these early historiographic sources strengthened the communal mythologies of Cordes, they also provided the foundations for future studies of the site, many of which would continue to propagate certain myths about the medieval village and its houses. For example, such historical misperceptions are particularly acute in Verdier and Cattois's discussion of Cordes in *Architecture Civile et Domestique au Moyen Age et à la Renaissance* (Paris, 1857-58). Furthermore, modern restorations of medieval domestic architecture in Cordes, as well as governmental methods of classifying historical monuments, reveal the same focused fascination with the façade and its sculpture.[82] In an effort to unify the façade of the monument, Yves Boiret, chief architect for the Commission des Monuments Historiques, added a sculptural frieze in the style of the fourteenth century to the second level of the Palais du Comte Raymond as late as 1972. Restored today as hotels, fashionable boutiques and restaurants, the medieval houses of Cordes demonstrate that even as the mystique surrounding Count Raymond VII was revised, the noble identities of the medieval houses of Cordes were simply replaced by other, equally invented identities.

NOTES

This article is derived from a chapter of my University of Chicago doctoral dissertation, *Constructing Cordes: The Idea and Invention of the Medieval House*, scheduled for completion this year. My research for this article was conducted with the financial assistance of the University of Chicago (1992-93) and the Samuel H. Kress Foundation (1994-1995). I would like to offer my great appreciation to Michael Camille, Linda Seidel, and Katherine Taylor of the University of Chicago without whose advice and longterm support this article could not have been achieved. In addition, I am indebted to Maurice Scelles of the Direction Régionale de la Culture, Midi-Pyrénées (Toulouse) and Mesdames Charnay, Franzetti, and Hubaut of the Departmental Archives of the Tarn, Albi, for their guidance and suggestions as I conducted the present research. Unless otherwise indicated, translations are mine.

1. A *bastide* was a type of free town, or commune, whose residents (largely artisans, merchants and the bourgeois) held unique urban privileges. The founder of a *bastide* (likely to be a noble figure) would use these privileges to attract rural residents, thereby establishing a strong population and fiscal base in the region.

146 Studies in Medievalism

Since many *bastides* are virtually depopulated today, some of the better known examples include the lower town of Carcassonne (Aude, fnd. 1247) and Libourne (Gironde, fnd. c. 1270), which lies due east of Bordeaux.

2. Over one dozen well preserved medieval houses remain in Cordes, making this one of the largest groupings of such houses in France, next to those of Figeac (Lot), Cahors (Lot), Cluny (Saône-et-Loire), Montpellier (Hérault), and Provins (Seine-et-Marne).

3. Jennifer L. Schuessler, ed. *Let's Go to France* (New York: St. Martin's Press, 1991), 358.

4. Despite the many historiographic contributions to this small settlement, particularly with regard to its medieval houses, the larger impact of Cordes's historiographic material on contemporary ideas of the medieval house and village, as well as the fundamental reasons why Cordes was at all studied and popularized, have not been sufficently examined. The most imporatant recent studies on the French medieval house include Pierre Garrigou-Grandchamp's *meures Médiévales* (Paris: REMPART, 1992) and Bernard Sournia and Jean ouis Vayssette's *Montpellier: La Demeure Médiévale* (Paris: Imprimerie Nationale, 1991).

Since no publication has significantly addressed the historiography of the medieval house, I have been compelled to study the work of several revisionist historians with a devotion to nineteenth-century historiography, including Pierre Nora's multi-volume *Les Lieux de Memoire* (Paris: Gallimard, 1984-1992) and Robert Gildea's *The Past in French History* (New Haven: Yale University Press, 1994). In addition, I am indebted to the many fine studies of nineteenth-century art and architectural historiography which have emerged in the past two decades, including the contributions to the exhibition catalogues *Le "gothique" retrouvé avant Viollet-le-Duc* (Paris: Caisse nationale des monuments historiques, 1979) and *Toulouse et l'art médiéval de 1830 à 1870* (Toulouse: Musée des Augustins, 1982). Although far from being a full picture of the period, these works offer some analysis of the nineteenth-century "reinvention" of the Middle Ages and its contribution to the larger historical memory of France.

5. In England, for example, the London Society of Antiquarians was founded in 1707.

6. Archaeological studies of Normandy by English authors include Andrew Colter Ducarel's *Anglo-Norman Antiquities* of 1767 and Cotman's *Architectural Antiquities of Normandy* (1810). By the early nineteenth century, Normandy had become the most prolific center for archaeological exploration in France, producing works such as Gerville's *Monuments de la Manche* (1810) and the first edition of Nodier, Taylor, and de Cailleux's *Voyages pittoresques et romantiques dans l'ancien France* (Vol. I, Normandy edition, 1820-25). The Société des Antiquaires de Normandie was part of a long list of *sociétés savantes* founded in France since the seventeenth century, including the Académie française (founded in 1638), the Académie des Sciences (1666), the Académie de Caen (founded in 1652, and further attesting to the local erudition of Normandy), the Société des Jeux-Floraux (1694), and the Académie de Toulouse (1746). Because the Revolution suppressed learned societies, it was not until the nineteenth century

Inventing the Medieval House

that they again proliferated in France. One of the first such learned societies founded after the Revolution was the Académie celtique (1804), which became the Société des Antiquaires de France in 1814. Four years later, the Institut de France was reorganized, signaling the appearance of many more societies devoted to the study of agriculture, the sciences and/or the arts.

Analyses of this historiography are rare and include Alain Erlande-Brandenburg's brief article "La Normandie à la recherche de son passé," *Monuments Historiques* 103 (June 1979): 2-5; Françoise Bercé, "Arcisse de Caumont et les Sociétés Savantes," in Pierre Nora, ed., *Les Lieux de Memoire*, Vol. 2, pt. 2 (Paris: Gallimard, 1986), 533-567; Paul Leon's *La Vie des Monuments Français: destruction, restauration* (Paris: Picard, 1951), 90-97; and Paul Yvon, "La renaissance gothique en Angleterre dans ses rapports avec la Normandie," *Bulletin de la Société des Antiquaires de Normandie* 38 (1929). According to Bercé (536), Normandy paid one quarter of all French taxes during the *Ancien Régime* and had a population which consisted of a powerful aristocracy and affluent *bourgeoisie*. Contemporary statistics for the Languedoc form an interesting comparison, suggesting that the reason for the relative paucity of *sociétés savantes* in southwestern France was directly related to its poor, agricultural population and high rate of illiteracy. There were also fewer landed gentry and the great population drain towards the cities had already begun following the Revolution, leaving fewer bourgeois behind. See the analysis of these statistics in Charles-Olivier Carbonell, *Histoire et Historiens: une mutation idéologique des historiens français, 1865-1885* (Toulouse: Privat, 1976), particularly the chapter entitled "Démographie et géographie historiographiques," 167-213. The Société des Antiquaires de Normandie was not the first organization devoted to the monuments of a single region, having been preceded by the Commission des antiquités de Seine-Inférieure, founded in 1818.

7. J. Lavallée, *Voyage Dans les departments de la France: Tarn* (Paris: Brion, l'an VII).

8. This manuscript is in the holdings of the Archives départementales du Tarn, Albi [CC193 1-3]. Although the text is undated, 1821 is argued in Emile Jolibois's publication of the introduction to the *Mémoire,* which appeared in the *Revue du Tarn* 2 (1878-79): 71-76; Jolibois dates the work on 74 fn., based on knowledge of the dates of Du Mège's official work in the Tarn.

9. Virtually nothing is known of Du Mège's mother; she is rarely mentioned in the biographical sources. For more on Du Mège's life, see Auguste d'Aldéguier, "Eloge à M.A. du Mège," in *Memoires de la Société archéologique du Midi de la France,* VIII (1865): 255-271, and Marcel Durliat, "Alexandre du Mège ou les mythes archéologiques à Toulouse dans le premier tiers du XIXe siècle," in *Revue de l'art* 23 (1974): 30-41. Two other important sources are Louis Soulé, "Le chevalier Du Mège de la Haye," in the *Bulletin municipal de la ville de Toulouse* (April 1940:245-278; May 1940: 363-377; July 1940: 401-426, and the catalogue for the exposition *Alexandre Du Mège, inspecteur des antiquités de la Haute-Garonne, 1780-1862* (Toulouse: Musée des Augustins, 1972).

10. Durliat, 30.

11. D'Aldéguier, 257.

12. Du Mège's interest in Egyptology must have been further enhanced by the discovery of the Rosetta Stone in 1799 and the ensuing conflicts which it aroused. Discovered northeast of Alexandria by a Frenchman named Bouchard or Boussard, the Rosetta stone remained in French hands until the surrender of Egypt to the British in 1801, roughly the same time Du Mège became a Mason. Southwestern France had a particularly strong fascination with the *Egyptomanie* which pervaded the country during the Empire and Restoration. The Egyptologist Jean-François Champollion (1790-1832), who translated the hieroglyphics of the Rosetta Stone between 1821-22, and his paleographer brother Jacques-Joseph Champollion-Figeac (1778-1867) hailed from the town of Figeac, only seventy-five miles northeast of Toulouse.

13. To my knowledge, no part of this *Pyramide Principale* was ever fulfilled. The plans and project description are maintained in the Bibliothèque municipale de Toulouse, Ms. 1194. The role of Pierre Sentetz in Auch paralleled that of Du Mège in Toulouse. Like Du Mège, he was a Mason and founded the local museum. In addition, he was professor of history at the Ecole Centrale, archivist and municipal librarian, conservateur of monuments des Arts du Gers, a member of the council for the cathedral works, and mayor of Auch during the *Cent Jours*. Images of the proposed pyramid are in Durliat, 32.

14. The pyramid and the ritual dress are described by Durliat (31).

15. Durliat, 32. Durliat cites Thomas Paine (1737-1809), the American expatriate to France and member of the Convention, as the greatest proponent of this theory.

16. See Jurgis Baltrusaitis, *La Quête d'Isis: Essai sur la legende d'un mythe* (Paris: Flammarion, 1967), and Durliat, 31 and 34.

17. Quoted in Durliat, 33, although he does not name the original sources.

18. Durliat offers this telling anecdote: "Il convient de souligner combien l'enquête menée sur le terrain était chose nouvelle. Lorsque, le 18 novembre 1803, Du Mège remet au préfet Richard un *Memoire sur les antiquités de la Haute-Garonne*, ce haut fonctionnaire voulant se renseigner sur l'authenticité des oeuvres signalées, s'addresse à l'administration du musée des Augustins. La réponse est édifiante. Aucun des artistes qui la composent n'a eu l'occasion de voyager dans les parties du département où se trouvent les monuments en question. Personne ne connait ni les objets ni les lieux" (33).

19. Durliat mentions this article (33). It was first published in the *Journal de la Haute-Garonne* on 6 August 1807.

20. From Maurice Caillet, "Un rite maçonnique inédit à Toulouse et à Auch en 1806," *Bulletin de la Société archéologique, historique, littéraire et scientifique du Gers* 50 (1959): 40, quoted in Durliat, 34. Du Mège states, "Si ces objets vous paraissent barbares . . . . et que vous ne jugiez pas à propos de les conserver chez vous, je m'en accommoderai. Je paierai leur valeur, leur port, etc. Mais surtout sauvez-les; les monuments du Moyen Age deviennent, grâce au vandalisme révolutionnaire et à l'ignorance des acquéreurs des domaines nationaux, d'une rareté extraordinaire."

21. Du Mège, *Mémoire*, fol. 1r.

22. For example, the monuments of important communities in the central and southern portions of the department, such as Castres, Lavaur, and Lacaune, were completely omitted.

23. Jolibois states that Du Mège began his studies in the Tarn in 1820, but the General Council, believing he was taking too long in his work, canceled his assignment in 1823 ("Mémoire," 74-75 fn.). Jolibois does not cite the source of his evidence.

24. *Mémoire*, Vol. I, folio 30r.

25. The text appears on folios 30r to 32r in Vol. I of the *Mémoire*.

26. In Du Mège's defense, such grasping at iconographical straws was not out of place when one considers his belief that these houses were built in the eighth century, an impossibility given Albi's history. It is more likely that the houses dated from the eleventh to thirteenth centuries.

27. Massol was the founder and first librarian of the municipal library of Albi. The first part of his book describes each of the more significant communes in the Tarn, with Cordes appearing on 140-143. Massol mentions only that there is important medieval architecture in Cordes and does not go further. The history of the region, which Du Mège evidently read closely and cites in the *Mémoire*, comprises the second half of Massol's work.

28. Du Mège makes these points on folio 20 r-v in Vol. I of the *Mémoire*. Raymond VII (1189-1249), the last Count of Toulouse, reigned from 1222-1249. As the founder of Cordes in the first year of his reign, he was thought during the early to mid-nineteenth century to have been the original owner of the finer properties in the village. Later in the century, Elie Rossignol was the first to argue that this theory was inconsistent with the actual date of the house, and chose to use its alternative title, the Maison du Grand Veneur. Rossignol is, however, uncritical of this equally misleading name. See Elie Rossignol, *Monographies Communales de l'arrondissement de Gaillac* (Toulouse: Delboy, 1864-66), 3:94.

29. *Mémoire*, Vol. I, folio 20r-v.

30. *Mémoire*, Vol. I, folio 20r.

31. The use of domestic decoration to create mythologies has a precedent in the historiography of Pompeii, where the tradition of "naming" houses (such as the House of the Vettii) continues to the present.

32. *Mémoire*, Vol. I, fol. 30r.

33. On the use of Pompeian motifs in modern architecture, see Robin Middleton and David Watkin, *Architecture du dix-neuvième siècle* (Paris: Gallimard, 1993; originally published in Italian in 1977). The authors note (88-89) that the discoveries at Pompeii were particularly influential in the area of mural painting, resulting in, for example, the "Pompeian Gallery" of Packington Hall in Warwickshire, England by Joseph Bonomi, 1782-86. It is notable that the Pompeian motifs were reintroduced into a domestic, albeit modern, setting.

34. That the *State of Europe* (London: John Murray, 1818) appeared in twelve editions before Hallam's death in 1859 attests to its long-lived popularity and importance as an historical text. The work was published in the United States as well as in German, Italian, and French (as *L'Europe au Moyen Age*) versions

150   Studies in Medievalism

between 1820 and 1821. From this larger work, Hallam published the work for which he is best known, *The Constitutional History of England, from the Accession of Henry VII to the Death of George II* (London: John Murray, 1827). He demonstrates a breadth of knowledge in his *Introduction to the Literature of Europe in the Fifteenth, Sixteenth and Seventeenth Centuries* (London: John Murray, 1837). Hallam received a doctorate of laws (L. L. D.) and was a foreign associate of the Institute of France. As a further testament to his connections with France, he is one of the few foreigners whose biography appears in Vapereau's *Biographie Universelle des Contemporains*. Hallam was also the father of the poet Arthur Henry Hallam (1811-1833) to whom Tennyson dedicated *In Memoriam*. For more on Hallam, see the chapter devoted to him in G. P. Gooch, *History and Historians in the Nineteenth Century*, 2nd ed. (1913; London: Longmans, 1952), 265-288.

35.   Hallam, *State of Europe*, 12th ed. (London: John Murray, 1872), 345-346.

36.   Hallam, 346.

37.   Hallam, 350-351. Aside from the condescension implied in this statement, Hallam named some of the earliest sources on French domestic architecture on these pages, including M. de Paulmy's *Mélanges tirés d'une grande bibliothèque*, Vols. 3 and 31 (n. d.) and Du Cerceau's *Les plus excellens Batimens de France* (1607). The latter's focus is the architecture of the sixteenth century. Hallam also cites Villaret as a further source for domestic architecture but offers no title or date of publication. Hallam notes in an accompanying footnote that "It is to be regretted that Le Grand d'Aussy never completed that part of his *Vie privée des Français* which was to have comprehended the history of civil architecture." He observes (in another footnote) that "Chenonceaux in Touraine was built by a nephew of Chancellor Duprat; Gaillon in the department of Eure by Cardinal Amboise; both at the beginning of the sixteenth century. These are now considered, in their ruins, as among the most ancient houses in France." The only house mentioned which could be considered "medieval" is that of Jacques Coeur in Bourges (fifteenth century). Notably, no images accompany this text, which mentions only monuments in northern France and is one of Hallam's more brief discussions of domestic architecture outside of England. Hallam devoted more than twice as much space to Italy, for example.

38.   According to Paul Meier in *William Morris: The Marxist Dreamer*, trans. from the French by Frank Gubb (Sussex: Harvester Press/New Jersey: Humanities Press, 1978), Hallam played a "pioneering role" in the historical revolution. "More jurist than artist, he concentrated mainly on the history of institutions. . . . But he had an insatiable curiosity and was not uninterested in any detail; yet he maintained a remarkable sense of synthesis . . . . Sweeping away the legends created by a mass of romantic literature, he brought out the simplicity of customs which obtained at all levels of society, even among the feudal nobility . . ." (108).

39.   Hallam, 268.

40.   Meier, 108.

41.   The quotation is on the first page of the 1869 edition of the *Abécédaire, ou rudiment d'archéologie* (Caen: Le Blanc-Hardel, first published in 1850).

42. Lawrence Luchtmansingh notes, "If late medieval artistic production spoke of the free expression of the worker and the spirit of the people at large, the work of the nineteenth century showed precisely their absence" ("Archaeological Socialism: Utopia and Art in William Morris," in *Socialism and the Literary Artistry of William Morris*, ed. Florence S. Boos and Carole G. Silver [Columbia: Mo.: University of Missouri Press, 1990], 14). This notion became important in the later nineteenth-century work of architect and architectural historian Eugène-Emmanuel Viollet-le-Duc, who saw the worker/commoner as the heart of medieval society and the most important of the traditional "three orders" (cleric, noble/warrior, and layperson).

43. *Mémoire*, Vol. I, folio 4v. He states that "chaque notice est accompagnée de plans ou de dessins faits avec soin." Indicating that he made the images himself, he adds, "[J]'ai levé leurs plans, dessiné leurs formes . . ." (folio 4r). Where Du Mège learned to draw is open to some question. No artistic apprenticeship or course in draughtsmanship is mentioned by his biographers. However, his autobiographical information in the *Mémoire* recounts that he was an *ingénieur militaire* prior to his visit in the Tarn. Although such a title has many interpretations, architectural and civil design may have been part of his curriculum.

44. Michel Barrère, "Historiographie en Cinq Tableaux," in *Archéologie et vie quotidienne aux XIIIe-XIVe siècles en Midi-Pyrénées* (Toulouse: Musée des Augustins, 1990), 15. Du Mège mentioned the number of plates, "in format de folio," on folios 5r-v of the *Mémoire*, Vol. I.

45. *Mémoire*, Vol. I, f.5v. Jolibois notes that Du Mège made several new plates which were intended to be included in the *Mémoire* before the project was canceled; these images were also sent to the Bibliothèque de l'Institut de France in Paris (75 note).

46. Jolibois (74-75, note) was the first to mention their transfer to Paris in his publication of the *Mémoire*. The drawings are catalogued in Ms. 4178 (I-III) at the Bibliothèque de l'Institut de France. Du Mège numbered these plates in the *Mémoire*. Plate 10 is the Maison Béziat, the so-called House of Sicard d'Alaman; plates 11 and 12, the Palais du Comte Raymond VII; plate 13, the Maison Auger; plate 17 depicts the Porte de Tournuiller. Illustrations 1-20 and 29-40 are smaller images of architectural or sculptural details.

47. Coincidentally, the prestigious Ecole des Beaux-Arts, which trained gifted young architects for government service, opened in 1819, a year or two before this image was drawn. The style of Beaux-Arts architectural drawing had its roots in the rationalism and geometric purism of late eighteenth century architectural drawing (e .g., E.-L. Boullée and C. Perrault) and Du Mège's style may derive from this tradition. That Du Mège, who was not trained at the Ecole, deliberately followed a newly official method of architectural drawing—perhaps in order to validate his own efforts--is an enticing possibility. Such a conclusion would require a thorough examination of his training and drawings, and precious little is known about the former. For more on the Ecole des Beaux-Arts, see Robin Middleton, ed., *The Beaux-Arts and Nineteenth-Century French Architecture* (Cambridge, Mass: MIT, 1982).

48. A report by the architect H. Jullien on 1 October 1943 indicates that restoration of the façade had not progressed very far: "Il est certain que pour rétablir les fenêtres du XIVe siècle au premier étage, il faudra non seulement modifier la distribution intérieure mais aussi le plancher haut de ce premier étage qui est trop bas pour permettre l'ouverture des fenêtres anciennes" (Paris, Archives des monuments historiques, File 1476, subsection *Maison du Grand Veneur*). The restoration of the first story windows, and the entire façade, was finally completed in 1972 by Yves Boiret, Architect en Chef des Monuments Historiques. Boiret later went on to supervise the restoration of St. Sernin in Toulouse and as of this writing he heads the restoration of the Cathedral of Reims. His prestigious later projects suggest the high status of the Grand Veneur restoration project by the 1970s.

49. Several scholars have attested to the accuracy of the images in the *Voyages pittoresques*, including Paul Guinard, who refers to the "valeur documentaire" of the images in his article "Le découverte du Languedoc par les dessinateurs romantiques: Dauzats et Chapuy à Albi," *Annales du Midi* 78 (1966): 458.

50. Taylor received a gold medal for his drawings in 1827 and became a member of the Académie des Beaux-Arts in 1847.

51. Vapereau, *Dictionnaire universel des contemporains*, 3rd ed. (Paris: Hachette, 1865), 1701. The lithographic process was invented in 1798 by Aloïs Senefelder.

52. Taylor began his exploration of the Languedoc in 1831, while completing his project on the neighboring region of the Auvergne. Paul Guinard suggests that Taylor chose the project not only for its proximity to the Auvergne, but also because he had a general interest in the region, traveling to Spain in 1835, and he saw this edition as juxtaposing gothic art in the south to the northern monuments he had already included in his previous editions. More importantly, Guinard suggests that Taylor and Du Mège had strong professional ties; Du Mège subscribed to the early editions of the *Voyages pittoresques* and Taylor was one of the first members of the SAMF. The attention to Toulouse and the Musée des Augustins in the Languedoc edition of the *Voyages pittoresques* offers evidence of Du Mège's considerable contributions to the publication. See Guinard, "Le Baron Taylor, la Société Archéologique du Midi de la France et le Languedoc des *Voyages pittoresques*," *Memoires de la Société Archéologique du Midi de la France* 34 (1968-69): 39-42.

53. Known today primarily as an orientalist, Dauzats accompanied Taylor on an 1830 expedition in Egypt and later the Duke of Orléans on a military campaign in Algeria. See Guinard, "La découverte de Languedoc," 453.

54. Guinard observes that Taylor was occupied by his official duties in Paris as the Royal Commissioner of the French Theater and could only serve "on site" for the *Voyages pittoresques* for a few days or weeks at a time. This indicates that instead of writing the *Voyages pittoresques*, Taylor was the figurehead of a large organization for which his assistants did most of the work. See Guinard, "La découverte de Languedoc," 454-455.

Inventing the Medieval House

153

55. Guinard, the only scholar to have examined Dauzats's work in the Midi, has not sufficiently explored the question of when Dauzats was in Albi. He states, "We have no details of Dauzats' séjour in the Tarn. . . . It is necessary to exclude the summer of 1832—when his father's death took him back to Bordeaux for two months—and of 1833, when he followed Taylor into the Roussillon, then to Spain. But it is possible that Dauzats worked in the Tarn in 1834, the year when we least know his movements" ("La découverte de Languedoc," 455). This is an impossibility as the section on Albi was published in 1833. Furthermore, Guinard contradicts himself by noting that Dauzats's "discovery" of Albi began in 1833 (455). Between 1834 and 1836, Dauzats exhibited his lithographs of Albi in salons (Vapereau, *Dictionnaire universel*, 473). Only the images of Toulouse surpassed in number those of Albi in the Languedoc edition of the *Voyages pittoresques* (Guinard, "La découverte," 451).

56. The image is plate 82 in Book 35 of this volume.

57. For this reason I take issue with Paul Guinard's assertion of the "documentary value" of Dauzat's images ("La découverte de Languedoc,"458).

58. Charles Portal, *Histoire de la Ville de Cordes en Albigeois* (1902; reprinted Toulouse: Privat, 1984), xiii.

59. For a recent study of Lenoir, see Deborah Jenson, "Monumental Wounds: The Musée des Monuments Français (1795-1816) and the Revolutionary Archaeology of French Romantic Medievalism," in *Medievalism and Romanticism 1750-1850*, ed. Leslie J. Workman, *Poetica* 39/40 (1993): 191-206.

60. For more on this, see *Biographie Nouvelle des Contemporains* (author unknown), 2: 352. Lenoir's museum is discussed at length in *Le "gothique" retrouvé avant Viollet-le-Duc*, 75-78.

61. *Biographie nouvelle des contemporains* (author unknown), 11:351-352. These monuments were later dispersed to the cemetery of Père Lachaise, but can be seen *in situ* in Guyot's engravings after Lenoir which were published in Lenoir's *Musée des monuments français ou description historique et chronologique des statues en marbre et en bronze, etc.* (Paris, 1806), Vol. 5, plates 196 and 204.

62. On Lenoir's false attributions, see Louis Dimier, *Les Impostures de Lenoir: examen de plusieurs opinions reçus sur la foi de cet auteur concernant quelque points de l'histoire des arts* (Paris: P. Saquet, 1903).

63. The quotation is from Linda Seidel, "A Romantic Forgery: The Romanesque 'Portal' of Sainte-Étienne in Toulouse," *Art Bulletin* 50 (1968): 33.

64. See Seidel, "A Romantic Forgery," 33-42 and images. Her argument is derived from her doctoral dissertation, *Romanesque Sculpture from Saint-Etienne Cathedral* (Harvard, 1964). The most vehement opponent of Seidel's theory is Marcel Durliat, whose response to her work can be found in the aforementioned "Alexandre du Mège ou les mythes archéologiques." For a viewpoint more sympathetic to Seidel, see Denis Milhau (Conservateur of the Musée des Augustins), "Restaurations et mythes du musée: Le Musée des Augustins," in *Restaurer les Restaurations*, Cahiers de la Section française du Conseil International des Monuments et des Sites (ICOMOS) 1 (proceedings from a conference held at Toulouse 22-25 April 1980), 85-88.

154   Studies in Medievalism

65. Milhau, "Restaurations et mythes du musée," 86.

66. The recollections of a youthful Jules Michelet, one of the more illustrious visitors to the Musée des Monuments français, provide a description of the museum space as experienced by a visitor in addition to a testimony of the museum's ability to spark one's curiosity in the Middle Ages. He states: "Je me rappelle encore l'émotion, toujours même et toujours vive, qui me faisait battre le coeur quand, tout petit, j'entrais sous ses voutes sombres et contemplais ces visages pâles, quand j'allais et cherchais, ardent, curieux, craintif, de salle en salle et d'âge en âge. Je cherchais quoi? Je ne le sais; la vie d'alors, sans doute, et le génie des temps. Je n'étais pas bien sûr qu'ils ne vécussent point, tous ces dormeurs de marbre entendus sur leurs tombes, et quand, des somptueux monuments du XVIe siècle, éblouissants d'albâtre, je passais à la salle basse des Mérovingiens, où se trouvait la croix de Dagobert, je ne savais pas trop si je ne verrais point se mettre sur leur séant, Chilpéric et Frédégonde." From Michelet, *Histoire de la Révolution française* (Book 12, Ch. 7), quoted in Georges Huard, "La Salle du XIIIe siècle du Musée des monuments français à l'Ecole des Beaux-Arts," *La Revue de l'art* 47 (Feb. 1925): 122-123.

67. Seidel, "A Romantic Forgery," 40.

68. Egotism played a certain role in Du Mège's endeavors. Linda Seidel has noted that he rarely received compensation for his painstaking work, receiving mostly honorary titles (*Romanesque Sculpture*, 78). Nevertheless, he did receive some prestige and acclaim from these titles as well as his discovery of important monuments for the museum's collection.

69. Durliat, "Mythes," 32. He observes that "Dans les deux cas [ref. Du Mège and Lenoir] la recherche de l'historien s'unit à la révélation mystique."

70. For more information on the role of the museum in defining and constructing culture and ideologies, see the work of Carol Duncan, particularly the article "Art Museums and the Ritual of Citizenship," in *Exhibiting Cultures: The Poetics and Politics of Museum Displays*, ed. Ivan Karp and Steven D. Levine (Washington, D. C.: Smithsonian Institution Press, 1991), 88-103.

71. Du Mège's mission in the southwest was a continuation of that prescribed on 27 January 1794, which ordered the administrations of each district to conduct a comprehensive inventory of historically important objects and monuments. For more information, see Durliat, "Mythes," 34. Seidel has argued that the historicist atmosphere of France under the July Monarchy was translated by Du Mège into a need to glorify the Toulouse region. According to Seidel, the invention of monuments like the Saint-Etienne portal would have only furthered a nineteenth-century belief in Toulouse's cultural greatness ("A Romantic Forgery," 38-40).

72. *Mémoire*, Vol. I, folio 1v.

73. That Du Mège received some remuneration for his work is suggested by the following statement: "J'ai parcouru, *par vos ordres et sous vos auspices*, au partie de l'arrondissement d'Albi, celui de Castres et surtout trente-deux communes de canton de Gaillac et celui de Lavaur." *Mémoire*, Vol. I, folio 4v.

74. *Mémoire*, Vol. I, folios 5v-6r.

75. Guinard, "La découverte de Languedoc," 456.

Inventing the Medieval House 155

76.   Given the nature of lithography, we can to some extent forgive Dauzats for the liberties he took with the architecture of Cordes. The strenuous work and heavy equipment involved in the lithographic process would not permit Dauzats, who did his own lithography, to complete his work on site. The hill upon which Cordes stands is so steep that Dauzats would have had to hire an expensive team of horses or oxen to move his equipment, an inconvenience which does not correspond with his peripatetic lifestyle. Instead, Dauzats must have worked from a single drawing or series of drawings. The amount of time which elapsed between initial drawings and finished project is questionable, perhaps accounting for a somewhat selective memory of the setting. Had he desired a more accurate "picture" of Cordes, however, there is no reason to doubt that Dauzats would have chosen to do so.

77.   Vaissète and Devic provide the earliest known historical information for Cordes. However, no descriptive information concerning the community is contained in their work.

78.   According to Paul Guinard ("La découverte de Languedoc," 458), Taylor composed the "banal" text which was compiled, with few changes, from earlier chronicles and histories. Apparently nothing was done to create greater correspondence between text and image in any portion of the work.

79.   Guinard, "La découverte de Languedoc," 458.

80.   Guinard, "La découverte de Languedoc," 458.

81.   These sculptures were thankfully preserved when the house was destroyed in the late nineteenth century. They can be seen in the Musée Lapidaire, Reims.

82.   In all cases, only the façades of the medieval houses of Cordes are currently classified as "monuments historiques." This has the practical advantage of allowing proprietors to easily make interior changes without governmental authorization.

Saint Louis and French Political Culture

Adam Knobler

On 25 August 1270, King Louis IX of France died outside the ancient city of Carthage and was laid out on a bed of ashes—a failed crusader whose memory and deeds were such that he was shortly canonized. Six hundred years later almost to the week, on 2 September 1870, Emperor Napoleon III was captured by the Prussians at Sedan—a failed crusader whose memory and deeds were such that he was deposed and sent to live out the remainder of his days in exile.

The legacy of Saint Louis, the crusader king, was profound. While his own crusading ambitions went largely unfulfilled, he remained an important iconic figure of valor and righteousness for the monarchs who followed him on the French throne for the next six centuries. Rulers of France saw the deeds of Saint Louis as means of contextualizing their own achievements. He became a political symbol by which traditionalist and anti-revolutionary forces in nineteenth-century France attempted to articulate their own legitimacy in the face of liberal and anti-clerical opposition. Through public commemorations of and references to Louis IX, politicians of the far right attempted to formulate in their political community and in the public at large a sense of collective memory, using Louis as a means of defining a mythical past with which they wished to be associated and, it can be assumed, with which the public would be invited to join for the greater glory of the nation.

Examination of the construction of this kind of political culture and collective memory is not a new phenomenon in French historical studies. Maurice Agulhon, for example, has investigated the cultural construction of "Marianne," the female personification of the French nation, as a potent

Studies in Medievalism VIII, 1996

St. Louis and French Political Culture   157

political and cultural symbol in nineteenth- and twentieth-century France; more recently, Robert Gildea has outlined the development of the historical symbols used to define "mythical pasts" in French society.[1] This essay will attempt to establish how nineteenth-century rulers of France chose to develop the image of the sainted crusading king of the thirteenth century to suit their own political needs.

The mythification of Saint Louis and the use of his image in royal propaganda date to the seventeenth century. Louis XIV had consciously made references to his royal predecessor. The Sun King's wars against the Ottoman Turks were proclaimed as a sign of his desire to follow in the footsteps of his crusading namesake.[2] Throughout his reign (1643-1715), we find him portrayed in painting and sculpture as the sainted crusader. Louis XIV's reign also saw the resuscitation of popular celebrations of the crusades and the crusaders through wide encouragement of celebrations on 25 August, Saint Louis' Day. Parisian confraternities of the period dedicated themselves to the royal saint with increasing regularity: fan-makers, jewelry traders, and gold-cloth embroiderers among them.[3] It was Louis XIV too who was responsible for establishing a military "cult" in honor of Saint Louis. Since the reign of Henry IV (1589-1610), devotion to Saint Louis had been elevated as an institution of state: Louis XIV continued this official cult in 1693 by creating the Military Order of Saint Louis to honor men whose deeds and chivalry were worthy of the name.[4]

The Revolution brought with it a new set of historical symbols--or, rather, created new symbols of its own. Streets were renamed; the *tricoleur* replaced the old white banners of the Bourbons; the monarchy and royal family were condemned and decried in the most extreme terms. However, by the time of the fall of the First Empire in 1830, Bonapartism and its postrevolutionary symbols had by and large fallen into disfavor with all but the most diehard members of the Parisian working classes and the rank and file of the military. Yet the scale of royalist enthusiasm which manifested itself upon Louis XVIII's entry into Paris on 3 May 3 1814 was striking—even to the most fervent supporters of the Bourbons. There would be, it seemed, no immediate need to develop any complicated royalist propaganda machine to fend off attacks on the regime and its legitimacy. Louis believed in his divine right to rule, and that, as far as the monarch was concerned, was that. Yet those who surrounded the new monarch knew full well that some provisions needed to be made to assure occupying allies of Louis' abidance by a recognized rule of law, while still safeguarding the king's own claims to legitimacy. And thus the preamble of the Constitutional Charter of 1814 noted the unbroken link with the past to which the current monarch was bound. Saint Louis was explicitly recognized as part of that long pedigree.[5]

The king's subsequent highhanded behavior regarding the privileges of the old nobility sat poorly in the provinces, and within a short time the monarchy was again on the brink of collapse. Napoléon returned from exile to a shortlived and initially popular reinstatement only to be dethroned once again following the debacle of Waterloo in 1815. It was from this point until the July Revolution of 1830 that the Ultraroyalists' mythic past—in contrast to Bonapartist, Orléanist, and especially liberal political factions—were brought to the fore of French political culture. The "calumnies" launched against the Bourbons during the Revolution were to be exposed by the Ultraroyalists and the honor of the Bourbon family and its antecedents restored.[6] The heroes of the past were resuscitated and recrowned as befitted their divinely ordained status. In particular, the past now valorized was not the absolutism of Louis XIV but a more romantic and medieval vision embodied by Louis IX.[7] Three *modele de tapisseries* on themes of Saint Louis's life were commissioned by the King from Parisian artist Georges Rouget between 1817 and 1820 for display in the Conseil d'État. Edouard Simon's preface to the 1815 edition of Pierre Le Moyne's epic poem *Saint Louys, ou la Sainte Couronne reconquise* noted with joy the "happy reestablishment of the august family of the Bourbons."[8]

Others were far more confrontational, issuing a challenge to the nation, and the symbols employed to reassert authority became more often medieval. "The throne . . . illuminated by the wisdom of Saint Louis" must not perish, as the Public Education minister Monsignor Frayssinous asserted in 1816.[9] The assassination in February of 1820 of the king's nephew the Duc de Berry, accused by the Ultras of being a liberal agent, served further to exacerbate political differences. The Archbishop of Paris, Hyacinthe Louis de Quélen, inveighed against the calumnies the dynasty had suffered. His oration at the Duc de Berry's funeral made the connection with the Middle Ages explicit: who, he asked rhetorically, were the enemies of France, "Saint Louis, the most perfect model that history offers," as the anti-royalists would contend?[10] Religious images and engravings replaced Revolutionary themes on the walls and in the homes of the middle classes. Paper woodcuts of Saint Louis were made available by the firm of Garnier-Allabre shortly after the Restoration, perhaps in keeping with a renewed interest in the popular religious cult surrounding the royal saint in their native Chartres.[11] Secret Ultra societies, such as the Chevaliers de la liberté, based on medieval crusading models, were formally incorporated while royal chivalric orders, notably the Order of Saint Louis, were revived.

This symbolism was further developed following Louis XVIII's death in 1824 by his more traditionalist brother, Charles X. Perhaps the most ostentatious public manifestation of the Bourbonist mythistorical medieval vision was to be found at Charles' own coronation on 29 May 1825 at Reims, an event steeped in a recreated aura of *ancien régime* splendor.[12] Charles' desire to be publicly proclaimed as a representative of a medieval crusading legacy was clearly demonstrated through his acts of royal patronage. Along with an additional piece in the Louis series of paintings from Georges Rouget, who had worked for his brother, Charles commissioned a painting in 1826 on the siege of Damietta from the painter Guillaume Guillon Lethiere. More striking, perhaps, was his patronage of the work of historian Joseph-François Michaud. Michaud, a staunch royalist, had pamphleteered for the Bourbonist cause from the time of the Revolution. Elected to the Chamber of Deputies following the Restoration, Michaud had already written in his *Histoire des croisades* (1825) how the crusades held important lessons for his own time. They were the roots of French grandeur and greatness: a fundamentally "French" undertaking whose participants and their descendants were still the nation's "noblest source of patriotism." In a subsequent work, the *Bibliothèque des croisades* (1829), Michaud made the connection between the crusades and the current monarchy manifest, noting that his work on crusading was "worthy of being encouraged by the descendants of St. Louis."[13]

But Charles' object was not simply royal beneficence. The public association of the king with the crusades and the great crusading king of the French past had its broader political implications as well. Having lost his majority in the Chamber following the election of 1827 election, and with the economy in grave trouble, Charles and his new Ultraroyalist ministry under the Duc de Polignac devised to revive French self-esteem with an invasion of Algeria, in imitation of Saint Louis' campaign of 1270. Since the eighteenth century, historians had developed a picture of the Muslims of North Africa as usurpers of a Byzantine and Romano-Christian heritage epitomized by Saints Augustine and Cyprian.[14] Western travelers to the North African coast commented fulsomely on the Byzantine monuments and heritage of the region's antiquity, often ignoring the presence of any Muslim monuments. Thomas Shaw (1694-1751), once chaplain to the English factory at Algiers, observed in 1738 that Arabs were suspicious of all foreigners because they believed that they were "sent to take a Survey of those lands which . . . are to be restored to the Christians."[15]

The logical conclusion of this suspicion, which harked back to Spanish designs of the sixteenth century, called for the conquest and recolonization of North Africa by Christians. "Where . . . is it possible," wrote one commentator, "to point out a more important acquisition to Europe than the northern shores of Africa? Which . . . would at once throw open the whole of that vast continent, and lead to its speedy civilization."[16] A leading French freethinker, l'abbé Raynal (1713-1796), also called for a conquest.[17] Again and again, the echoed theme was the legitimate right of Christians to rule on the North African coast. French commentators went to great lengths to prove the Christian descent of the pre-Arab peoples of the region, most particularly the Kabyle mountain Berbers. Their blue eyes and their use of cross-like figures in facial tattooing were cited as proof of their Nordic or Vandalic origin.[18] Some went so far as to believe that they might even be Christians, secretly practicing their faith in the mountains where the Muslim authorities would not see. Some even posited that they might have been descended from some of Louis IX's crusaders, lost after his death in Tunisia. And it was to the great monarchial past that the royal minister of war would turn in proclaiming the the French people as "le fils de Saint-Louis" whose duty lay "venger a la fois la religion . . ." for any wrongs done Christians in Algiers.[19] A clear appeal—not to democratic or liberal values, but to the older, absolutist ideal of "un roi, une foi, une loi."

Tensions between France and Algiers had existed well before the incident in April 1827 where the Dey of Algiers struck the French Consul in the face with a flyswatter. Charles, a champion of the Ultra-royalists, was well disposed to any action that would bring glory to the army and its *émigré* leadership. The electoral successes of the bourgeois opposition an invasion could also be used to placate the commercial classes, who would see the capture of Algiers as a possible means of revitalizing the Mediterranean trade that had been flagging since the beginning of hostilities in Greece in 1821. To this support could be added that of the conservative members of the clergy, who viewed the king as their champion since his reintroduction of the Sacrilege laws early in his reign and who would glory in the religious symbolism of a war against Islam.[20]

As the power of the opposition increased, Charles increasingly looked to Saint Louis, the greatest historic hero of French conflict with Algiers, for his inspiration, as a potent symbol of traditionalist, anti-Revolutionary values.[21] As mentioned earlier, the Order of Saint Louis, dormant during the Revolution, had been revived by Louis XVIII and was fully active by 1830; Bourmont, the minister of war, was himself appointed its Commander. Charles proudly announced before the National Assembly that reparations from the Dey of Algiers would be obtained to the "profit de la chrét-ienté."[22] Polignac issued a circular endowing his king with lofty crusading motives and virtues symbolic of the monarchy's glorious past and, one would assume, its glorious present.[23]

The invasion itself, orchestrated by the king and Polignac, was short-lived—swift and direct—and while resistance continued for more than a decade, the coast and its Christian heritage were, it was claimed, liberated from the usurpers. As the song "Solitaire de la Touloubre" announced proudly, "A nos guerriers Alger vient de se rendre/La croix s'élève ou brillait le croissant."[24] The monarchy itself was not so successful. Charles, overplaying his hand in the midst of the euphoria over the success of the invasion, issued the Ordinances of 25 July, revealing his earlier appeals to the commercial classes as sham.[25]

With the July Revolution, the Orleanists began a thorough revision of public political culture. The *tricoleur* again replaced the *fleur-de-lis*. Bourbon street names were replaced with others more revolutionary and liberal. Appeals to the past, necessary to insure a symbolic legitimacy of the new dynasty, had to be couched in such a way as not to glorify the deeds of the recently deposed *ancien régime*. The French nation was to be the object for pride. A national policy of restoring historical monuments was undertaken under the directorship of the author and historian Prosper Merimée. However, the greatest public memorial to France's grand past was to be the conversion of the royal palace at Versailles to a museum dedicated "to all the glories of France."[26]

Of the nearly one hundred-thirty paintings on medieval topics com-missioned for the monarchy by Louis Philippe (reigned 1830-48), nearly fifty were on crusading themes.[27] Four works dealt specifically with Saint Louis himself. While the largest and perhaps most renowned of these was undoubtedly Delacroix's depiction of the Battle of Taillebourg, commis-sioned in 1834 and still hanging in the grand Salle des batailles, the majori-ty of crusading scenes were commissioned between 1838 and 1842, corre-sponding to Louis Philippe's renewal of Charles X's "croisade" in Algeria. The exploits of crusaders, hung on the walls of France's new "national" museum, publicly affiliated military action against a Muslim power with the Orleanist dynasty without needing to be associated with Charles' Ul-traroyalist politics. Any renewed action in the Maghrib could be undertak-en in the name of the new French nation and would invoke ancient and noble grandeur rather than Bourbonist excess and whimsy.

Renewed public interest in Algeria was not difficult to generate. With a rather languid domestic policy, Louis Philippe could enhance his own rather tenuous legitimacy through glories achieved overseas. Charles' crusade would be dechristianized and turned into a new glory for the new rulers. The Church, however, did not fail to encourage the king in his venture. Cardinal Luigi Lambruschini, the papal secretary of state, tried to persuade the French to install the Knights Hospitaller—perpetual crusaders, to be sure—in Algiers.[28] They had, after all, been evicted from their home base on Malta by Napoléon Bonaparte in 1798, and their restoration would be seen by conservatives as a clear, anti-Revolutionary, anti-Bonapartist action and perhaps allay fears regarding Louis' possible liberal personal sentiments. The Pope, Gregory XVI, created a bishopric for Caesarea, the former Roman capital of Mauretania (now Cherchel, Algeria), in 1836. Its first occupant accepted the honor of "the seat of Saint Augustine" as the definitive beginning of the restoration of Christianity to North Africa. Traditionalism and royalist sentiments were still very strong in certain regions of the country—the south, for example—and the appeal to history remained strong throughout the century.[29]

Napoleon III (reigned 1852-70) was a master of political propaganda and of the manipulation of collective historical memory. His own seizure of power in 1851 was choreographed to fall upon the anniversary of the coronation of his illustrious namesake and his victory at Austerlitz. While Marx called him a mere *remplaçant* for the original Bonaparte, he skillfully combined liberalism and reaction, reform and repression, democracy and dictatorship, to hold power in France for twenty-two years—the longest of any French head of state since the death of Louis XV in 1774.[30] David Kulstein, in a seminal work, has demonstrated the ability of Napoleon III to use propaganda geared toward the working class. His attempts to appeal to the most conservative elements of society—the clergy, royalists, and wealthiest members of the commercial and banking classes—skillfully used the press, through the agency of the ultramontanist journalist Louis Veuillot among others, to recall a time when social order reigned supreme and revolutionary ideology was oppressed with swift and brutal efficiency.[31]

The clergy were, of course, a powerful electoral force, capable of bringing a wide number of traditionalist voters into the Bonapartist fold, and therefore it is not surprising that we find the Emperor repeatedly promoting religion and "traditional" values as a political tool. Foreign policy, the flexing of French muscle, would be a convenient means of connecting the grandeur of the royalist past to a Bonapartist present, without offending the sensibilities of the broader public.

Conflict in Lebanon, for example, gave birth to schemes in the conservative Catholic press in the summer of 1860 demanding that the emperor intervene militarily in defense of the Christians of Syria and Lebanon.[32]

St. Louis and French Political Culture   163

Clerics, such as then chairman of the Oeuvre des Ecoles Charles-Martial Allemand-Lavigerie, were sent to Syria to distribute aid and solace to Maronite refugees. The possibility of a crusade was posited.[33] The Emperor himself, like Charles and Louis Philippe before him, invoked the great crusading precedent of the French past as the basis of his right to protect the Holy Places of Palestine in the face of Turkish and Russian claims to the contrary.[34] As French troops left for the Levant in 1860, his words rang with crusading imagery:

> Vous partez pour la Syrie. . . . Sur cette terre lointaine, riche en grands souvenirs . . . vous vous montrerez les dignes enfants de ces héros qui ont porté glorieusement dans ce pays la bannière du Christ.[35]

The observer Gabriel Charmes looked across the Mediterranean at Syria and noted how everything of the Syrian past reverberated with the deeds of the crusaders—and that at the core of French responsibility to the memory of the medieval crusaders was the protection of Syrian Christians and the establishment of French colonial control over Syria.[36]

An obvious example of Emperor Napoleon's clever deployment of crusading imagery as a means of appealing conservative domestic political forces came in his decision to intervene militarily in southeast Asia. The "martyrdom" of missionaries and the persecution of Christian converts in Vietnam, coupled with British economic success in South China, gave the Emperor the perfect pretext. By intervening, he could appeal to and appease the reactionary Catholic forces at home, while giving the banking and commercial community a foothold in Asia. Responding to calls from clergymen such as the orientalist Father Evariste Huc, Napoleon and his Spanish-born empress Eugenie declared "il faut venger nos martyrs."[37]

As the Emperor no doubt hoped, the arch-conservative press broadcast these calls for intervention across France with great vigor. Louis Veuillot led the call to crusade. His newspaper *L'Univers*, which had great influence among the French clergy, called for intervention in the strongest possible crusading terms. His brother Eugene wrote in *La Cochinchine et le Tonkin* that the motives of the French were generous and Christian and that those who fight are men of the cross.[38] In keeping with this sentiment, the Emperor himself continually strove to emphasize the religious character of the expedition. "France," he insisted, "has duties to fulfill to herself, to religion and to civilization . . . these circumstances justified our forcible intervention . . . for the good of religion."[39]

The call for crusade and detailed plans for holy war were voiced in the conservative print media. Intervention in Burma, as well as Indochina, was discussed openly—possibly in conjunction with the British in India. Prosper Dumont called for the establishment of Christian protectorates in Indochina, the Bay of Bengal, Cambodia, and Tonkin.[40] This would be followed, he proposed, by a joint Franco-British expedition from Burma into Yunnan province in China, and thence on to Canton and Hue. It was a plan supported by General d'Orgoni, and it was announced as a full "croisade" by the official newspaper, *Le Moniteur Universel*, in 1858.[41]

The following year, the Catholic *Annales de la Propagation de la Foi* declared that the actual expedition to Vietnam—conducted by a joint Franco-Spanish force—was a "genereuse croisade" in the name of civilization and the faith.[42] The participation of the Spanish, who had only recently launched a "crusade" into Morocco, was seen by many contemporary observers as a religiously motivated decision. The Spanish chaplain of the mission pointed out that the expedition was purely a religious matter.[43] Louis-Adolphe Bonard, the French governor of Cochin China (1861-3) and a veteran of the 1830 Algeria campaign, went so far as to state that some of the Spanish Dominicans had "taken up the sabre and musket with the crucifix and are committed body and soul to the revolt affecting Tonkin."[44] As for the French, colonial minister Prosper de Chasseloup-Laubat noted his desire to "create for my country a veritable empire in the Far East. I want our Christian civilization to have in its new conquest a formidable establishment from which she can radiate [her influence] over all those territories."[45] In a memorandum to Foreign Minister Drouyer de Lluys, Chasseloup-Laubat wrote that no other western powers in Asia had had the opportunity of controlling a region so open to Christianity as the French. Echoing the feelings in the Maghrib, Captain Gabriel Aubaret (1825-94) expressed the belief that "Cochinchina will never really belong to us until it is Christianized." "It is a wholly religious expedition," wrote Monsignor Lefevre, the apostolic vicar of West Cochinchina, and "the government and its principal agents have no other purpose than to serve Providence."[46]

Napoleon's appeals to crusading tradition, as symbols of his true conservatism, were able to appease the ultramontanist press and public for only a short time. His decision to intervene militarily in Italy, and the threat that this posed to the integrity of the Papal States, soon turned the Church against the Emperor, whom the ultramontanists branded as a traitor to the Faith, weakening his already unstable political base.

During the republican period which followed the collapse of the Empire in 1870, there was little use for governmental crusade imagery in

St. Louis and French Political Culture

order to reassure an uneasy, traditionalist clergy. It was, however, the clergy itself which again became the bulwark of antirevolutionary traditionalism. And it was the clergy, in the person of Charles-Martial Allemand-Lavigerie, archbishop of Algiers from 1867 and cardinal from 1882 to his death in 1892, who came to use the imagery of crusading, whose legitimist political sensibilities were conjoined with an attempt to restore the preeminence of Christianity as a political and moral force in an increasingly secular world.[47]

Lavigerie had been appointed to the See of Algiers in 1867 after a brief tenure as Bishop of Nancy, where he had gained a reputation for outspokenness and ambition. By the time of the Empire's collapse, his activist, anti-Muslim proselytizing had brought him into conflict with Algerian Governor-General Patrice MacMahon, whom the cleric came to detest. When MacMahon became President of the Republic (1873-79), the conflict became a matter of public record. Lavigerie, a traditionalist to his very marrow, sought to reassert the authority of the French Church, damaged as it was under republicanism, by appealing to the crusading exploits of Saint Louis. In doing so, he hoped to revitalize the Church's fortune in North Africa—both as the moral superior of Islam and as a leader of a new "crusade" against Muslim slavery. As such, Lavigerie's entire career in North Africa was dedicated to the restoration of Christianity in its full glory and to extending its sway into the rest of the continent.[48] Yet despite his ardent views, Lavigerie was no crackpot. A favorite of Pius IX and a personal friend of Leo XIII, he came to be recognized as a leader of the French church, surviving during the Third Republic while many anticlericals around him faltered and faded away. Like Napoleon, he was clever in his use of the media and politically and rhetorically quite adept.

Part of Lavigerie's language derived from a deeply personal anti-Muslim bias. Echoing some of the writers of the early part of the nineteenth century, "the Christians of North Africa" were, he wrote, the first victims of Muslim aggression.[49] Their lost honor needed to be restored. His master plan, outlined in an 1877 letter to Pope Pius IX, was to restore the Catholic See at Carthage, to gain a foothold for Christianity in Jerusalem, and to fight the slave trade.[50] Each of these goals he pursued with vigor that both amazed and annoyed his contemporaries. Hoping to spark French interest in restoring Christianity to Carthage, in Tunisia, he repeatedly appealed to the memory of Saint Louis. Whether in private meetings with Charles X's grandson (and heir presumptive) Henri, Comte de Chambord, in public appeals to Bourbonist monarchists and members of the French titled aristocracy, or in his sermons before French troops in North Africa, Lavigerie invoked the memory of the king who died fighting for Christianity in Tunisia.[51] And, like those who had preceded him, he too believed in the true Christian origin of the Kabyle Berbers.[52] When French rule was established in Tunisia in 1880-1881, he made special effort to insure that the memory of Saint Louis was regularly (if not, indeed, ostentatiously) flaunted before the Muslim populace of the country through parades and festivals in the saint's honor. In these actions, he was acting as a French Catholic patriot, calling for the restoration of what he felt was rightfully France's and Christendom's by historical precedent. In essence, he was seeking the practical revitalization of medieval crusading in the modern world.

Lavigerie held his most striking crusading language for his hoped-for war against African slavetrading. In this, he went beyond parochial, national concerns—returning, in essence, to the pan-Christian call for crusade of the Middle Ages. His appeals were addressed to all Catholic Christians who, in the name of the faith and of civilized society, should take up the rifle with the cross and march against the Muslim slave-traders of the African interior. His grand scheme was to establish a Christian kingdom in Uganda or Tanzania in order to fight the slavers at the source. To do so, he seized upon the idea of sending papal Zouave troops to Africa to accompany missionaries as an elite fighting force.[53] In the late 1870s he ordered missionaries to make forays across North Africa as a sign of the force of the Church! In trying to establish a new military order of fighting preachers, Lavigerie's discussion turned to the restoration of one of the original orders, using the Hospitallers as a model.[54] A rule for the order, based on that of the Hospitallers, was in fact drawn up. Finally, Lavigerie wrote to the Holy See proposing the use of the Hospitallers themselves, specifically that the Order be recommissioned so that its members might accompany missionaries to Tanganyika. Pope Leo XIII appeared to approve of the scheme. But it became clear that the Knights had long abandoned their martial functions and lost their battle skills. Once this was apparent, Lavigerie abandoned the project, regretting that he was absolutely incapable of, as he put it, "galvanizing these paralytics."[55] Yet Lavigerie did not abandon his campaigns entirely. Pressing Leo XIII, he requested a crusading bull against slavery and slavers—for the liberation of Africa and of its native inhabitants. In 1888, before the Anti-Slavery Society in London, he called for five hundred volunteers for his new chivalric order. In Belgium, he lauded King Leopold for his own "crusading" against slavery and Islam.[56]

This language proved to be a two-edged sword for Lavigerie. Some ultramontanist journalists, and authors of children's stories like Georges Demage, still urged French intervention against slavery and in North Africa in the name of St. Louis as suitable vengeance for his death six centuries before.[57] But others saw these calls as mere fantasy on the part of a deluded cleric, doubly dangerous given the increasingly large Muslim population in France's new African overseas empire.[58] Lavigerie's unabashedly romantic view of the Church's role in the Empire sat very poorly with a republican régime supported by non- and anti-clerical elements of the electorate that came to see his rhetoric as outmoded and anachronistic. It was not until his 1890 "Toast of Algiers" and Leo XIII's explicit call in 1892 for French Catholics to "rally" to the republican cause, that Lavigerie bowed to modern political and imperial realities.[59] Yet Lavigerie continued to have his followers and emulators, even after his death in 1892. The writer Louis Bertrand—whose scholarly concern with patristics gave him a special interest in Augustinian North Africa—carried on Lavigerie's call for a crusade.[60] Bertrand often wrote of his admiration for the Cardinal, and he modeled his character of Monsignor Puig after him in his 1901 novel *La Cina*.[61]

In conclusion, the two attempts to revitalize monarchial rule in post-revolutionary France provided a new life for the imagery of the crusades. Given the rise of a liberalizing *bourgeoisie* that could look to the Revolutionary images of Marianne and the *tricoleur* as their own, the traditionalist forces in society—monarchists and clerics—gravitated toward images of their own which had a much older and, in some respects, even more romantic provenance: a sainted king in a holy war. As Paul Léon phrased it, "dans le respect du passé, dans le culte de l'ancienne France, les garanties de stabilité qui manquaient à [leurs] origines."[62]

While the effectiveness of these images in generating political support might be questionable, they certainly were quite durable. And by the time of the Second Empire, the image of "croisade" is being broadcast, not merely in official circles, as it was during the Restoration, but also in the popular media—journals and newspapers whose readership was drawn from several layers of French society, from several regions of the country. We must suppose, therefore, that among editors and propagandists, at least, the image was felt to have some potency.

And indeed, even after the collapse of all monarchial rule in France, there continued to be a certain romantic appeal of the crusades as a representative of a simpler time, when international justice and diplomacy was undertaken, or so the stories went, with divine sanction and under a rather uncomplicated set of moral absolutes. For many, the appeal of this image in the late nineteenth, and even into the early twentieth century, was unmistakable in a world where even the Pope felt it necessary to comment on the conditions of labor (as in Leo XIII's encyclical *Rerum Novarum*)

168 Studies in Medievalism

and the traditional hereditary leaders of Europe were to be replaced by fractious commoners. And while few looked for a literal revival of the practice of holy war as advocated by Cardinal Lavigerie, the image of the knight in shining armor still represented for many of the French people, as for others in Europe, a powerful symbol of justice, honor, and Christian virtue. This might then serve as an explanation for the statement attributed to the first French military governor of Syria, General Henri Gouraud, who upon arriving in Damascus in 1920 was heard to have said, "Behold, Saladin, we have returned!"[63]

NOTES

Earlier versions of this paper were presented at the 1995 Conference of the Arizona Center for Medieval and Renaissance Studies and at the Eighth International Conference on Medievalism in September 1993. I should like to thank Professors Dennis Sweeney, William C. Jordan, and James R. Farr for reading drafts and for their most constructive comments.

1.   Maurice Agulhon, *Marianne into Battle: Republican Imagery and Symbolism in France, 1789-1880*, trans. Janet Lloyd (Cambridge: Cambridge University Press, 1981), and *Marianne au pouvoir: l'imagerie et la symbolique republicaines de 1880 à 1914* (Paris: Flammarion, 1989); Robert Gildea, *The Past in French History* (New Haven: Yale University Press, 1994). On French collective memory in general, see Pierre Nora, ed., *Les Lieux de memoire*, 3 vols. (Paris: Gallimard, 1984-92).

2.   Nicole Ferrier-Caverivière, *L'image de Louis XIV dans la littérature française de 1660 à 1715* (Paris: Presses universitaires de France, 1981), 82. Cf. Jacques Bénigne Bossuet, "Oraisons funèbre d'Henriette de France," in *Oraisons funèbres de Bossuet*, ed. Jacques Truchet (Paris: Garnier, 1967), 105. The same comparisons with Saint Louis had been made regarding Louis XII (1498-1515): cf. Peter Burke, *Popular Culture in Early Modern Europe* (New York: Harper and Row, 1978), 151,170.

3.   Peter Burke, *The Fabrication of Louis XIV* (New Haven: Yale University Press, 1992), 28, 115; Colette Beaune, *The Birth of an Ideology: Myths and Symbols of Nation in Late-Medieval France*, trans. Susan Ross Huston, ed. Fredric L. Cheyette (Berkeley: University of California Press, 1991), 120.

4.   On the development of the official cult of Saint Louis from Henry IV's reign onward, cf. *La Renaissance du culte de Saint Louis au XVIIe siècle* (Paris: Musée national de la Legion d'honneur et des ordres de chevalerie, 1971); on the edict of creation (10 April 1693), cf. 22-23. Peter Burke (*Fabrication*, 113) calls this event the "climax" of identification between the two kings.

5.   For the text of the Charter, see Jean Duvergier, ed., *Collection complète des lois . . . de 1788 à 1830*, 2d ed., 106 vols. (Paris, 1834-1906), 19: 59-73.

6. On the use of the familiar metaphor in the French Revolution, cf. Lynn Hunt, *The Family Romance of the French Revolution* (Berkeley: University of California Press, 1992). On the royalist use of the French "family" before the Revolution, cf. Jeffrey Merrick, "Patriarchalism and Constitutionalism in Eighteenth-Century Parliamentary Discourse," *Studies in Eighteenth-Century Culture* 20 (1990):317-30. On the desire of the Ultras and other Conservatives to glory in the monarchial past, cf. Stanley Mellon, *The Political Uses of History: A Study of Historians in the French Restoration* (Stanford: Stanford University Press, 1958), Ch. 4.

7. On this, cf. René Rémond, *The Right Wing in France, from 1815 to de Gaulle*, trans. James M. Laux (Philadelphia: University of Pennsylvania Press, 1966), 49-50.

8. Pierre LeMoyne, *Saint Louys ou la Sainte Couronne reconquise* (Paris, 1816), ix-x, quoted in William Chester Jordan, "Saint Louis of France: the Modern Image" (unpublished paper). I wish to thank Professor Jordan for sharing his paper with me.

9. Baron Henrion, *Vie de M. Frayssinous* (Paris, 1844), 1:84, 125.

10. François-Rene de Chateaubriand, *Mémoires, lettres et pieces authentiques touchant la vie et de la mort de S.A.R. Monseigneur Charles Ferdinand d'Artois, fils de France, duc de Berry* (Paris, 1820), 9.

11. See illustration 161 in Jean Adhemar, *French Popular Imagery* (London: Arts Council of Great Britain, 1974), 34. On Chartres and other centers of the cult, cf. Beaune, 327-30.

12. See Landric Raillat, *Charles X: Le sacre de la dernière chance* (Paris: Orban, 1991); Vincent W. Beach, *Charles X of France: His Life and Times* (Boulder: Pruett, 1971), 197-205.

13. Joseph-François Michaud, *Histoire des croisades*, 4th ed., 6 vols. (Paris, 1825-29) 1:510, and *Bibliothèque des croisades*, 4 vols. (Paris, 1829) 1: xv. For much of my discussion of Michaud, I am indebted to Kim Munholland, "Michaud's History of the Crusades and the French Crusade in Algeria under Louis-Philippe," in Petra ten-Doesschate Chu and Gabriel P. Weisberg, ed., *The Popularization of Images: Visual Culture under the July Monarchy* (Princeton: Princeton University Press, 1994), 144-65.

14. Poiret claimed that the great North African empires of the past had been succeeded by ignorance and despotism; cf. Jean Louis Marie Poiret, *Voyage en Barbarie, ou Lettres écrites de l'ancienne Numidie pendant les années 1785 & 1786, sur la religion, les coutumes & les mours des Maures & des Arabes-Bedouins; avec un essai sur l'histoire naturelle de ce pays*, 2 vols. (Paris, 1789), i-ii. On this theme generally, cf. Ann Thomson, *Barbary and Enlightenment: European Attitudes towards the Maghrib in the 18th Century* (Leiden: Brill, 1987), and "Arguments for the Conquest of Algiers in the Late Eighteenth and Early Nineteenth Centuries," *Maghrib Review* 14 (1989): 108-18.

15. Thomas Shaw, *Travels, or Observations Relating to Several Parts of Barbary and the Levant* (Oxford, 1738), viii. Shaw, like Bournichon after him, believed that a fear of Christian return was instilled in Algerine children from birth. Cf. Joseph Bournichon, *L'invasion musulmane en Afrique suivie du réveil*

de la foi chrétienne dans ces contrées et de la croisade des nous entreprise par S.E. le cardinal Lavigerie, archevêque d'Alger et de Carthage (Tours, 1890), 244-9.

16. Filippo Pananti, *Narrative of a residence in Algiers: comprising a geographical and historical account of the regency; biographical sketches of the dey and his ministers; anecdotes of the late war; observations on the relations of the Barbary states with the Christian powers; and the necessity and importance of their complete subjugation* (London, 1818), 413, 412. Pananti even makes parallels with Cortez's conquest of Mexico (414).

17. Abbé Raynal, *Histoire philosophique et politique des établissements et du commerce des Européens dans l'Afrique septentrionale*, 2 vols. (Paris, 1826), 1: 106f, 137.

18. Shaw, 120; William Shaler, *Sketches of Algiers, political, historical, and civil: containing an account of the geography, population, government, revenues, commerce, agriculture, arts, civil institutions, tribes, manners, languages, and recent political history of that country* (Boston, 1826), 91. On this in general, cf. Charles-Robert Ageron, *Les Algériens musulmans et la France (1871-1919)*, 2 vols. (Paris: Presses universitaires de France, 1968), 268ff.

19. Marquis de Clermont-Tonnerre to Charles X (Paris, 14 October 1827), in Paul Azan, ed. "Le rapport du Marquis de Clermont-Tonnere ministere de la guerre sur une expédition a Alger (1827)," *Revue africaine* 70 (1929), 215, 253; similar statements are cited by Marwan Buheiry, "Planat de la Faye: A Critic of France's Algerian mission in the 1840s," *al-Abhath* 26 (1973-77): 20. The minister's words were remembered fondly by Cardinal Lavigerie many years later, in a speech at the Algiers cathedral for the Algerian army, stating that the invasion "C'eut été une croisade, la derniere, la plus noble, la plus digne de la France et des inspirations de l'Evangile." Charles M. Allemand-Lavigerie, *Oeuvres choisies, I*, 2 vols. (Paris, 1884), 1: 42-3.

20. A good, brief description of the forces at work here can be found in Pierre Lévêque, *Histoire des forces politiques en France, 1789-1880, tome 1* (Paris: A. Colin, 1992), 161-222.

21. Saint Louis had also become a common part of the speeches made by royalist prefects sent from Paris to the provinces, though as one critic, Pons de Villeneuve, noted, while speaking nicely of Saint Louis they did nothing to strengthen public resolve against revolution. Cf. David Higgs, *Ultraroyalism in Toulouse from Its Origins to the Revolution of 1830* (Baltimore: Johns Hopkins University Press, 1973), 57-8.

22. Address of Charles X (2 March 1830) in *Archives parlementaires* 61 (July 1829-August 1830): 543; Charles André Julien, "La question d'Alger devant les Chambres sous la restauration," *Revue africaine* 63 (1922): 451. On the Order in Algeria, cf. briefly the examples noted in *La Renaissance du culte*, 54-55.

23. This was included in the Third Protocol of the Anglo-French agreement of 3 February 1830, where the French monarch's rights as protector of the Catholic population of the Ottoman empire was reasserted. See Louis de Viel-Castel, *Histoire de la restauration*, 20 vols. (Paris, 1860-80), 20: 214. See also Norman

Daniel, *Islam, Europe and Empire* (Edinburgh: Edinburgh University Press, 1966), 327.

24.   Pierre Guiral, "L'opinion marseillaise et les débuts de l'entreprise Algérienne (1830-1841)," *Revue historique* 214 (1955): 12.

25.   A translation of the text may be found in Beach, 442-6.

26.   See Irene Earls, "Restoration of the National Monuments of France," *Proceedings of the Consortium on Revolutionary Europe 1992* (1993), 1-8; Thomas W. Gaehtgens, *Versailles, de la résidence royale au musée historique. La galerie des batailles dans le musée historique de Louis-Philippe*, trans. Patrick Poirot (Antwerp: Fonds Mercator, 1984); Michael Marrinan, "Historical Vision and the Writing of History at Louis-Philippe's Versailles," in Chu and Weisberg, 113-43.

27.   Calculated from Claire Constans, *Musée national du chateau de Versailles: catalogue des peintures* (Paris: Editions de la Reunion des musées nationaux, 1980).

28.   Roderick Cavaliero, *The Last of the Crusaders: The Knights of St. John and Malta in the Eighteenth Century* (London: Hollis and Carter, 1960), 267.

29.   Marcel Émerit, "La lutte entre les généraux et le prêtres aux débuts de l'Algérie française," *Revue africaine* 97 (1953): 74-5; see Andre Jardin and Andre-Jean Tudesq, *Restoration and reaction, 1815-1848*, trans. Elborg Forster (Cambridge: Cambridge University Press, 1983), 234-7.

30.   Karl Marx, *The Eighteenth Brumaire of Louis Bonaparte*, in his *Selected Writings*, ed. David McLellan (Oxford: Oxford University Press, 1977), 321.

31.   David I. Kulstein, *Napoleon III and the Working Class: A Study of Government Propaganda under the Second Empire* (Sacramento: California State Colleges, 1969). On Veuillot, cf. Marvin L. Brown, Jr., *Louis Veuillot: French Ultramontane Catholic Journalist and Layman, 1813-1883* (Durham: Moore, 1977).

32.   Xavier de Montclos, *Lavigerie, le Saint-Siège et l'Église: de l'avènement de Pie IX a l'avènement de Léon XIII, 1846-1878* (Paris: E. de Boccard, 1965), 142-3.

33.   "Napoléon III n'est pas seulement l'Empereur des Français, il est le chef de la dernière croisade . . . comme à une autre époque; la France dit à son souverain: 'Dieu le veut! Dieu le veut!'" *La question d'Orient* (Paris, 1860), 48.

34.   Barbara W. Tuchman, *Bible and Sword: England and Palestine from the Bronze Age to Balfour* (New York: New York University Press, 1956; reprinted New York: Ballantine, 1984), 255ff; Harold Temperley, *England and the Near East: The Crimea* (Hamden, Conn.: Archon, 1964), Ch. 11. Later commentators continued to note the distinctly "French" aspect of the crusades; cf. Louis Madelin, "Le Syrie franque," *Revue des deux mondes* 87/vi.38 (1917): 316.

35.   Quoted in Taxile Delord, *Histoire du second Empire*, 6 vols. (Paris, 1869-75), 3:31. See also Joseph Hajjar, *L'Europe et les destinées du proche-orient II: Napoléon III et ses visées orientales, 1848-1870*, 3 vols. (Damascus: Dar Tlass, 1988), 2: 1104f.

36.   *Journal des débats* (17 June 1880) and Gabriel Charmes, *Politique extérieure et coloniale* (Paris, 1885), 1-103, 305-428; Agnes Murphy, *The Ideology of French Imperialism, 1871-1881* (Washington, D. C.: Catholic University Press, 1948; reprinted New York: H. Fertig, 1968), 183-4.

172   Studies in Medievalism

37. Evariste Huc to Emperor Napoleon III (January 1857), in Georges Taboulet, *La geste française en Indochine; histoire par les textes de la France en Indochine des origines à 1914* (Paris, 1955-6), 404-5, 411.

38. Taboulet, 411; Eugène Veuillot, *La Cochinchine et le Tonquin: le pays, l'histoire et les missions* (Paris, 1859), ii, xiv-xv.

39. "Appendix to the minutes of the 7th meeting of the Cochinchina Commission (Paris, 18 May 1857)" in *French Catholic Missionaries and the Politics of Imperialism in Vietnam, 1857-1914: A Documentary Survey*, comp. Patrick J. N. Tuck (Liverpool: Liverpool University Press, 1987), 48.

40. Prosper Dumont, *Le général d'Orgoni, sa mission en France et a Rome, et plan de campagne pour une croisade française en Indo-Chine et en Chine* (Nancy, 1858), Ch. 3; Taboulet, 412-3.

41. Étienne Vo-Duc-Hanh, *La place du catholicisme dans les rélations entre la France et le Viet-Nam de 1851 à 1870*, 3 vols. (Leiden: Brill, 1969), 1: 16-17. On Napoleon's use of *Le Moniteur universel*, cf. Kulstein, 44-78.

42. "Expédition franco-espagnole en Cochinchine," *Annales de la propagation de la foi* 31 (1859), 75; Vo-Duc-Hanh, 1:19.

43. Fr. Francisco Gainza to Fr. Antonio Orge (Bay of Tourane, 5 September 1858) in *Annales de la propagation de la foi* 31 (1859), 93.

44. Rear Admiral Louis-Adolphe Bonard to Colonial/Naval minister Prosper de Chasseloup-Laubat (Saigon, 24 July 1862), in *French Catholic Missionaries*, 67. Later scholars, notably Truong Buu Lam (*Patterns of Vietnamese Response to Foreign Intervention, 1858-1900* [New Haven: Yale University Press, 1967], 5) and Milton E. Osborne (*The French Presence in Cochinchina and Cambodia: Rule and Response [1859-1905]* [Ithaca: Cornell University Press, 1969], 29), state their belief that the Spanish were purely engaged for religious purposes. However, James W. Cortada's study "Spain and the French Invasion of Cochinchina" (*Australian Journal of Politics and History* 20/3 [1974]: 335-45) seems to show that the Spanish government did *not* in fact view the operation as crusading.

45. Chasseloup-Laubat (Paris, 15 February 1862), in *French Catholic Missionaries*, 72.

46. Chasseloup-Laubat to Drouyer de Lluys (Paris, 10 December 1863), Aubaret to Admiral/Governor Bonard (note on Cochin China, c.1862-3), Mgr. Lefevre to Directors of the Société des Missions étrangères (Saigon, 2 February 1860), all quoted in *French Catholic Missionaries*, 73, 83, 62.

47. On Lavigerie's life and career, cf. Joseph Dean O'Donnell, *Lavigerie in Tunisia: The Interplay of Imperialist and Missionary* (Athens: University of Georgia Press, 1979); François Renault, *Lavigerie, l'esclavage africain, et l'Europe, 1868-1892*, 2 vols. (Paris: E. de Bocard, 1971), and *Le Cardinal Lavigerie, 1825-1892: l'Église, l'Afrique et la France* (Paris: Fayard, 1992).

48. Cf. Lavigerie, *Oeuvres choisies* 1: 8-9, 97ff.

49. Pastoral letter in Lavigerie, *Oeuvres choisies* 1: 5.

50. In A. C. Grussenmeyer, *Vingt-cinq années d'épiscopat en France et en Afrique. Documents biographiques sur son éminence le cardinal Lavigerie archevêque*

de Carthage et d'Alger primat d'Afrique a l'occasion de son jubilé épiscopat, 2 vols. (Algiers, 1888), 2: 111-12.

51.   See his letter (20 November 1890) in Jules Tournier, *Le cardinal Lavigerie et son action politique (1863-1892) d'après documents nouveaux et inédits* (Paris, 1913), 40; Charles Alfred Perkins, "French Catholic Opinion and Imperial Expansion, 1880-1886," Diss. Harvard University 1964, 69.

52.   In a speech at Algiers cathedral for the opening of a religious service for the Algerian army in Lavigerie, *Oeuvres choisies* 1: 47. Other contemporaries of the Cardinal such as the Algerian deputy François Gastu (1834-1908) echoed this sentiment. Cf. Ageron, 274.

53.   Cf. letter from Lavigerie to Charmentant (25 March 1879) in Renault, *Lavigerie, l'esclavage,* 1: 238ff.

54.   Renault, *Lavigerie, l'esclavage,* 1: 252-3; he is, in fact, compared by one scholar to Grand Master Albert of Buxtedhude of the Teutonic Order. Cf. Waldemar Von Bock, "Cardinal Lavigerie, Erzbischof von Karthago und Albert v. Buxhöwden, Bischof von Livland oder die Kirche gestern (1201) und hente (1892) eine deselbe," *Frankfurter zeitgemässe Broschüren,* n.f. 14 (1892): 181-99, especially 190.

55.   Renault, *Lavigerie, l'esclavage,* 1: 253 (rule is outlined 254-5); 1: 257-60; 1: 260-1, 266-7.

56.   Bournichon, preface, 326. Leopold had called for a crusade in Africa at his Geographical Conference in 1876, before a gathering of the leading European explorers. On Leopold's relationship with Lavigerie, cf. J. Perraudin, "Le Cardinal Lavigerie et Léopold II," *Zaire* 11 (1957): 901-32 and 12 (1958): 37-64, 165-77, 275-91, 393-408.

57.   Cf. G. Demage, "A Plunge in the Sahara," *Boy's Own Paper* 16 (1893/4), 757.

58.   Renault, *Lavigerie, l'esclavage,* 2: 364-7.

59.   Ralph Gibson, *A Social History of French Catholicism, 1789-1914* (London: Routledge, 1989), 220.

60.   Daniel-Henri Pageaux, "Le mirage latin de Louis Bertrand," in *Espagne et Algérie au XXe siècle: contacts culturels et création littéraire* (Paris: Editions L'Harmatten, 1985): 119. This theme is echoed by other authors, notably Ernest Psichari, who also called for an outright crusade against Muslim power in the Maghrib. Cf. Martine Astier Loutfi, *Littérature et colonialisme: l'expansion coloniale vue dans la littérature romanesque française, 1871-1914* (Paris: Mouton, 1971), 80-1.

61.   Louis Bertrand, *La Cina: roman* (Paris, 1901), 436-40; Loutfi, 76-7; Pageaux, 118.

62.   Paul Léon, *La Vie des monuments français* (Paris: Picard, 1951), 115.

63.   Note the reference to this incident made by Gamal Abdul Nasser, in a speech of 20 March 1958, Goumhoura Square, Cairo, in *President Gamal Abdel Nasser's Speeches and Press Interviews, 1958* (Cairo: Information Department, 1958), 129.

Saint Louis in French Epic and Drama

William Chester Jordan

> Françoise in her kitchen was wont to hold forth about St Louis as though she herself had known him, generally in order to depreciate, by contrast with him, my grandparents whom she considered less "righteous." One could see that the notions which . . . the mediaeval peasant (who had survived to cook for us in the nineteenth century) had of classical and of early Christian history, notions whose inaccuracy was atoned for by their honest simplicity, were derived not from books, but from a tradition at once ancient and direct, unbroken, oral, distorted, unrecognisable, and alive.

In these few words, Marcel Proust interweaves the discourse of a peasant cook—and her iconic imagined Saint Louis—into the wondrous tapestry of recollections that constitute his masterpiece, *A la recherche du temps perdu*.[1] "Unbroken" and "oral" though her tradition is, it is nevertheless "distorted, unrecognisable, and alive." So too the unbroken literary tradition, of which the passage in Proust's novel is only a late example, distorted the received scholarly image of the king and saint and would have been puzzling, if not unrecognizable, to his contemporaries. Yet precisely because it was possible to build on the core of that image for a myriad of purposes and create multiple representations of the holy king, the cultural memory of Louis IX remained powerfully alive for centuries.

This paper constitutes an attempt to recall some aspects of this once "living tradition" in French epic and drama and to chart their history. Saint Louis was principally employed as an image of probity in all literary constructions of his character, but in the seventeenth and early eighteenth centuries it was the dynastic implications of his probity that authors emphasized. In the tumult of the later eighteenth century, polemicists on the right—monarchists or not—turned the image against what they regarded as

Studies in Medievalism VIII, 1996

Saint Louis in Epic and Drama 175

revolutionary excesses, urging either a return to monarchy or a moderation in the pace and direction of political change. In the confusing long aftermath of the Napoleonic era down to the end of the nineteenth century and even beyond, polemicists and apologists refashioned the image of the saint-king in diverse ways, but playwrights chose predominantly to create a character and story that, depending on circumstances, embodied a critique of cynical political conventions, irreligion (including toleration of Jews), class hatred, and social injustices.

The tradition began with the epic poem of Pierre Le Moyne, *Saint Louis ou la Sainte Couronne reconquise*, which enjoyed immediate success after its initial publication in 1658.[2] The author was a prolific Jesuit writer most noted for his *Gallérie des femmes fortes* (1647) and for earning Blaise Pascal's quasi-Jansenist disgust for another popular book, *La Dévotion aisée*.[3] The poem on Saint Louis, though incredibly long (nearly eighteen thousand lines), was republished over and over again in the decades after 1658 and, as we shall see, set the tone and standard (and occasionally served as the whipping boy) for several much later treatments of the life of the saint.

Le Moyne drew upon Jean de Joinville's inspiring *Histoire de saint Louis*, the memoir of the king's personal friend, widely available in printed editions from the mid-sixteenth century.[4] The publication of Joinville's loving portrait concurrently encouraged a vigorous scholarly literature on the reign and character of Saint Louis, many of whose authors would probably have agreed with Le Moyne that Louis IX as Christian hero offered a better subject for an epic poem than shameless Helen and the crown of thorns a better trope for spiritual quest than the golden fleece.[5] As Le Moyne wrote in the *Dissertation du poëme heroïque*,

> I could not choose a more accomplished hero than [Louis]: and, moreover, the choice I have made gives honor to France, which produced him, to our kings who descend from him, to the royal house which is of his lineage, to the nobility which has him for a patron and model, to the entire nation for which God has given him as a protector; to the whole church which has received him in the litany of the saints that it reveres. And I believe that my poem which bears his name, is like unto a temple where his image and his relics will always be visible, where the wonders of his life will be sung throughout the ages, where his virtues will be preached to all princes, where his memory will receive the devotion and praise of all people.[6]

176   Studies in Medievalism

French scholars of the period, no matter how much they endorsed a heroic image of Saint Louis, remained nevertheless faithful to the basic *materia* of Joinville's memoir: a fine young man grows up in difficult circumstances after the premature death of his father, but under the able tutelage of his mother who acts as regent. He overcomes baronial rebellions, but is neither vindictive nor cruel. He becomes his own man by launching a great crusade (against his mother's wishes) which fails and leads to his brief captivity in Egypt. After his release and subsequent return to France his life is one long penance expressed by acts of justice and mercy, before he decides once more to go on crusade (to Tunis) where he will die.

Le Moyne and his imitators were inspired by but not limited to this narrative line. Le Moyne's Louis, for example, wins rather than loses the crusade in Egypt. Le Moyne's Louis goes on crusade in the first place to rescue the crown of thorns.[7] In fact the king had purchased what purported to be this relic ten years earlier and had already had the Sainte-Chapelle in Paris built to house it before the crusade.[8] Le Moyne concocts a scene in which Louis is taken to heaven by a chariot of fire in the midst of the crusade—indeed almost in the midst of battle—in order to enjoy a discourse with Christ through which he obtains a revelation of the future kings of France, hearing each of them praised in turn down to and including the young Louis XIV (93-96). Le Moyne also invents a story of poisoned armor given to Louis by evil Saracens. Unknowingly, the king dons the armor in order to protect himself as he prepares to slay a dragon, whereupon a lightning bolt strikes him, separating him from the armor and burning the venomed iron clothing to a crisp (119-20). Heaven's defense of the king is manifested also at the very end when a ray from on high identifies which of two crowns of thorns discovered is the genuine relic. If Louis chooses the wrong crown, legions of demons in league with the Saracens will be set free to strike his army with plague. Thanks to the benevolent beam Louis chooses correctly and is rewarded by being crowned himself with the crown of thorns.[9]

Le Moyne's justification for these changes is important for the history of literary genres; and his apologia in the *Dissertation* has sustained interest among critics.[10] It is hard to say, however, what is the real focus of the poem, for its length demands a number of extended plots. Considerable space is given over to the vision of future kings, that is, to a vision subservient to royalist historiography; and a persistent theme is the glories of the Bourbons, which is to say, of the cadet branch of the Capetian family.[11] In many ways Archembaud de Bourbon, the king's companion in arms, is a major hero. When Louis, somewhat befuddled by the cathartic lightning bolt—as any man might be—rethinks his intention of slaying the dragon, the fairy-tale task is vouchsafed by heaven, through a female prophetic intermediary, to the Bourbon companion of the king. And Archembaud too is prophetically informed at a different place in the poem of his lineage's glorious future in quite specific terms.[12]

There is in all of this much toadying by Le Moyne; and, indeed, on the whole, the poem reads like an attempt to curry favor with the contemporary ruler and to show the essential harmony between papal and royal interests. (Le Moyne routinely suppresses references to church-state struggles in his futuristic revelation of history.) There is here nothing of Joinville's stubborn, sometimes irascible king; nothing of the king who gave in to his emotions or exasperated his wife; none of that occasional sense of self-doubt and self-criticism.[13] Louis simply prays, performs his "spiritual exercises," and everything comes out all right. He is in every way a victorious Christ on earth, crowned with Jesus's own crown, a model Jesuit, but of the thirteenth century.

The theme of Saint Louis on crusade persisted in the eighteenth and early nineteenth centuries, fed in part by the spirited Egyptomania of the period.[14] Le Moyne's poem, as mentioned, continued to be reworked. There exists, for example, an unfinished or deliberately truncated prose version of 1774 by an otherwise anonymous classicizing author who employed the title "Louisiade."[15] The epic was also to be abbreviated after the Revolution by Edouard-Thomas Simon, who published his version in 1816. Like the Vicar of Bray in the English ditty, Simon was one of those men who changed smoothly with the times. The great monarchy of Père Le Moyne's day having fallen in 1792, Simon became a revolutionary of whatever stripe required by the regime in power; yet at the age of eighty, following the Bourbon restoration in 1815, he republished Le Moyne's *Saint Louis* with a prefatory notice of "the happy reestablishment of the august family of the Bourbons on the hereditary throne of the French."[16]

Simon's version reduces Le Moyne's poem by about three-fourths and divides it into eight *chants* or books instead of the original eighteen. He retains the overall series of plots, but parades his knowledge of the true story with historical and explanatory footnotes. As Lionel Gossman has shown, this was an age when the scholarly study of the Middle Ages in France was enjoying a spectacular flowering;[17] by stressing the difference between history properly so-called and what he was doing, Simon hoped to avoid carping scholarly criticism. For Simon's aims were transcendent: to achieve the apotheosis of monarchy and to restore awe. Where "facts" might get in the way he acknowledged their shadowy existence but otherwise ignored them. The king is a victor, not a loser, and his enemies (the enemies of the faith) are the enemies of the state. It is remarkable that Le

Moyne's overbearing epic, even in abridged form, was believed capable of serving these purposes reasonably well for readers down to the early nineteenth century.

Two apparently original Restoration works deserve discussion here, one by Jacques Ancelot, the other by Népomucène-Louis Lemercier, for they represent the shift from employment of the saint-king for dynastic reinforcement to his use, seen faintly in Simon's work, as a polemic against revolutionary excess. Ancelot, in full Jacques-Arsène-François-Polycarpe Ancelot, born in 1794, was the author of *Louis IX*, his first important and evidently his most important play, considered something of a *tour-de-force* on technical grounds. Performed for the first time on 5 November 1819, it caused a stir partly because another play, *Louis IX en fers* of the year before, was named by some hostile critics as Ancelot's unacknowledged source, a slur he denied vehemently.[18] More important, Ancelot's play took its place as the legitimist-royalist answer to Casimir Delavigne's "liberal" play of the same year, *Vêpres siciliennes*, which used as its backdrop the overthrow of the oppressive rule of Louis IX's brother Charles of Anjou by a conspiracy in Sicily in 1282 and which, despite Delavigne's enormous popularity, had excited spirited official opposition.[19] (Delavigne's play is well known even now as source for the libretto of Verdi's opera *I Vespri Siciliani* of 1855.)

Royalist opposition to Delavigne's play four years after Bonaparte's definitive fall might have been expected: after all, this was a play that fed on the desire for regicide. The first reference to the Sicilian king, Saint Louis's brother Charles, makes him a regicide of the former rulers, Manfred and Conradin of the house of Hohenstaufen. The speaker of the words that follow wonders aloud whether the miscreant, whom he describes pointedly, is nearby.

> . . . the conqueror of Manfred,
> The executioner, the assassin of our last king?
> . . . this unworthy brother
> Of the pious Louis whom France reveres? (14)

This is a play, too, that insistently invokes "the people" and their oppression by tyrants—"O despotisme horrible!"; "O joug insupportable"— and it promises "Guerre aux tyrans." There is even one part, the ringing end of Act IV, where the conspirators evoke the Marseillaise with cries of "Marchons! Marchons!" (48, 87, 92).

Of course *Vêpres siciliennes* is far more than a liberal squib. It ends with an equivocal scene in which one of the Sicilian conspirators reflects on his acts and laments murder of the French even in a good cause; and the play features another poignant scene in which an old French *chevalier* counsels an hubristic young knight against his lust to humiliate the Sicilians. He tells him that if he had known Saint Louis (who died in 1270; the play is set in 1282), he would realize that military prowess, even courage, are not the highest virtues; rather, greater admiration is due to justice and compassion for the poor and the oppressed. To earn the love of a people is, in his words, "the most sublime perfume (*encens*) that a king might breathe" (36). All this, of course, falls on the deaf ears of the posturing and haughty young warrior, whose behavior would in no small measure provoke the Sicilians' inordinately violent uprising as depicted in the play.

Whether Ancelot wrote his play directly in the spirit of opposition to Delavigne's or deliberately to develop its image of Saint Louis may never be known, but he dedicated his work to the saint's namesake Louis XVIII, no friend of conspiracies or of the overthrow of French regimes.[20] Ancelot's play includes in fact only two themes: loyalty and coming of age. In the epic tradition he completely alters the historical details. He makes Louis IX, his wife Margaret of Provence, and their son, the future Philip III, appear all together as captives in Egypt in 1250. Margaret in fact was never captured. Philip, who is treated as heir and as an adult if youthful knight, was only a small child at the time of the crusade to Egypt; the presumed heir was Prince Louis who had remained in France during his saintly father's expedition. It was not until 1260 that this prince would die, thus leaving the succession to Philip. But as with Le Moyne in the seventeenth century, there is a purpose to the welter of changes. This is a play about how a young man sees his father bear suffering heroically and, it is implied, how the same young man comes to maturity all the better for having done so. In that sense it is the cryptograph of Louis XVII, the story of what might have been if the son of the executed Louis XVI had lived to rule in the Restoration.

It is also, as suggested, the story of absolute loyalty. The king is the father of his country. And though not every one can understand why any king or father acts in the specific ways he does, it is every subject's duty to accept the monarch's fatherly will: in the king only resides the hope of preventing anarchy and arresting petty tyranny, the tyranny of upstarts (I. iii; II. iv). Interestingly, the staging of the play or at least the iconography of its published text, as Barbara Cooper shows, reinforces these strong patriarchal images—in an era when the existence of political patricides constituted the core of governmental paranoia.[21]

In Ancelot's play, Louis IX demands the loyalty inherent in this conception of kingship, and he defends the ideal of loyalty above all ideals save devotion to the Christian religion itself. The exposition of the theme commences when Almodan, the sultan, breaks the oath he had made to release the Christians for ransom. Louis deplores the oath-breaking, not principally because it deprives his men of their freedom, but because it is inherently sinful (II. ii, iii). We are not to be surprised, therefore, that the king refuses to escape when an uprising erupts against the sultan. Louis is on his earlier word of honor not to escape, which is to say, he holds faith even with those who are faithless (oath-breakers and infidels). The knight who urges him to flee entreats, "Come, or under my very eyes Almodan will kill you. Follow me." The king replies, "The sultan has received my word of honor." The knight will not be put off: "He has broken his oath." No matter, the king responds, "I will heed mine." Desperate, the knight implores the king once more to flee, but Louis stands firm with the words (III. viii), "I am French, a knight, and a Christian" (*Français, chevalier et chrétien*). There can be no effective retort to this trinity.

Again, after the king is condemned to death but while armed resistance remains possible, he refuses to resist or even allow resistance from others under his command, since it was by oath that he gave his fate into Almodan's hands (IV. iv). When finally the Saracen rebels themselves, in clear sight of victory over Almodan, offer their services and obeisance (*honneurs*) to Louis, he persists in his refusal, imploring them to abandon their rebellion against their ruler, tyrant though he may be, and to beg his forgiveness: "Muslims, away from me with these sinful honors; / Respect your king, above all in his misfortunes" (V. iv; see also V. iii). It is the sultan alone whom Louis can permit to be generous to himself.

Lemercier, whose tragedy *Louis IX en Egypte* soon followed, was older than Ancelot, having been born in 1771 of noble parentage. A critic of absolutism, he embraced the Revolution as he entered into manhood, but like many of his titled contemporaries he desired a "legal" revolution, the monarch's authority defined by new negotiated constitutional arrangements voluntarily ratified by the crown itself. Events after 1792 left him further and further behind. Briefly Lemercier saw the emerging Bonaparte (opponent of the "petty tyrants" of the Terror) as a possible restorer of the true (or Lemercier's idea of the true) revolutionary spirit, and they became close friends.

As Bonaparte grew increasingly autocratic, however, he and Lemercier parted company, with Lemercier's paranoia increasing in proportion. Though Lemercier was elected to the Academy in 1810, the Empire became hateful to him, Bonaparte odious, and the emperor and his henchmen, or so he felt, determined upon his murder. This was not entirely delusive; someone did try to assassinate the playwright but failed in the

Saint Louis in Epic and Drama 181

attempt. Lemercier blamed the Imperial party. Bonaparte's decisive fall and distant exile in 1815 were therefore blessed events. And Lemercier became strident in execrating the memory of the Empire and Napoleon's legacy; he would lead opposition to the return of the emperor's bones to France after the exile's death in 1821.

Nonetheless, the years after 1815 were no panacea for Lemercier. His play, performed for the first time on 4 August 1821, may have been offered as an antidote to pro-Bonaparte nostalgia in the months after Napoleon's death (5 May).[22] However, it proves on reading a vehicle for the expression of opposition both to the legacy of Bonapartism and to the renewed pretensions of Bourbon absolutism. The play opens with Louis already a captive, and it expands an incident recorded by Joinville, the murder of the sultan and the subsequent *coup d'état* that put the fate of the captured crusaders at risk. The sultan alive has been depicted as a vicious tyrant by the playwright; yet at an opportune moment when an innocent but vengeful victim of his tyranny manages to hatch a plot, it is Louis (also a victim of the sultan's cruelty) who shouts a warning to the sleeping tyrant, thus saving his life. The explanatory thread in this behavior is explicit in the drama. The Louis IX of Lemercier's tragedy acknowledges himself a "plaything of a cruel despot" (*jouet d'un despote cruel*), but what he has learned from the yoke of cruelty and the madness of despotism is "how much tyranny is execrable to men, / And that a monarch, enamored of false splendors, / is nothing without equity, the source of his greatness" (IV. v).

Enduring the tyranny of one in authority is regarded by Louis as an obligation. Tyrannicide does not exist in the king's vocabulary of political virtue even when under the heel of a tyrant himself. The successful killing of the sultan by his Egyptian subjects later in the play provides Louis with the opportunity to speak with indicative (but in fact normative) force on the difference between savagery (Egypt) and civilization (France): "You [Egyptians] butcher your rulers; the French defend them." Such stoic forthrightness and putative moral superiority are, of course, rewarded in the end—by the grudging admiration of the Saracens and by the release of the king's army (V. vi).

Lemercier died in 1840, the year of the return of Napoleon's bones in honor to France, while still another monarchy was grappling with the complex French political tradition and employed or was forced to confute a wide variety of images and political symbols to do so. Louis-Philippe, who had come to power as a result of the Revolution of 1830 and styled himself the "citizen-king," ushered in a period marked by efforts at co-optation and reconciliation. This is most apparent in the story of the creation of the great museum at Versailles, the old symbol of Bourbon absolutism. The museum was to showcase the accomplishments of all dynasties and regimes in France. The return of Napoleon's bones complemented this effort: even the arch-enemy of royalist sensibilities was to be incorporated into the pantheon of French heroes along with Saint Louis, the paragon of Catholic and monarchist values.[23]

The era of reconciliation endured even beyond the July Monarchy into the Second Empire. Upstart usurpers fed on images of military prowess celebrated in the vast panoramic historical paintings at Versailles. Books and prints were relentless in their insistence that Louis was a symbol for all good subjects (whether of kings or emperors); proof positive was the installation of the saint's picture in government-owned monuments and administrative buildings.[24] The Pantheon in the course of its various "secularizations" and "desecularizations" achieved the same purpose almost by accident later in the century in the latitudinarian acceptance of royal, imperial, and republican heroes in its burials and artistic scheme.[25] But the hero-worshipping equipoise of the mid-century in general gave way, after the violence of the Commune, to the sectarian battles of the Third Republic.[26] The image of Louis IX became a weapon against the secularist and egalitarian proclivities of the state. Nowhere was this virulent strain of partisan manipulation of the saint's image more vivid than in drama.

Victor Delaporte, with whom we shall begin, joined the Jesuit order in 1866 at the age of twenty. During his long career he wrote plays and books mostly on religious or historico-religious themes. His point of view may be inferred from the title of a book he wrote in 1893 on Louis XVI: *Le Roi-Martyr*. This offputting volume, published to coincide with the hundredth anniversary of Louis XVI's execution and republished the same year with other Louis Seize memorabilia, constitutes an apology for that king who, in Delaporte's hands, becomes a gifted and tragically misunderstood saint.[27] It is relevant to the present discussion because of the way Delaporte conflated Louis XVI with Louis IX. On page after page he reports the resemblances between the two and the devotion of the later for his ancestor: incidents Louis XVI experienced on Louis IX's feast day are reported as symbolic revelations, and so on.

Many of Delaporte's plays and biographies were meant to be read or performed by children; he himself was a party to the ongoing debate in the Third Republic about the relative merits of an education based in the Christian or pagan classics. As Janine Dakyns notes, Catholic criticisms of education could be severe (like those of Abbé Gaume).[28] On this point, however, Delaporte was a moderate. What he really wanted to see was the creation of a set of modern juvenile texts that incorporated a continuing

Christian vision of social order and that would not be considered subversive by the state. (To be sure, he was not happy with the republican state as it existed, but that was another matter.)[29]

Delaporte's major play pertinent to our theme is *Saint Louis 1242*, published in 1894, the year after *Roi-Martyr* made such extensive use of the saint's image. In September of that year the Dreyfus affair began. While I think it unlikely that the play speaks directly to the affair, it expresses sentiments that help situate some Catholic attitudes. Père Delaporte dedicated his play to the "young Christians of France"; and he acknowledged in his preface that he had largely depended on Joinville (an acknowledgment by then typical of fiction writers) but had also consulted Latin chronicles of the period.[30] In his footnotes to the play he occasionally took on the great expert on Saint Louis, the rather conservative Catholic scholar and ardent republican Henri Wallon, whose bulky two-volume study is now considered a dated but masterful piece of nineteenth-century French historiography. The problem was that Wallon, although a practicing Catholic, was dedicated to scientific history in the nineteenth-century sense; and he emphasized some themes in Louis's life—his disputes with the church, for example—in a way that offended certain Catholic traditionalists who were self-appointed guardians of the saint's memory.[31]

Delaporte's play itself does not make interesting drama, but it is particularly important given its intended audience of children. Set in the difficult period around 1242 when Louis put down a major challenge to royal authority by barons of the southwest, the play opens on the eve of the battles that subdued these barons, when the outcome is still uncertain. Early on we encounter two characters in Paris discussing the distressing political situation: what will happen in the revolt of the barons? One suggests that Paris itself might join the revolt, but this is denied by the other. Paris, he claims (3), will remain loyal to the king, except for a few "outlaws, gallows meat; / and Jews" (*malandrins, gibier de piloris; / Sauf les juifs*). These will be the traitors.

Jews are frequently mentioned in the fictional work on Louis IX, but it was the Third Republic that witnessed Louis's treatment of the Jews as central to the retelling of his story. To some degree—and this is the significance of this dreadful play—Père Delaporte led the way. Images of the Jew traitor are invoked again and again in his play. In *Roi-Martyr* he had several times quoted approvingly the story that a *sans-culotte* had dipped his hands into the blood of the executed Louis XVI and sprinkled the drops on the heads of the crowd, mocking the evangelist's report of the Jews' scorn for Christ, "His blood be on us and on our children" (Matth. 27.25). This emblem of Jewish guilt transferred to the regicides fascinated

Delaporte in *Roi-Martyr*. In *Saint Louis 1242*, he evidenced his absolute consumption with Jew-hatred. At decisive moments in the play he set his biting anti-Jewish sentiments over against the refrain of *Montjoye*, the French battle cry associated with the crusader ideal of the conquest of Jerusalem. It was a battle cry that had, by then, a long history in the service of cultural critics—whether anti-semitic or not.[32]

The play's subplot (elaborated from a medieval tale) pursues a similar theme. It concerns a much maltreated sculptor, Olivier, so skilled that the jealous master of the *atelier* in which he labors does not wish examples of his work, particularly a stunning statue of the Virgin, to be seen by nobles who might recommend the young man to the king. Olivier, gifted though he is, is a sculptor by necessity, not choice. In fact, he is the son of a nobleman imprisoned at the behest of a wicked Jewish usurer and denied his birthright—this even in Saint Louis's reign. (Delaporte, who parades his knowledge of history, seems to have been unaware that under Louis IX distraint of Christians' persons for arrears was forbidden to both Jewish and Christian moneylenders.)[33] The justice of Olivier's recovery of his birthright from the grasping Jew and the theme of patriotism over against traitorous Jews are really at the core of this play. Dedicated to the "young Christians of France" and offered as an improved part of the curriculum in the year the Dreyfus affair began to consume the Republic, the play was all the more *au courant*: for in the eyes of the anti-semites the Republic had itself betrayed France to the Jews by permitting them positions of power and authority.

A more searching social critique of the same period, for which the image of Saint Louis was decisive, occurs in the work of the Nobel Prize-winning author Romain Rolland, one of the more complex figures in turn-of-the-century literary history.[34] Rolland's was a meandering odyssey from traditional Roman Catholicism to an indifferently Catholic but intensely evangelical attitude toward the world; from there to an almost free-thinking, anti-Christian, and pro-communist cast of mind; and from there to profoundly Catholic but lukewarm communist inclinations. This description neglects his various passing enthusiasms for Indian mysticism, Judaism, anti-Judaism, pacifism, and Leninism. Rolland was also a visionary in the clinical sense: he experienced visions which he regarded as supernatural and wrote fiction and criticism in response to them. Once, for instance, he visited Voltaire's house on the Swiss border and toured it. Coming out, he saw a distant mountain and felt—or so he expressed it in an oddly repulsive passage—as if he were a virgin being raped by Mother Nature. As his biographer Harold March comments, "It is not given to every man to look at a mountain and feel like a violated virgin."[35]

Saint Louis in Epic and Drama

It was in response to another "vision," a short visit from God in October 1894, that Rolland wrote his play *Saint Louis*. March sees the play and indeed perhaps the vision itself as a reaction on Rolland's part to his failed marriage to a Jewish woman.[36] He had married her partly in penance, from a sense of guilt that developed when this small-town boy came to Paris and discovered that Catholicism was not simply the cold mornings at early mass, the smell of incense and the comfort of familiar rituals, but also the locus of a vicious anti-semitism. Clotilde was a kindred spirit on many levels, but Rolland wanted especially to redeem Christianity by protecting her from anti-semitic calumnies. What Rolland discovered after his infatuation wore off was that the Judaism of his wife and her family was worn very lightly indeed. They were progressives, connected to wealthy bankers and holding university positions, and they had nothing but disdain or at best indifference for the so-called superstitions of Judaism. They turned out to be insufficiently oppressed to have returned to their religious roots or to have made a courageous defense of Judaism *per se*; and therefore they became in his view unworthy of his compassion. Rolland came to loathe both Clotilde (though they did not separate until 1901) and French Jews of her class.

Rolland waffled in the Dreyfus affair. According to William Herzog, he "was connected with both camps," but in 1903 in the play *Les Loups* he definitively threw his lot in with the Dreyfusards.[37] It was somewhat different earlier: in 1895 he wrote, "I feel in them [the Jews] the (unconscious) enemies of the thought, the beliefs, the underlying soul of the nation, arrogant and crude enemies, against whom a reckoning is coming."[38] Yet Rolland's *Saint Louis* of the previous year, rather than forming a diatribe against Jews in the manner of Delaporte, is a studied attempt to create a kind of mystically elegant Christian vision which, in his view, is so superior to anything else, including Judaism, that nothing else bears mentioning. So odd is the play that it was quite unpopular with publishers. It was not until 1897 that it appeared in print in the *Revue de Paris*.[39] And yet it hurt Rolland to see it appear, because he owed its publication to his Jewish wife's powerful influence in business and literary circles.

To say that Rolland's *Saint Louis* is marked by historical error would be an understatement. After a prologue in France the venue rapidly shifts to southern Europe and the Holy Land. Louis will die on this crusade, but not in Tunis; his wife Margaret will die with him, although she did not go on her husband's last crusade and outlived him by twenty-five years. The plot, such as it is, is simple. The king goes on crusade. A motley group of crisis-ridden people accompany him. They are defeated.

186 Studies in Medievalism

All is character analysis. Most of the *dramatis personae* suffer from *fin-de-siècle* neuroses, elevating the play to a form of social criticism. Rosalie de Brèves, the wife of a man who always puts his knightly duties first, is the very type of the constrained woman, oppressed by polite society, longing for a Bohemian existence ("Ah! le devoir! le devoir! Des ordres! . . . Jamais libre!"). And she sums up the mood of the play. "We have," she intones in one peroration, "one and the same [enemy], the cruelest of all . . . it is the heavy despotism of this society which keeps us all enchained" (112, 129).

We have Manfred, the perpetual cynic, who goes on crusade to subvert it (he is also a spy) and to make money. He ridicules religious sentiment and ends up insane (584-86). We have Gaultier de Salisbury, the man of extremes—at one time with an exaggerated fear of hell and of his own unworthiness, at another with an exaggerated desire for another man's wife and an egotistical sense of his own role as a man of action and destiny. Yet he is the same man who will die in a fit when the king of France looks at him with the penetrating gaze of a saint and seems to foretell Gaultier's eternal damnation (393-94). The bored, the cynics, the unrestrained pleasure-seekers, the supermen without moral scruples—in fine, the end products of nineteenth-century rationalism and bourgeois society in the fashionable critique of the pundits—are repeatedly tested against the transcendent spirituality of Louis IX and a few other "healthy" types. These latter can still have visions, unlike the victims of bourgeois *ennui*, though they do not need them. They still possess spiritual goals. They want ultimately to share with Christ the joy of overcoming the world.

Even most of these fail the test in Rolland's play. Nonetheless, the recovery of transcendence and, more concretely, the willingness to denounce social class as a barrier to spiritual community are the bold markers of the heroes of the play who have set out to create a new or heavenly society on earth. Not, to be sure, a society led by kings. Rolland is no monarchist flunky. The society he imagines is one in which the true moral kingliness of each person may inspire others. For in the climactic closing scene of the play, as Louis and his utterly defeated troops climb Zion, it is the king who dies before the ascent is completed (593). And although references throughout the play raise questions about whether any of his high crusader ideals can survive him, it is the army of the poor that continues to climb the mountain inspired by his effort.

Rolland's *Saint Louis* seems universally regarded a dramatic failure. Less stodgy and funnier is *Le Lit de saint Louis* (1911), a one-act farce by Augustin-Thierry and Eugène Berteaux. Berteaux seems to have been something of an iconoclast; he collaborated while quite young on at least

Saint Louis in Epic and Drama

187

two plays with Augustin-Thierry and was productive down to about 1950. Augustin-Thierry, born Gilbert Augustin in 1843, was the nephew of the great medievalist and *homme de politique* Augustin Thierry, whose name he adopted with the added affectation of the hyphen. The nephew, who published some of the great man's writings, was rather an eccentric mixture. Far older than Berteaux, he had been active in the regime of the Second Empire when Napoleon III sent him to England for research preparatory to a collection of the extant correspondence of Napoleon I. Despite his modest role as a scholar Augustin-Thierry remained basically a playwright and novelist, drawn to Romantic and grossly *outré* subjects, especially the occult.[40]

Le Lit de saint Louis opens in a provincial museum run by an officious director, Monsieur Mirabelle, who spends a considerable part of his time spouting laws as the justification for his actions.[41] His only staff is comprised of a guard who doubles as janitor, an uncouth fellow with the barbarian name Odoacer who speaks a mean unlettered French, frequently lacking in vowels, except when his punctilious boss makes him recite laws proving that his performance of the tasks they mandate is as barbaric as his name implies. Odoacer's main duty is to keep the jewel of the museum's collection from getting dusty; and that special centerpiece is none other than the bed of Saint Louis. It is not quite a complete bed; it lacks its original supports. Hence, it has remained only a provincial jewel in the crown of a provincial museum. Notwithstanding, it is still a real plum—a gift to the museum from the personal collection of Monsieur Mirabelle ("Mr. Plum-Tree").

This delightful play also functions as a brutal satire on French bureaucracy and Republican "historicity," officialdom's attempt to incorporate all heroes of the past. The only reference to the bed of Saint Louis that was more than passing in the medieval sources, let alone that would have been known to educated Frenchmen, was, of course, Joinville's. Louis, he said, deliberately held court and dispensed justice sitting informally at the end of his bed to avoid the ceremonial oppressiveness of the normal judicial setting.[42] A more obscure reference to a *lit de saint Louis* is equally piquant: there was a tradition reported continuously from at least the sixteenth century at the Hospital of Vernon in Normandy, which Louis endowed, that he kept a bed there so that he might sleep *incognito* among the poor and the sick.[43] The play, however, contains no allusion to either of these beds. Indeed, Monsieur Mirabelle cannot quite decide on the significance of the museum's prize. He is willing to believe that it was meant for sleeping, that being, in a precious syllogism, what all beds are

188   Studies in Medievalism

for, but whether for Louis as a child or as an adult, the pressing question to him, he always finds it difficult to decide.

In any case, we learn that Monsieur Mirabelle has been sent a new administrative assistant with the noble but placeless (perhaps mock Corsican) name, de Val d'Ajol. In fact, de Val d'Ajol is a nobody. Uneducated and unprepared for a job in museum administration, he has been appointed by preferment. He even plans to steal valuable objects from the museum and, later that night, breaks in with his mistress Marguerite (Saint Louis's wife's name), whom he affectionately calls Margot. Margot is the only really sympathetic character in the play. Of the earth earthy, she wants to make love on Saint Louis's bed as soon as she lays eyes on it. She gets her timid paramour to lie on the bed with her, and under the covers they find a chastity belt, unused, they speculate, since the halcyon days of the Seventh Crusade. In the spirit of the tryst Margot ecstatically shouts out phrases like "Tu es mon maître, mon roi, mon croisé" and my favorite expression, uttered at the peak of pleasure, "Montjoye Saint-Denis," the Capetian battle cry. Her lily-livered lover, afraid of being caught, can only reply, "Damiette . . . Mansourah"—not very appropriate (one the site of the victory, the other of the colossal defeat of the French army on crusade under Saint Louis). In one of their many tumbles the bed collapses. The ever cheerful and ever resourceful Margot fixes up a makeshift set of supports, an act that causes de Val d'Ajol to bewail her ignorance in "fixing" the bed, since, as he learned that very morning from Monsieur Mirabelle, one was not supposed to "fix" monuments but "restore" them—again, a pointed barb at Third Republic policies of historical preservation.

In the end, of course, Odoacer overhears their lovemaking and hastens to inform the director, who hurries to the museum and catches the lovers still undressed. De Val d'Ajol chivalrously tries to take all the blame, but Monsieur Mirabelle upbraids them both. Ultimately, however, he agrees not to report them. His change of heart is the result of Margot's plea that her life will be ruined if he turns them in, for she is a married woman whose passion for de Val d'Ajol has blinded her to her duty. She asks Mirabelle to search his own past and remember that he too must have taken headstrong actions when young and in love.

At last the *dénouement*. Just as Monsieur Mirabelle agrees to be lenient, the pompous and insufferable Inspector-General of Historical Monuments arrives, with the perfect hyphenated bourgeois name Dupont-Durand. Since he is also the husband of Margot, Margot quickly hides in an Egyptian sarcophagus. Monsieur Dupont-Durand, suspecting nothing and spouting a law to the effect that he can inspect at any time of the day or night, praises Mirabelle for being in the museum at night, attending, so he thinks, to business. Then he notices the famous bed of Saint Louis with the makeshift supports. He asks Mirabelle to explain whether he "restored" it. Monsieur Mirabelle denies everything, an act that prompts de Val d'Ajol to take responsibility. Dupont-Durand, however, has nothing but praise for the attractive young man with the noble name; the restoration in his view is perfect. Such a bed, Saint Louis's bed, with such a restoration, a perfect restoration, is no longer appropriate for a mere provincial museum. He will authorize its removal to the Louvre; and he will see to it that de Val d'Ajol gets the promotion such a handsome young man obviously deserves. With this resolution, the Inspector-General, the director, and the absolutely dumbfounded Odoacer depart, leaving de Val d'Ajol standing alone. Relieved that the ordeal is past, he never wants to enter the dreadful museum again, but Margot replies that lying in the sarcophagus has rather turned her on, and she implores her lover to return with her the next night for another go. Curtain.

Le Lit de saint Louis is a funny play, sending barbs against the double standard, Republican posturing around the symbol of a royal hero, the persistence of preferment over rewards for talent in French bureaucratic circles, and the insufferable self-satisfaction of bourgeois life (cruelly mocked in Dupont-Durand's slavish and arguably homoerotic toadying to the handsome would-be nobleman de Val d'Ajol). Along with Delaporte's *Saint Louis 1242* and Rolland's *Saint Louis* it reveals the range of uses to which the holy king's image might be put in fiction in the generation before the First World War. It also throws into high relief the seismic shift from the earlier epic and dramatic tradition, which employed the saint-king's image to praise the royal lineage or to exalt monarchy as a form of government (and denounce rebellion), to mid- and late nineteenth-century works—principally but not exclusively of political rightists and moral traditionalists—that engaged Saint Louis to indict ethical laxity, social disorder and pretension, and perceived injustices. The transition from the one form of criticism to the latter was, as we have seen, the long attempt beginning in the 1830s to co-opt all "French" heroes of the past, however they differed in their political and religious persuasions, into one universal and corporate nationalist pantheon.

Much more could be said about Louis IX in French epic and drama and in fiction in general in the periods covered by this essay and especially in the period after the Great War. There are other plays, like the academician Henry Bordeaux's *Mystère de saint Louis* of 1950, a very old man's apprehension over a Europe brought low for the second time in his memory.[44] A long and loving personal portrait of the saint—less sharp perhaps but in the tradition of Rolland's work—the *Mystère* testifies to the enduring

190   Studies in Medievalism

moral force of the image of the king in a society still nearly half peasant and with relatively strong monarchical movements. But there are novels, too, such as Hubert Villez's titillating *Mémoires de Shadjar, les amours secrètes d'une reine d'Egypte*, with a second subtitle, *La Tentation de saint Louis*, illustrated (Paris, 1969). This suggests that another perhaps even more decisive shift was completed by the mid-twentieth century in which Louis IX and his story became curiosities, escapist fantasies in the hands of playwrights, novelists, and film makers, with about as much social and political thrust as a musical based on King Arthur. It is somewhat sad, this erosion. A "tradition at once ancient and direct, unbroken, oral, distorted, unrecognisable, and alive," in Proust's wonderful words, is no more.

NOTES

A very early version of this essay was prepared for the millennium celebration of the accession of the Capetians to the French throne held at the Twenty-Second International Congress on Medieval Studies, Western Michigan University, 1987. I would like to thank the chair, Elizabeth Brown, participants Donna Sadler and Harvey Stahl, and commentator Jacques Le Goff for their kind response. I would also like to acknowledge the help of Professor Adam Knobler, who provided extensive comments on earlier drafts.

    1.   Marcel Proust, *Swann's Way*, vol. 1 of *Remembrance of Things Past*, trans. C. K. Scott Moncrieff and Terence Kilmartin (New York: Vintage, 1989), 164-65. Brief allusions to remembered images of Saint Louis, like comforting evocations of a dreamy past, appear in several other places in the novel as well (see, for example, 65, 66). The device, if this word captures the image, was employed by other French authors; cf. Gustave Flaubert's picture of Emma Bovary in the nunnery of her youth where her knowledge of the famous women of the past "stood out for her like comets upon the dark immensity of history, along with certain more shadowy and mutually unrelated phenomena such as St. Louis and his oak-tree" (*Madame Bovary*, trans. Alan Russell [Harmondsworth: Penguin, 1950], 50).
    2.   I consulted the luxury Paris edition of 1671 in *Les Oeuvres poétiques du P. Le Moyne*, 1-235 (with three preliminary unpaginated leaves); all citations are from this edition. Some bibliographic sources suggest that this is the fifth edition, but the book itself refers to the existence of only three previous editions. Le Moyne's poetic works are very rare in the United States. I owe a great debt of thanks to John Logan, Romance Languages and Literatures Bibliographer at Princeton University, for expeditiously securing a copy of this volume for my examination.

Saint Louis in Epic and Drama

3. For discussions of his work, see Esther Gross-Kiefer, *Le Dynamisme cosmique chez Le Moyne* (Zurich: Juris, 1968), and Richard Maber, *The Poetry of Pierre Le Moyne (1602-1671)* (Berne and Frankfort-am-Main: Peter Lang, 1982).

4. See the publishing information assembled in A. de La Bouralière, "L'Imprimerie et la librairie à Poitiers pendant le XVIe siècle," *Mémoires de la Société des antiquaires de l'Ouest* 23 (1899): 105-06, 128-29. (I owe this reference to Hilary Bernstein, a Ph. D. candidate at Princeton.) The standard critical edition of Joinville's book is J. Natalis de Wailly, *Histoire de saint Louis* (Paris, 1872). My citations are to this edition. A newer critical edition is Noel Corbett, *La Vie de saint Louis* (Sherbrooke, Que.: Nauman, 1977). The most accessible English translation is Margaret Shaw, "The Life of Saint Louis," in *Joinville and Villehardouin: Chronicles of the Crusades* (London: Penguin, 1963), but the translation is very free. More literal is René Hague's *Life of Saint Louis* (London: Sheed and Ward, 1955), translated from Wailly's edition.

5. The greatest product of this tradition was the churchman Louis Sébastian Le Nain de Tillemont's work, which remained in manuscript until the nineteenth century: *La Vie de saint Louis*, ed. Julien de Gaulle, 6 vols. (Paris, 1849). Important works that followed were Paul François Velly's monumental *Histoire de France*, which was cribbed by Richard de Bury (or Buri) for his enormously popular *Histoire de saint Louis, roi de France*. The latter went through no fewer than twenty-two reprints or editions from 1755 to the twentieth century. The final "new" edition was published at Tours in 1902. For the biographical information on de Bury, Velly, and the other authors discussed in this essay I have consulted, in addition to the authors' works themselves, the great multi-volume compendia *Biographie universelle (Michaud) ancienne et moderne*, new ed., 45 vols. (Paris, 1843-65); *Nouvelle biographie générale*, 46 vols. (Paris, 1845-66); *La Grande encyclopédie*, 31 vols. (Paris, 1866-1902); and the still ongoing *Dictionnaire de biographie française* (Paris, 1933-).

6. "Je ne pouvois donc choisir vn Heros plus accompli que celuy-là [Louis IX]: & d'ailleurs le choix que j'en fait, est honorable à la France, qui l'a éléve; à nos Rois, qui sont nez de luy; à la Maison Royale, qui est de sa Race; à la Noblesse, qui l'a pour Patron & pour modèle; à toute l'Eglise, qui l'a receu au rang des Saints qu'elle revere. Et j'ai crû, que mon Poëme qui porte son nom, pourroit estre comme vn Temple, où son Image & ses Reliques seroient toûjours exposées; où les merveilles de sa vie seroient chantées à tous les Siècles; où ses Vertus seroient preschées à tous les Princes; où sa Mémoire recevroit le culte & l'encens de tous les Peuples" (*Oeuvres poétiques*, unpaginated). In this essay, as in the excerpt just quoted, I have unless otherwise noted provided my own translations.

7. "Roy de France . . . extimant qu'il estoit de l'honneur de Jesus Christ, que la Sainte Couronne autrefois teints de son sang, ne demeurast plus au pouvoir des Sarrasins, à qui vn Renegat Grec l'avoit venduë, entreprend de la retirer de leurs mains, & de l'apporter en son Royaume" (*Oeuvres poétiques*, unpaginated).

8. William Jordan, *Louis IX and the Challenge of the Crusade: A Study in Rulership* (Princeton: Princeton University Press, 1979), 107-9.

192   Studies in Medievalism

9. Because the work is so rare in the United States, it may be helpful to refer the interested scholar to William Calin, *Crown, Cross and "Fleur-de-Lis": An Essay on Pierre Le Moyne's Baroque Epic, "Saint Louis,"* Stanford French and Italian Studies 6 (Saratoga, CA: Anima Libri, 1977), which includes a detailed synopsis.

10. August Buck et al., eds., *Dichtungslehren der Romania aus der Zeit der Renaissance und das Barock* (Frankfurt-am-Main: Athenäum, 1972), 299-301, 459-65 (the latter pages with excerpts from Le Moyne's "Dissertation"). I owe this reference to John Logan.

11. Similar intrusive devices would be used to the same purpose by later authors, such as Jacques Ancelot (discussed below); see Barbara Cooper, "Creating a Royal Stand-In: History, Politics and Medievalism in a French Restoration Tragedy," *Medievalism and Romanticism 1750-1850*, ed. Leslie J. Workman, *Poetica* 39-40 (1994), 236-37.

12. For a selection of relevant passages, see Le Moyne, *Oeuvres poétiques*, 93-96, 119-20, 131-31.

13. See William Jordan, "The Case of Saint Louis," *Viator* 19 (1988): 209-17.

14. One can mention in passing the Jesuit Josèphe du Baudory's play, *St. Ludovicus in vinculis*, which may also have existed in a French version, *Saint Louis en fers* (1747). It was acted in the Collège Royal de Henry le Grand at La Flèche on 2 September of that year. The received opinion—at least with regard to the Latin version—is that it was something of a failure. The play is listed in Clarence Brenner, *L'Histoire nationale dans la tragédie française du dix-huitième siècle, University of California Publications in Modern Philology* 14.3 (1929), 226, 325. The title, referring to St. Louis's captivity in Egypt, suggests a more realist approach to the saint's biography than we find in Le Moyne's poem. The episode of Louis in Egypt also became the subject of a musical extravaganza performed before the Royal Academy of Music in 1790; see Jean Mousset, *Saint Louis* (Tours: Maison Mame, 1950), 15-16.

15. *Les Quatres premiers chants de Louisiade, poème héroique, proposé aux amateurs* (Avranches, 1774).

16. Edouard-Thomas Simon, *Saint Louis* (Paris, 1816), ix-x.

17. See Lionel Gossman, *Medievalism and the Ideologies of the Enlightenment: The World and Work of La Curne de Sainte-Palaye* (Baltimore: Johns Hopkins University, 1968), 175-324.

18. Jacques Ancelot, "Louis IX: Tragédie en cinq actes," *Suite du répertoire du Théâtre français: Tragédies*, XII (Paris, 1823), 1-75. His vigorous denial of plagiarism is at 3-5.

19. For the play, see Casimir Delavigne, *Vêpres siciliennes, tragédie en cinq actes*, new ed. (Paris, 1829); further citations in text. The contemporary debate between "adherents" of this play and Ancelot's is addressed in Cooper, 231-34.

20. The obvious connection to the representation of Louis XVIII is the main theme of Cooper's article. The success of Ancelot's play, such as it was, garnered for the author ennoblement, a lucrative sinecure, and a two-thousand-franc pension, but fortune soon soured. The Revolution of 1830 and the institution of the "Bourgeois Monarchy" were calamities for Ancelot, although except for

Saint Louis he always had indifferent success among theatre-goers as opposed to other playwrights. He made do for the first ten years of the new regime, did not abandon his royalist-legitimist views, and began to re-emerge from obscurity in the later 1830s. His production was at all times prodigious and technically impressive. He failed twice of election to the Academy, once in the 1820s, once in the 1830s, but was finally chosen in 1841. Ironically for a man accused of plagiarism, his last major undertaking was an embassy after the Revolution of 1848 to several European countries to arrange protocols on the protection of literary property, that is, early copyright, which laid the foundation for many of the conventions which still govern us. He died soon after.

21. Cooper, 237-43.

22. Népomucène-Louis Lemercier, "Louis IX en Egypte: Tragédie en cinq actes," *Suite du répertoire du Théâtre français: Tragédies*, X (Paris, 1822), 283-359.

23. For a fascinating discussion of the issues surrounding the location and building of the tomb for Napoleon's remains (the final decision was for the Church of the Invalides) and to explore the resonances of this discussion for broader issues in nineteenth-century French politics, see Michael Driskel, *As Befits a Legend: Building a Tomb for Napoleon, 1840-1861* (Kent: Kent State University Press, 1993). The changing fortunes of the cult(s) of Napoleon are nicely chronicled in Robert Gildea, *The Past in French History* (New Haven: Yale University Press, 1994), 89-111. Related political issues are treated in detail in Professor Knobler's article in this volume of *Studies in Medievalism*.

24. For example, the picture by Alexandre Cabanel (1823-1889) of the "Glorification of Saint Louis" which hung in the Château of Vincennes in 1855 (it was later moved to Versailles); see Claire Constans, *Musée national du Château de Versailles: Catalogue des peintures* (Paris, 1980), s.v. "Alexandre Cabanel."

25. On the Pantheon, see Roger-Armand Weigert, *Le Panthéon* (Paris: Éditions du Cerf, 1948). Cabanel did the three frescoes of Saint Louis at the Pantheon, one of which is reproduced in Weigert, 15.

26. For more on this in various genres, I refer the interested reader again to Professor Knobler's article.

27. I consulted the edition with the Louis Seize memorabilia, *Le Roi-Martyr* (Paris, 1893). The eponymous essay is at 5-69; introductory remarks on Louis XVI as a misunderstood saint may be found on 1-2. For a brief treatment of centenary commemorations of the beginning of the French Revolution and of subsequent revolutionary events, like the execution of Louis XVI, see Gildea, 17-19.

28. Janine Dakyns, *The Middle Ages in French Literature, 1851-1900* (Oxford: Oxford University Press, 1973), 76. Jean Joseph Gaume (1802-1879) wrote immensely popular work on educational issues in which he favored the suppression of pagan authors in favor of the Church Fathers. He also wrote a catechism, a comparison of communism and Christianity (and their relation to the workers' movement), and a polemic on the evil of revolution.

29. A curious feature of the memorabilia attached to *Roi-Martyr* is a list (205-10) glorying in the miserable fate of the Republican regicides of 1793. Delaporte tried to show in delicious detail how each had met a particularly horrible

but well deserved death. Although he was certainly adopting a common device here, the point is that his hatred of the First Republic was a reflex of his hatred for the Third.

30. Victor Delaporte, *Saint Louis 1242, drame historique en cinq actes, en vers* (Paris, 1894), v-vi; further citations in text.

31. The work of Henri Wallon at issue is *Saint Louis et son temps*, 2 vols. (Paris, 1875). For some of Delaporte's criticisms, see *Saint Louis 1242*, 23, 85. Delaporte, as indicated, was not alone. Charles Verdier wrote a contemptible set of articles trying to rebut Wallon for the journal *Etudes religieuses, philosophiques, historiques, et littéraires*, vols. 7 and 8 (1875).

32. Dakyns, 5.

33. William Jordan, *The French Monarchy and the Jews from Philip Augustus to the Last Capetians* (Philadelphia: University of Pennsylvania Press, 1989), 134, 162.

34. For the repertory of Rolland's works, see William Starr, *A Critical Bibliography of the Published Writings of Romain Rolland* (Evanston: Northwestern University Press, 1950). For a critical assessment of his work, see Harold March, *Romain Rolland* (New York: Twayne,1971).

35. March, 22.

36. March, 43-46.

37. William Herzog, *From Dreyfus to Petain: "The Struggle of a Republic,"* trans. Walter Sorell (New York: Creative Age, 1947), vii. See also Gildea, 40-41.

38. Quoted in March, 43.

39. Romain Rolland, "Saint Louis," *Revue de Paris*, March-April 1897, 87-137, 358-95, 571-93; further citations in text.

40. The major biographical sources offer little on Berteaux as opposed to Augustin-Thierry; I have therefore constructed what little I can of Bertraux's biography from the hints in his published works.

41. Augustin-Thierry and Eugène Berteaux, *Le Lit de saint Louis, pièce en un acte* (Paris: Librairie Théatrale du "Nouveau siècle," 1911).

42. Joinville, Chap. 12.

43. Referred to in Georges Goyau, *Saint Louis: Louis de Poissy—Louis de France* (Paris: Plon, 1928), 88.

44. Henry Bordeaux, *Le Mystère de saint Louis, drame en 4 actes et 15 tableaux* (Paris: Plon, 1950). The play is novel length, with narrational "tableaux" and songs (many of which the author was willing to see changed or shortened to meet performance requirements). The play reads like a rather dull history book. Only the word portraits of Louis's wife, Margaret of Provence, are lively and humorous.

Asceticism, Masochism, and Female Autonomy: Catherine of Siena and *The Story of O*

Suzy Beemer

In her book *The Body in Pain*, Elaine Scarry investigates the infliction of pain as a means of empowerment, arguing that torture is used not primarily to hurt the victim but to highlight and empower the agent of pain. The semantics of torture, which function not to effect sympathy for the victim but to conflate pain with power, and the literal tools used to effect torture, are emphasized, thereby accentuating agency, the subject who tortures rather than the object who is tortured.[1] Similarly, Michel Foucault contends that torture as a public spectacle—pain made visible, often with an emphasis on the tools of agency—translates into a reaffirmation of the power of the state, the body functioning as a site of the reinscription of the sovereign's power: the spectacle of the victim renders the agent, not the victim, most significant.[2]

But what happens to power when agency is not so easily located, when the boundaries between torturer and victim, subject and object, are blurred, as for example, in female asceticism and masochism? In these cases too a preoccupation with agency exists, as evidenced by the often regimented routine of the ascetic or the carefully crafted script of the masochist. This emphasis on agency works to direct authority toward the agent/torturer rather than her pain, putting her in a position of power as the executor of her own bodily harm. Paradoxically these self-mortifying behaviors function to empower the female they are directed against, since

Studies in Medievalism VIII, 1996

she herself is the director of the action. She remains object, but is also simultaneously subject.

One manifestation of this phenomenon is the disease anorexia nervosa, an almost exclusively female disorder. In his book *Holy Anexoria*, Rudolph Bell notes a connection between modern-day sufferers of anorexia nervosa and holy women in late medieval times. Many of these pious women, as part of their ascetic practices, simply refused to eat: a phenomenon Bell terms "holy anorexia." He concludes that both twentieth-century anorexia and holy anorexia are manifestations of the same phenomenon: in each case these females are striving for autonomy—because, living for and according to the standards of others (the former for parents and teachers, the latter for parents, priests, and confessors), they do not feel they have an identity of their own.[3]

Bell notes but does not especially emphasize the very gendered nature of this behavior and its probable patriarchal cause, which forces women to seek autonomy via seemingly curious avenues. Since women continue to exist directly or indirectly for men, having relatively little access to political or economic power, and since even a woman's own body may be outside her jurisdiction (consider, for example, male ownership in previous centuries of women and the children they bore, abortion rights debates and rape in our own), dominion of the body may carry particular significance for females. The anorexic may subconsciously perceive that if she can at least govern her "own" (a debatable issue) body, she may in some sense gain subject status, by objectifying her self, her body.

Significantly, most of Bell's "holy anorexics" were nuns or at least tertiaries. The convent, of course, provided European women with a significant amount of autonomy, since it released them from home- and child-care labors and separated them, their bodies, and their sexuality from male dominion.[4] The cloister afforded women an intellectual freedom unavailable to them in any other late medieval societal arena. Although these women were answerable on occasion to male clergy, immediate male dominion of fiscal and social law did not exist in the cloister: the result was a degree of female self-government which never could have existed in the outside world. Their "self-willed unavailability [to men]" put such women in "control over their lives."[5]

It was nuns and tertiaries, as well as pious laywomen who took vows of chastity—in other words, women who removed themselves from patriarchal dominion and who arguably were struggling for autonomy—who engaged in the behavior Bell labels holy anorexia. But ordinarily these women engaged in other types of bodily abnegation as well. I would argue that not only holy anorexia but other kinds of holy asceticism, various

Asceticism and Autonomy

types of pious bodily negation, can be seen as manifestations of the female's struggle to gain autonomy in a partriarchal society. Caroline Walker Bynum observes that the cultures in which "women are more inclined than men to fast [and] to mutilate themselves . . . are all societies that associate the female with self-sacrifice and service."[6] It follows then that conquest of the body—not only through anorexia but through asceticism—may be the result of the medieval female ascetic's quest for autonomy, an attempt to govern, to establish dominion over her "own" body. She is, as suggested by Scarry's theory, empowered as the agent of her own pain.

One of Bell's main case studies is St. Catherine of Siena (1347-1380). A Dominican tertiary who refused to marry, Catherine wielded extraordinary political influence in the Church, lobbying hard for Urban VI during the schism when his papacy was threatened. Her desire for autonomy already obvious and to a measurable degree procured, Catherine was nevertheless a female "satellite," rallying support for a male pope from his male electorate, a system of which she was not a part. According to Bell, Catherine exhibited the symptoms of a holy anorexic: following the holy anorexia pattern, she gradually decreased her food intake until by the age of twenty she would eat nothing but raw vegetables, generally just chewing them and then spitting them out.[7] Ultimately she starved herself to death. But Catherine's extreme asceticism included more than just inedia. She was known to flagellate herself with chains for an hour and a half three times daily. At one time she wore a hairshirt, but later replaced it with a chain bound so tightly about her that it embedded itself in her flesh. She reduced her sleep to approximately one half hour every two days, and used only a board for her bed. In the hope of curing Catherine of the extremity of her austerities, her mother once took her for a course of baths, but even then Catherine found a way to mortify herself: under the pretense of obtaining the full effect of the baths she edged toward the canals where boiling sulfuric water entered the pool, and intentionally scalded herself.[8]

One might assume that dualistic theology is responsible for Catherine's extreme self-mortifying behavior. Such a stance implies that through bodily abnegation some degree of autonomy is gained: conquering the flesh gives women the opportunity to exercise dominion over and/or transcend their bodies, resulting in spiritual empowerment. Bynum, however, discredits the notion of dualism as an explanation for medieval women's asceticism and instead favors the concept of *imitatio Christi*. By Catherine's lifetime, the notion of imitating Christ had moved beyond the idea of meditating on the events of his life and was now seen much more literally: to imitate Christ's life was not to remember it, but to live it physically, suffering as he had suffered on the cross. Bynum asserts that Catherine's

198 Studies in Medievalism

penitential practice, particularly in the instance of drinking pus from the breast sores of a dying woman for whom she was caring, was an example of *imitatio Christi*, suffering in conjunction with service.[9] Indeed, considering that several of Catherine's fasts lasted forty days, as did Christ's, and that she died of self-induced starvation not only, as she claimed, to expiate the sins of the Church, but also at the age of thirty-three, the *imitatio Christi* seems a logical explanation for her behavior.

But while Catherine's alimentary habits may seem an obvious example of the *imitatio*, her other penitential practices do not fit quite so easily into this category.[10] Bynum's view of the breast-sore incident, for example, is not supported by the account of Raymond, Catherine's confessor. Raymond, appearing to favor not an *imitatio Christi* but a more dualistic approach to the incident, explains Catherine's act as an example of mind over matter, a spiritual conquest of the flesh: he writes that she "rebuked her own body" for standing in the way of her service to the woman by holding her mouth and nose against the sore until "she had stamped out the rebellion of the flesh against the spirit."[11] Catherine's letters, virtually filled with exhortations to their recipients to kill the self-will, also seem, at times, theologically dualistic. She often chided others for misusing bodily mortification as an end in itself rather than what she clearly states is its proper purpose, to annihilate the will. Despite rather frequent discussion of ascetic practice throughout her letters, Catherine does not assert that such penance is to be carried out in *imitatio Christi*. Both Raymond's account and Catherine's own letters thus cast doubt on the notion of *imitatio Christi* as the grounds for her own ascetic practices.

Bynum is quite right in asserting that the *imitatio Christi* played a significant role in medieval women's piety. Catherine, for example, prayed that she might be allowed to assume the burden of her dying father's sins, suffering for him so that he might bypass purgatory and be allowed direct passage into heaven. In another instance, she prayed that she might be made a stopper in the mouth of hell to prevent other souls from entering.[12] But these Christlike instances are not examples of active asceticism. Bynum's allegations that *imitatio Christi* is responsible for the asceticism of medieval women may be true in some cases, but with the exception of specifically inedic asceticism, it is simply not borne out in the instance of Catherine of Siena, whom Bynum uses as an example to support her argument.

Although the goal of Catherine's austerity is ostensibly a pious and therefore selfless one, we should not overlook the fact that she in turn profits from her ascetic behavior, at least in her own perception. Catherine believed that in giving up her own will in order to adopt God's will

Asceticism and Autonomy

she became subject to him, necessitating her absolute obedience to his authority. But paradoxically, and according to traditional Christian doctrine, this resignation of autonomy results not in a loss of freedom but in ultimate liberty. In her letters, Catherine invokes a common metaphor for the will, describing the liberty of the unbridled horse which is free *because* it has severed itself from the will and its appetites.[13] In Catherine's view, her asceticism, while a denial of her will, functions paradoxically as a means for her to gain freedom and autonomy.

At least three explanations are possible, then, for Catherine's self-infliction of pain. Yet it could be argued that any one of the three affords, or seems to her to afford, some degree of autonomy. Catherine's own perception of the purposes of bodily suppression maintains that penance performed to kill self-will paradoxically results in freedom. Somewhat more dualistic is Bell's "holy anorexic" argument, which by extension suggests that "holy ascetics" sought autonomy by exercising dominion over their own bodies. In contrast to dualistic proposals, Bynum's theory of Catherine's asceticism as *imitatio Christi*, if correct, also affords autonomy. If, as Bynum asserts, medieval women through suffering in *imitatio Christi* made themselves "parallel" to, "merged," and "fused" with Christ, this would lead them undeniably to subjective status and beyond: they became in their own eyes the ultimate Sovereign Being. The body thus functions, says Bynum, not as a "hindrance" but an "opportunity" for the "soul's ascent."[14]

Female asceticism in the Middle Ages has also been studied by Jane Tibbetts Schulenberg, who has gathered extensive documentation of the particular self-mortifying practice of amputating the nose and lips. According to Schulenberg, this self-disfiguring act was a specifically female behavior and a relatively common practice, documented in various areas of Europe and in at least the eighth, ninth, and twelfth centuries. Neither a penitential conquest of the body nor a fusion with Christ's suffering, this self-disfiguring act, even more overtly than the bodily abnegation of Catherine, was unequivocally a quest for or protection of autonomy for the female—in this case, sexual autonomy. The nose and lips were cut off by these women for two quite specific reasons: to protect themselves from rape (perceived as based on attraction) which often occurred during violent invasions of convents, or to avoid unwanted impending marriages.[15]

In one such "self-disfigurement in defense of chastity," St. Margaret of Hungary (d. 1270), upon hearing reports that the Tartars (reputedly assailants of virgins) were invading, believed that if she cut off her lips she would be left untouched. Having previously refused to marry the Duke of Poland, the King of Bohemia, and the King of Sicily, Margaret threatened again to mutilate her face upon learning that despite her prior refusals the pope had arranged for her to be married.[16] Other women not only threatened but actually did disfigure their faces to prevent marriage.

Except in cases of sexual assault such as those noted above, lurid or violent sexual practices hardly come to mind when considering the reputed virtue and chastity of the medieval ascetics, many of them now sainted. However, despite the differing contexts, the parallels between medieval asceticism and present-day heterosexual masochism are striking. When, as is often the case, the medieval ascetic or contemporary masochist is female, the language of either practice focuses on the denial of the will so that a male will, either a male human's or a male god's, may be assumed.[17] Both asceticism and masochism are forms of bodily abnegation, and both, I would argue, offer manifestations of the female's struggle for subject status. These parallels are noted infrequently in psychology and psychiatry texts, but are occasionally discussed in the fields of literary criticism and women's studies: and the text invoked repeatedly in these discussions is *The Story of O*.[18] While it may seem incongruous to compare an ostensibly fictional novel with the ostensible historical reality of Catherine's asceticism, this distinction is actually quite nebulous. Catherine's austerities, while they probably did exist, are also, like O, literary: we learn about them from her confessor's writings, which, it should be remembered, were composed with the hagiographic agenda of effecting canonization.

The Sadean *Story of O* caused quite a stir upon its original publication in France in the mid-1950s. Because of its explicit sexual and sadomasochistic content, the book has been considered scandalous by both the religious right and the feminist left. Most disconcerting to some feminist critics is the fact that the book was apparently written by a woman—a fact which has finally, forty years later, been confirmed. Because the author's name, Pauline Réage, is a pseudonym, controversy abounded regarding the writer's sex. Some maintained that Réage was female; others, particularly feminists, refused to believe that a woman could write such an allegedly pornographic "male-fantasy"-type book, claiming that the female pseudonym functioned to perpetuate the myth that women desire their own debasement.[19] In her book on rape, Susan Brownmiller reported that she was "vehemently hostile to suggestions that . . . popular sex fantasies attributed to women are indeed the product of a woman's mind . . . ." While reading the "scurrilous, anonymous pornographic classic *The Story of O* by 'Pauline Réage,' a pseudonym that many men delight in believing masks the name of a real woman," Brownmiller "nearly retched" and was understandably disturbed that one of her male colleagues suggested the book to

Asceticism and Autonomy

201

her as "'the truest, deepest account of female sexuality" he had ever encountered.[20]

Despite Brownmiller and camp's objections, it is now known that *The Story of O* was indeed written by a woman. Long suspected as the author, Dominque Aury, a French journalist, editor, translator, and literary critic who is now eighty-seven, has finally come forward. Her current testimony supports her previous anonymous interviews with Régine Deforges and the account in *A Girl in Love* (which precedes the main text of Réage's *Return to the Chateau*), in which she claims that *The Story of O* is not autobiographical; she wrote it, she says, without intending publication but as a personal gift for her male lover—now known to be the deceased French intellectual Jean Paulhan, who was often suspected as O's author. It was Paulhan who urged Aury to let him find a publisher and who wrote the book's preface.[21] In it, insisting the author's identity is unknown to him, he posits that she must be a woman, claiming the quaintly essentialist "proof" that a male writer could never have conceived of, for example, O's being concerned about the condition of her lover's frayed slippers as he continues to torment her (xxiv-xxv).

In the Deforges interviews, published in 1979 as *Confessions of O*, Réage (Aury) does not denigrate O's nor her lovers' behavior, does not find the book "scandalous," and seems to avoid the whole issue of masochism; her purpose in writing the book was apparently not political, neither an anti- nor pro-feminist gesture. She claims, however, to be a feminist, and touches on feminist issues throughout her interviews with Deforges.[22] And not all critics dealing with (anti-)feminist issues raised by the book have objected to it on that basis: Nathaniel Brown and Rebecca Blevins Faery, who before Aury's "revelation" assumed her to be O's author, see a possible feminist subtext to the work. Although they realize they may be interpreting counter to the author's intent, it is perhaps (and I stress *perhaps*) because they assume female authorship that Brown and Faery read O quite differently than does Brownmiller. In a manner similar to that suggested by Judith Fetterley's *The Resisting Reader*, which challenges traditional readings of certain male-authored texts, arriving often at interpretations apparently the inverse of ostensible authorial intent, Brown and Faery see O as a sort of feminist manifesto, a warning to women of the dangers of patriarchal marriage pushed to its logical extreme.[23] Erica Jong, on the other hand, has recently proposed that while equality may be what women desire outside the bedroom, when it comes to sex, they want to be dominated. She challenges any "politically correct lover" to read *The Story of O* and not be turned on.[24] (I did. I wasn't.)

202 Studies in Medievalism

The novel depicts its "heroine's," O's, voluntary submission to sexual atrocities and physical torture administered by her lovers, René and Sir Stephen, who also prostitute and eventually completely own her. Near the text's beginning, O is brought by her lover to Roissy Castle, "an establishment organized by men for the ritual violation and subjugation of women."[25] Upon arriving, she is given the following instructions, which illustrate the extent to which she will be completely subjected and objectified:

> You are here to serve your masters . . . . At the first word or sign from anyone you will drop whatever you are doing and ready yourself for what is really your one and only duty: to lend yourself. Your hands are not your own, nor are your breasts nor most especially, any of your orifices, which we may explore or penetrate at will. . . . You have lost all right to privacy or concealment . . . you must never look any of us in the face. If the costume we wear . . . leaves our sex exposed, it is not for the sake of convenience . . . but for the sake of insolence, so your eyes will be directed there upon it and nowhere else so that you may learn that there resides your master . . . . [Your] being whipped . . . is less for our pleasure than for your enlightenment. . . . Both this flogging and the chain attached to the ring of your collar . . . are intended less to make you suffer, scream or shed tears than to make you feel, *through* this suffering, that you are not free but fettered, and to teach you that you are totally dedicated to something outside yourself. (15-17)[26]

Note that, illustrating Elaine Scarry's hypothesis, the language used here and the intent of the torture is to emphasize not O's suffering but the power of the male agent. The remainder of the novel is really nothing more than the ensuing enactment of these instructions: daily forced vaginal, anal, and oral sex, prostitution, whippings, etc. O's objectification becomes complete when Sir Stephen has her buttocks branded with his insignia and her labia pierced with heavy iron rings which cannot be removed, marking her as his property. She dreads these processes and finds them to be extremely painful, but ultimately experiences "inordinate pride" as a result of the irons and the brand (158-67). Throughout the text, O not only willingly assents to but desires her subjugation, concerned only that Sir Stephen continue to "love" her.[27]

Already the parallels to religious asceticism are apparent: desiring the love of their subjugators, O and Catherine endure and even use physical annihilation in order to negate their own wills and to assume the will of

Asceticism and Autonomy

one who is perceived as powerful: the male René, the male God. Susan Sontag notes the connection between the pious ascetic and the masochist:

> The "perfect submissiveness" that her [O's] original lover [René] and then Sir Stephen demand of her echoes the extinction of the self explicitly required of a Jesuit novice or Zen pupil. O ["Catherine" could be substituted here] is "that absent-minded person who has yielded up her will in order to be totally remade," to be made fit to serve a will far more powerful and authoritative than her own.[28]

Indeed, the medieval comparison to another St. Catherine—St. Catherine of Alexandria (patron saint, significantly, of unmarried [relatively autonomous?] women)—is overtly made as Sir Stephen arranges a sort of torture chamber: "it was a handsome panoply, as harmonious as the wheel and spikes in the painting of Saint Catherine the Martyr . . . ." In characteritic *imitatio Christi*, the passage continues: "as harmonious . . . as the nails and hammer, the Crown of Thorns, the spear and scourges portrayed in the paintings of the Crucifixion" (171). O's torture likens her both to the martyred saints and to the crucified Christ.

The Story of O is replete with such religious imagery: Brown and Faery cite several references from *O* in which O is "depicted in the position of a nun, the cloistered bride of her god-like lover," while Jessica Benjamin compares O's story to "the surrender of the saints."[29] The difference is that O's gods are her male lovers. As a child, she had read a biblical text, "it is a fearful thing to fall into the hands of the living God" (Hebrews 10:31), but as an adult involved with René, she now disagrees with this, believing instead "what is fearful is to be cast out of the hands of the living God," meaning that she is afraid of being left by René. Reminiscent of Catherine's letters on the absence of consolation from God, O laments that René, like a god who has cast her out, loves her but neglects her: she fervently "prays," "Oh, let the miracle continue, let me still be touched by grace, René don't leave me!" (96-97). That René is O's god and she his religious subject is apparent earlier in the text as well. As three men look on, she is forced to perform fellatio on René:

> tears streamed down her ravaged face each time the swollen member struck the back of her throat and made her gag, depressing her tongue and causing her to feel nauseous. It was this same mouth which, half gagging on the hardened flesh which filled it, [repeatedly] murmured . . . "I love you" . . . . O felt that her

> mouth was beautiful, sincer her lover condescended to thrust himself into it . . . since, finally, he deigned to discharge in it. She received it as a god is received . . . . (19)

The parallels to a medieval religious context are obvious. Here in this sexualized context the Eucharist becomes semen, and O most definitely "suffers in conjunction with service," Bynum's description of the *imitatio Christi*.

Just as Catherine and other medieval women who mutilated their own bodies can be seen as trying to move toward subject status, toward autonomy, either through *imitatio Christi*—amalgamating themselves with the power and sovereignty of Christ—or more dualistically, by achieving dominion over their bodies, so too is the masochist like O striving toward a position of relative autonomy which is not afforded her as a female. Since subject status seems unobtainable, it is only by embracing objectification, annihilating self and fusing with the male subject, that she perceives access to power. Simone de Beauvoir extends this argument beyond the masochist to include more generally a woman in love, who exhibits the same loss of self as does the medieval ascetic:

> Shut up in the sphere of the relative, destined to the male from childhood, habituated to seeing in him a superb being whom she cannot possibly equal, the woman who has not repressed her claim to humanity will dream of transcending her being toward one of these superior beings, of amalgamating herself with the sovereign subject. There is no other way out for her than to lose herself, body and soul, in him who is represented to her as the absolute, as the essential. . . . She chooses to desire her enslavement so ardently that it will seem to her the expression of her liberty; she will try to rise above her situation as inessential object by fully accepting it. . . . Love becomes for her a religion.[30]

The perhaps oxymoronic self-effacing Subject is also examined by psychoanalyist and literary critic Jessica Benjamin, who observes as she explores the dynamics of the sadomasochistic relationship that autonomy is sought through masochistic behavior.[31] Benjamin's claim is supported by the work of psychoanalyst James Sacksteder, who asserts that a "masochistic identity is a type of negative identity, which, however costly and pathological, nonetheless represents for some individuals their best possible effort at creating and maintaining a separate and autonomous sense of self."[32] Benjamin glosses *The Story of O* as "a tale . . . in which the desire for autonomy and the desire for recognition can only be resolved by total renunciation [and therefore transcendence] of self" but is careful to point out that the Freudian concept of masochism as a simple pleasure-in-pain paradox has been revised by current psychoanalytic theory: pain can result in pleasure "only when it involves submission to an idealized figure." O's submission, as noted earlier, is most definitely to idealized figures; she considers her lovers to be gods. As males, they, not she, are sovereign. If she forsakes her own will to assume theirs, she becomes them and obtains, vicariously, authority. "In losing her own self," as Benjamin remarks, "she is gaining access, however circumscribed, to a more powerful one."[33]

Psychologist Roy Baumeister also points to the autonomy of the masochist, partly through submission as Benjamin notes, but also because often it is the masochist rather than the "sadist" who is actually in control. The masochist often writes the script to be enacted, and insists on going back to the beginning if it is not followed exactly. Dominant partners, says Baumeister, "sometimes imply that they are basically catering to their masochistic partners," monitoring responses carefully so that all is exactly as the masochist desires. Controlling his or her own pain, the masochist may use what Baumeister calls "safe words" (previously agreed on verbal signals) to indicate that the pain is too much and the dominant partner should stop; and, "the very entry into S&M is often initiated by the masochist." Similarly, O is free to leave the chateau at any time; Catherine initiated her own ascetic behavior. Since masochism involves a considerable degree of "fiction and illusion," Baumeister is careful not to come to definitive conclusions regarding control; he does suggest, however, that the assumed power dynamic of sadomasochism is turned upside down, implying the masochist's considerable autonomy.[34]

The question of agency, then, is integral in examining masochistic behavior. As with the ascetic, dominion of the body is at issue; even though bodily subjugation occurs at the hands of another, the masochist has voluntarily put her body in the situation and thus her will is of consequence. Baumeister suggests an even more explicit agency on the part of the masochist which puts all activities directly under her (his) control, rendering the sadist's role as subject almost negligible. But even if the sadist is primarily in control, the masochist comes vicariously to power though amalgamation. By making herself extinct, the female masochist then moves, by fusion with the sadist, to his, the subject's, position. Says Réage: "O is trying to see how far she can go, to test the limits of herself; she seeks to attain the absolute that life denies her. . . . O is looking for deliverance . . . ."[35]

Studies in Medievalism

Similarly, the medieval ascetics, either by establishing jurisdiction over their bodies or in fusion with Christ through *imitatio*, aligned themselves with sovereignty. Pearl Chang finds O's situation "hardly different from the case of the nun or other holy woman who, through self-mortification, claims communion with stronger and more comforting agencies than had been available to her through her own, independent means."[36] When questioned about O's excessive submission as a possible method of domination, Réage claims that "women use the weapons given them. It's not as though they have a very wide range. . . . Submissiveness can [be] and is a very formidable weapon, which women will use as long as it isn't taken from them."[37]

Whether the female "weapons" of medieval asceticism and contemporary masochism are effective is dubious at best, but despite the differing contexts, each is the possible manifestation of a woman's desire to achieve autonomy in the subjugated female world. Given the inefficacy of confrontation in the face of such overwhelming dominion apparent, she chooses weapons which embrace rather than challenge her subjected status, co-opting male domination for the purpose of liberating herself. Asceticism or masochism may be the only avenue some women—medieval or contemporary—perceive in their quest for autonomy under patriarchy.

NOTES

An earlier version of this paper was presented at the Eighth International Conference on Medievalism, University of Leeds, September-October 1993.

1. Elaine Scarry, *The Body in Pain: The Making and Unmaking of the World* (New York: Oxford University Press, 1985), 3-4, 18, 27-28.

2. Michel Foucault, *Discipline and Punish: The Birth of the Prison*, trans. Alan Sheridan (New York: Vintage, 1979), 47-48, 58 *et passim*.

3. Rudolph M. Bell, *Holy Anorexia* (Chicago: University of Chicago Press, 1985), 17-21. While some sources I cite use the word "autonomy" and others do not, I have chosen to use it—but with some hesitation. Its humanist connotations and lack of reference to any theory of social, ideological, or semantic construction are to me disturbing; I am more comfortable with Catherine Belsey's notion of agency in which the subject is neither autonomous nor overly determined but in a dialectical relationship with language and ideology. See Catherine Belsey, *Critical Practice* (London: Routledge, 1980) and *The Subject of Tragedy: Identity and Difference in Renaissance Drama* (London: Methuen, 1985).

4. See, for example, Caroline Walker Bynum, *Holy Feast and Holy Fast: The Religious Significance of Food to Medieval Women* (Berkeley: University of California Press, 1987), as well as Bynum's "The Female Body and Religious Practice in

Asceticism and Autonomy 207

the Later Middle Ages," in vol. 3 of *Zone: Fragments for a History of the Human Body*, ed. Michel Feher (New York: Urzone, 1989), and *Jesus as Mother: Studies in the Spirituality of the High Middle Ages* (Berkeley: University of California Press, 1982); Electa Arenal, "The Convent as Catalyst for Autonomy: Two Hispanic Nuns of the Seventeenth Century," in *Women in Hispanic Literature: Icons and Fallen Idols*, ed. Beth Miller (Berkeley: University of California Press, 1983), 147-83; Susan Carlson, "'Fond Fathers' and Sweet Sisters: Alternative Sexualities in *Measure for Measure*," *Essays in Literature* 16 (1989): 13-31; Emily James Putnam, *The Lady: Studies of Certain Significant Phases of Her History* (1910; rpt. Chicago: University of Chicago Press, 1970).

  5. Carlson, 16.

  6. Bynum, "Female Body," 173-74.

  7. Raymond of Capua, *The Life of Saint Catherine of Siena*, trans. Conleath Kearns (Wilmington, Del.: Michael Glazier, 1980), 55-58.

  8. Raymond, 64; Bell, 44.

  9. Bynum, *Holy Feast*, 171-72.

  10. Catherine was reportedly *unable* to eat (Bell, 25-28), which indicates that she had no choice in the matter and therefore casts doubt on a penitential theory of her fasting practices. In spite of this inability, to avoid criticism by those who accused her of vainglory (Raymond, 166), Catherine would force herself to eat at least once a day. The food in her stomach caused her acute pain, and she would habitually vomit (this was usually self-induced) after eating (Raymond, 170-71). She considered it more painful to eat than not to eat, and viewed the suffering inflicted by eating as a punishment for her sins. In this view, then, the eating rather than the abstaining could be considered asceticism. Bynum calls her own *imitatio Christi* argument into question by pointing out that Catherine referred to her inability to eat as an "infirmity," thereby reducing it to an abnormal physical condition rather than any type of religious practice (*Holy Feast*, 168, 170).

  If this was truly Catherine's perception, then of course penance (i. e., asceticism) is not even relevant to the matter, and her inedia could be discounted as an ascetic practice. However, Raymond says that referring to her inability to eat as a weakness or defect was just her way of saying, "This is God's doing in me, not my own," and he adds, "but far from making this a boast she insisted it was the result of her sins" (168). This does not necessarily mean that Raymond perceived her abstinence as self-abnegation, but, to him, it certainly was not just a physical condition devoid of any religious context. Of course the physical reason that eating was so painful to Catherine was that her system had adapted itself to functioning with little or no food. When she first began her abstinence from food, her system would not yet have made such an adaptation; at one time it was probably more painful for her to abstain than to eat. Perhaps her abstention was begun as a penitential practice, but as her system gradually adjusted, eating rather than denying food became more painful and was consequently viewed as asceticism.

  11. Raymond, 149.

  12. Raymond, 210; *Saint Catherine of Siena as Seen in Her Letters*, ed. and trans. Vida D. Scudder (London: Dent/New York: Dutton, 1927), 340. All refer-

ences to Catherine's letters are taken from this edition. A newer translation of several of Catherine's letters is available: *The Letters of Saint Catherine of Siena*, trans. Suzanne Noffke (Binghamton, New York: Medieval and Renaissance Texts and Studies, 1988). I refer to Scudder's earlier edition, however, because Noffke's selection is different.

13. Catherine, *Letters*, 100.

14. Bynum, *Holy Feast*, 171-72, 211-12; "Female Body," 162, 170.

15. Jane Tibbetts Schulenberg, "The Heroics of Virginity: Brides of Christ and Sacrificial Mutilation," in *Women in the Middle Ages and the Renaissance: Literary and Historical Perspectives*, ed. Mary Beth Rose (Syracuse: Syracuse University Press, 1986), 53, 55, 42.

16. Schulenberg, 49-50. Schulenberg quotes from *De B. Margarita Hungarica, AA.SS.*, Januarius, 3:518 (Jan. 28).

17. This is not to say that asceticism and masochism are in any way essentially or biologically inherent to the female sex.

18. Pauline Réage, *The Story of O*, trans. Sabine d'Estrée (1956; New York: Ballantine, 1975); further references in text.

19. See, for example, Janis L. Pallister, "The Anti-Castle in the Works of 'Pauline Réage,'" *Midwest Modern Language Association* 18.2 (1985): 3-13.

20. Susan Brownmiller, *Against Our Will: Men, Women, and Rape* (New York: Bantam, 1975), 359-60.

21. John de St. Jorres, "The Unmasking of O," *New Yorker*, 1 August 1994: 42-50. Interestingly enough, the translator of the third English edition of *The Story of O* also has a mysterious identity, and again gender plays a primary role. "Sabine d'Estrée" claims in "her" Translator's Note (included in the U. S. version of *O* published by Grove Press (1965), that the text required a woman translator who would "humble herself before the work" in order to render it faithfully without intruding upon the work and altering it, as a previous male translator had done *because*, she suggests, he was male. D'Estrée compares herself as translator to O, who "humbled" herself before her lovers (xi-xii). But St. Jorre (49) is convinced that d'Estrée is not a woman at all, but New York publisher Richard Seaver, thus undoing the essentialist argument that humility is a characteristic possessed inherently by women.

22. Régine Deforges, *Confessions of O: Conversations with Pauline Réage* (New York: Viking, 1979), esp. 39.

23. Nathaniel Brown and Rebecca Blevins Faery, "The Total 'O': Dream or Nightmare?" *Mosaic* 17 (1984)189-206; see also Judith Fetterley, *The Resisting Reader: A Feminist Approach to American Fiction* (Bloomington: Indiana University Press, 1978).

24. Erica Jong, "Freud Didn't Know What Women Want: But I Do . . .," *Esquire: British Edition*, October 1994: 62-65.

25. Jessica Benjamin, *The Bonds of Love: Psychoanalysis, Feminism, and the Problem of Domination* (New York: Pantheon, 1988), 56.

26. I am indebted to Benjamin for her excellent condensation of this passage.

Asceticism and Autonomy

27. See also Réage's *Return to the Chateau* (New York: Grove, 1971).

28. Susan Sontag, *Styles of Radical Will* (New York: Farrar, 1969), 68.

29. Brown and Faery, 196 (Brown and Faery touch on this only briefly, but conclude that the religious language in the novel represents an inversion rather than a parallel to monasticism); Benjamin, 60.

30. Simone de Beauvoir, *The Second Sex*, trans. and ed. H. M. Parshley (New York: Vintage, 1989), 643. For directing me to this most appropriate passage, I am indebted to Brown and Faery.

31. There is much controversy regarding the issue of female masochism—whether it is reality or myth, biologically based, externally or internally induced, etc. See, in addition to Benjamin, Paula J. Caplan, *The Myth of Women's Masochism* (New York: Signet, 1985); Judith Lewis Herman, "Masochism Unmasked," *Women's Review of Books*, 3.5 (February 1986):10.

32. James L. Sacksteder, "Thoughts on the Positive Value of a Negative Identity," in *Masochism: The Treatment of Self-Inflicted Suffering*, ed. Jill D. Montgomery and Ann C. Greif (Madison,Conn.: International Universities Press, 1989), 106.

33. Benjamin 55, 60-61.

34. Roy F. Baumeister, *Masochism and the Self* (Hillsdale, New Jersey: Lawrence Erlbaum, 1989), esp. 12-13; see also Caplan, particularly 172.

35. Deforges, 142.

36. Quoted in Brown and Faery, 191.

37. Deforges, 140.

Closing the Circle: Medievalism in Today's Occitan (Provençal) Literature

William Calin

The juxtaposition of the terms "Occitan" and "Provençal" in my title, necessary for reasons of communication ("Occitan" is the correct designation, yet a number of people are more familiar with "Provençal"), also has a symbolic function. The two terms, which in one sense are identical and in another in fierce opposition, mirror *en abyme* a Southern French cultural and linguistic entity fascinating in its precarious yet vociferously dynamic survival today.

Occitan, eight centuries ago, was the language of the troubadours, poets who created, as it were, courtly love and the medieval courtly lyric, one of the high points of western civilization. Occitan was (is) also the spoken vernacular of people in the South of France, its history extending from the breakup of Latin to our own times. Over the centuries Occitan never died out, though it did evolve (decline) from a literary *koine* and high court speech to the level of local patois; today all speakers of Occitan are also bilingual in French, and most of them are literate only in French. Over the centuries the literature fell into decline, yet the periods of decline alternated with a number of renascences: during the Baroque age, in the nineteenth century, and, perhaps above all, over the last twenty-five or thirty years, which have witnessed one of the richest and most exciting literary revivals in the history of modern Europe. It is this contemporary revival and its relationship to the past, for our purposes the medieval past, which is my subject.

For present-day Occitan intellectuals, as is the case in other minority cultures, we find, on the one hand, the desperate need for cultural roots,

Studies in Medievalism VIII, 1996

Medievalism in Occitan Literature   211

for a "usable past," which, as often as not, will be a medieval past: given that, as Leslie Workman argues, medievalism lies at the heart of and forms perhaps the essence of romanticism, and given that so many minority cultures were reborn, with a renewed sense of identity, during the Romantic period or under the influence of romanticism.[1] On the other hand, nothing in the history of cultures is simple or univocal. We can observe, along with the call for a usable past, sundry degrees of reaction against too strong or too stultifying a past, including romanticism with its accompanying medievalism.

Harold Bloom's theory of "anxiety of influence" functions here.[2] So does, I believe, what I elsewhere have called the "structure of repudiation" or "structure of refusal": the phenomenon, especially prevalent in the history of French, going back to Ronsard and the Pléiade, perhaps even to the first romancers of courtly love, whereby young writers consciously denigrate their immediate predecessors and the fashionable literature of their and their parents' generation, proclaiming the desire to be new and original; in order to do so, they seek inspiration in writers distant in space and time.[3] Rejecting the fathers, they turn instead to grandfathers and ancestors—perhaps Greek and Roman, certainly long since dead and buried. The phenomenon of classico-centrism denounced by Barthes contributes to this structure of repudiation: the vast majority of literary generations imagine a Golden Age situated in the past, condemns their immediate predecessors, and flatter themselves for having chosen such truly "golden" forebears.[4]

In the literature of Southern France, written in Occitan, the central public phenomenon of renewal occurred in the nineteenth century: it is associated with the Félibrige, the Avignon Reniassance, Mistral and his circle (Mistral, Aubanel, Roumanille, and others), the "empire of the sun," the "Latin race," and *Mireiho*: all the myth and imagery, also the concrete literary achievement, of a true renascence, and a renascence that exalted the Middle Ages. And afterwards? Afterwards, we find both the epigones, the obedient sons, the ephebes (as Bloom would say) who perpetuate the forms, ideas, and mindset of the great fathers; and those who rebel, the strong sons who seek their own kingdom.

In the regions of Languedoc, as in Scotland, as in Russia, Hungary, and Romania, the renascence is a school and movement of romanticism, saturated with all the elements that characterize European romanticism: relative formal traditionalism, the exaltation of nature and the individual, a certain rustic primitivism, nostalgia for the national past (including the Middle Ages), and, in a number of major figures, a political stance on the right or, at the least, resolutely apolitical and oriented toward art for art's sake. Therefore, in all of these lands, modernism was to take the form of antiromanticism and to adopt its generic traits: formal innovation, social realism, an urban decor, the refusal of sentimental nostalgia for the past, the refusal of what the French call, with distaste, *du folklore*, and, in many, a political stance resolutely on the Left.

In Eastern Europe intellectuals are so conscious of culture and of the need to extol the national past that they have had a tendency to consider, rightly or wrongly, Mayakovsky and Brodsky as the natural inheritors of Alecsandri and Eminescu. Perhaps the best they could do, under the Red Terror, was to think of the national patrimony as harmonious and one, and to defend it with passion.

In Scotland and the South of France the situation is, in certain respects, more complex. Here we find, in striking historical similarity, two old cultures in which, in the Middle Ages—with the troubadours and the Makars—the language was the medium for a high court culture in no way inferior to those of Paris and London. In both lands the language and the culture, having over the centuries become mere patois, were then reinvigorated by the supreme artistic achievements of a Romantic school: Burns and Scott, Mistral and Aubanel. However, the succeeding decades gave rise to a literature and culture of cliché: kailyard novels, bonny lassies, and Bonny Prince Charlie; or the bourrée and the farandole, pretty Arlésiennes, and charming braggarts from Marseille. Ephebes of genuine talent contributed to the myths of nostalgia: Stevenson and Pagnol, to cite the best. Yet the most serious of the minority intellectuals recognized that the myths of nostalgia were adopted by the dominant culture (London, Paris) in a spirit (conscious or unconscious) of condescension, the bagpipes and the farandole offering no promise of a serious movement for political autonomy or cultural renewal. For these reasons the moderns in Scotland and in Occitania proclaimed their modernity by thrusting away Burns and Mistral—fathers whose weight threatened to be mortal—and by rehabilitating an older, more authentic cultural past, closer to the totality of life and to the language in its vital totality. Hence the structures of repudiation, hence the strong sons of modernism throwing off the fathers and reclaiming worthy grandfathers from the Middle Ages. The cry in Scotland was "Dunbar! not Burns." Since the 1930s, in the South of France, the cry was or could have been: "Guilhem, Bernat, Arnaut, Guiraut, Peire! et non ce couillon de Mistral!" The similarity in career, doctrine, politics, personality, and *oeuvre* between Hugh MacDiarmid and Robert Lafont is stupefying.

The modernist rebellion, in Occitania as in Scotland and Brittany, did not occur without opposition, fierce and righteous opposition from the

Medievalism in Occitan Literature

disciples of the old Romantics who considered the new literature and the ideology to be, at best, an aberration, at worst an act of treachery. In the South of France the disciples of the old Romantics were and are the Félibrige: the inheritors of Mistral and the standardbearers of Provençal tradition. They have defended their tradition and their authority with passion: they also have their writers, and some very good ones indeed. As a result, we find today two schools, currents, or forces in the regional culture: the majority Occitan and the minority Provençal, that is the modernist Occitan and the neoromantic Provençal, hence the two words, the two terms I referred to earlier. Furthermore, each movement has its own distinct writers, publishing houses, journals, university departments, summer schools, and systems of normative orthography. Each makes a claim for hegemony and totality.

The division and subsequent rivalry have in many ways proved to be conterproductive, in a land where power is centered in Paris and provincial culture, even when speaking with one voice, is viewed with suspicion. The Occitan phenomenon, in its modernity, in its contemporary achievements and contemporary relevance, remains unknown to the general literary public including the educated bourgeoisie and sympathetic foreigners. One of my colleagues, a specialist well informed on French affairs, was curious as to my little secondary field of research: What is Occitan? he asked me, sympathetically. Since Provençal is obviously dead, he assumed, Occitan must be something different, perhaps in the Pyrenees, perhaps like Basque? How many families, French or English, returning from a holiday in the Dordogne with "OC" pasted on their bumpers, are aware that this "OC" is a language and has something to do with the troubadours? More to the point, and more seriously, among some families I know in Rouergue and Quercy, little people, the father a foreman in the factory or a minor state functionary, where the grandmother speaks patois in the home and the granddaughter is learning Occitan in school, I have no evidence, direct or indirect, that the family recognizes that *Bonne-maman*'s patois and little Fabienne's Occitan, in some respect, are or ought to be the same thing.

Having sketched the historical situation and set out what I hope is a valid comparative and theoretical contextualization, let us now proceed from the general and theoretical to the particular. Let us envisage contemporary writers, five case histories of major contemporary figures and what they do with the past, with their medieval heritage.

Case history 1: Max-Philippe Delavouët, the greatest poet in the Mistralian or Provençal school, who spent much of his adult life tending his farm in the hills of Provence, a bit of a recluse who cut himself off from all but a few intimate friends; meanwhile, he read most of world literature

214   Studies in Medievalism

and published, from 1971 to 1983, four volumes (a fifth appeared posthumously) of a vast lyrico-epic panorama entitled simply *Pouèmo* (*Poem*).[5]

Pouèmo adheres to the literary mode of celebration or incantation. Delavouët joins, intentionally I believe, Pindar, Ronsard, Hölderlin, and St.-John Perse: needless to say, he didn't always receive rave reviews from a Parisian establishment committed to the *Verbum in principio* proclaimed by Mallarmé which then became incarnate in the flesh of Valéry.

The Speaker of *Pouèmo* is a voice entitled the Prince: he also assumes the roles of Adam, Odysseus, Tristan, Roland, Mistral's Prince of Orange, and, no doubt, the implied author Max-Philippe Delavouët. The Prince leads a hieratic existence, grounded to a large extent in the Middle Ages or, if you prefer, in our literary myth of the Middle Ages. He undergoes quests, encounters dead cities, hermits, buffoons, or his alter ego, another prince, but more often a version of the Eternal Feminine. The dominant archetypal structure of *Pouèmo* is erotic, the thrust of desire, the yearning for two entities, one of which I call the Lady of the City, the other the Lady of the Sea.

The Lady of the City is the subject of "Courtege de la bello sesoun" ("Procession in Spring"), in which a Princess sleeps in her castle, dreaming of her love. The love in question is the Prince, who sets out on horseback, grasping a rose, under a white flag with a crimson heart. At the end of his quest the Prince discovers a white castle and city on the edge of the sea. He shakes his rose, the petals rise and scatter, and a flock of birds rises and scatters from the battlements. The Princess, who had already offered the holy Grail to her dream love, presents her chalice to the Prince, who pours into it his wine and drinks.

The phallic and vaginal imagery—the Prince, his horse, his rose, his wine, his procession through the countryside, and the color red, versus the Princess, her stone castle, her city, her dream, her cup, her immobility inside the stone walls, and the color white—plus the long, slow roll of the text—all contribute to a rite or ritual that evokes man and woman in the throes of desire and also the satisfaction of desire.

Less satisfaction, only the anguish, is evident when the Prince, metamorphosed into Tristan, wounded by the Morholt, alone on a boat, ill and half-mad, gives himself to the waters and to his dream of a love-death with a Lady of the Sea from afar. Or when, following a medieval Occitan elaboration of the Roland story, the Speaker, in the voice and person of Roland, seeks the love of a Saracen queen in Saragossa, and she seeks his love, yet their union can only be one of spiritual, pure, incandescent desire.

These reiterated scenes of Eros contribute to a pattern of union (desired or consummated), nuptials or a fertility rite between man and woman, yet on other, symbolic levels god and goddess, fire and water, gold and quicksilver, the sun and the earth, the masculine and feminine principles of the cosmos, and, because one of the most powerful vignettes describes Adam fecundating Eve on the shore, the birth of our planet and the history of mankind.

Delavouët expresses his cosmic vision in a series of metaphors and a pattern of imagery taken from the Middle Ages: the ideal of *fin' amor*, proclaimed by the troubadours, and the ideal of the quest, proclaimed by northern French romancers. No less medieval is the temporal nexus: a Speaker-Hero named Adam, who sleeps for centuries and is reawakened as the Prince (or Tristan or Roland), both (all) of whom seek the eternal Eve. In a structure that recalls medieval typology yet remains powerfully secular, the age of Adam, *vetus homo*, prefigures the age of the Prince, *homo novus*, all past ages culminating in the actual duration of Max-Philippe Delavouët poet, *hic et nunc*, which crowns and fulfills them. The four seasons and the four ages of man are conceived as the evolution of the race, from creation (by man) to judgment (by Delavouët), a judgment that is provisional not final, given that the present, which contains the past, throbs with its own Eros and Ever-becoming.

Case history 2: Jean Boudou, by general acclaim the greatest writer of prose in Occitan, the first and best modern novelist, a tragic, solitary figure with a tragic, solitary vision of life, who spent much of his adult existence as an itinerant schoolteacher and committed suicide in his fifties. After a superb novel, *La Grava sul camin* (*The Gravel on the Roadbed*), in the behaviorist mode *à la* Hemingway or Camus, Boudou turned to something approximating the magical realism of Latin America. The narrator of *Lo Libre dels grands jorns* (*The Book of the Last Days*, 1964) is a man dying of cancer who, for no conscious reason, gets off the train and wanders about Clermont-Ferrand. This intellectual quotes and alludes to the troubadours and to great figures in the history of Auvergne: Vercengetorix, Sidonius Apollinaris, Pope Urban II, and Pascal. His private myth of Auvergne is grounded in one dream of victory (the First Crusade) and in the multiple reality of defeat: the Gauls crushed by Rome, then, still worse, the Occitan world crushed by Northern France at the time of the Albigensian Crusade, for, the narrator implies, good crusades lead inevitably to bad ones, and evil always triumphs over good.[6]

The quotations from Jaufre Rudel and Raimbaut of Orange structure a thematic of courtly love and chivalry, which is then undercut by the contemporary story of the dying narrator, who lives an ironic anti-quest

216 Studies in Medievalism

in the manner of Kafka and Beckett. The protagonist wanders aimlessly in the maze of little passages, bars, and brothels nestled about the train station; he encounters whores, a defrocked priest, and a half-communist half-shepherd. Among the more prominent "demonic" counter-symbols prove to be: the fountain, a dried-up spring that emits noxious gas or which petrifies, actually transforming water into rock; and the "Other World," Marxilhat (Marxville), a metaphoric science-fiction hell inhabited by decapitated heads kept alive by a mad scientist. Both motifs are taken from Chrétien de Troyes: the fountain in *Yvain* and the severed heads in *Erec et Enide*; the mad scientist also reflects Merlin and, in more recent fantasy, Stalin or Maurice Thorez. The modern, both tragic and burlesque, parodies and undercuts the Middle Ages as well as the modern, proposing that our modern hell is the outcome of medieval folly and the failure of medieval dreams. And, always, in counterpoint, the motif of the narrator, an Occitan writer exploring one of the great cities of the South, the home of troubadours, who finds no one who can speak his tongue, who sets down his miserable tale in simple prose (versus *trobar clus*, the *genus grande* of hard verse, back then), and who, dying, creates one of the last texts of a dying language and a dying culture that will finally bring to an end, in the flesh, the language and culture which began to die centuries ago in the spirit.

Case history 3: René Nelli, a scholar and teacher who was never given a university position. Nelli was one of the early adherents to the new Occitan movement; more than any, he insisted that a minority literature has to grasp the modern world in its modernity (no bagpipes, no farandole) and has, therefore, to partake totally of modernism. Nelli wrote hard, difficult, arcane verse in the style of Valéry and Char, Montale and Quasimodo. Like them, he sought to attain a new Mediterranean classicism, a *monumentum aere perennius* that would fuse the rigor of Greece and Rome with the rigor of high modernist *trobar clus*. And, because he was a medievalist, the author of an important book on courtly love (*L'Erotique des troubadours*) and a number of volumes on the Cathars and Catharism, the Middle Ages is his dominant inspiration and preoccupation. The complete *Obra poëtica occitana* (*Poetical Works in Occitan*) contains two brief texts composed in medieval Occitan.[7] *Arma de vertat* (*Soul of Truth*), Nelli's most important collection, is many things, but most of all, a powerful meditation on and proclamation of *fin' amor* as he conceives it: a burning, spiritual longing for the Other, in fire, that will never be satisfied, because good love, by its very nature, in its essence, cannot be physical; yet, out of the body, crucible of Eros, will be born, purged of its dross, the work of art.

Medievalism in Occitan Literature   217

No less central to Nelli's vision is Catharism, the heresy stamped out by that Albigensian Crusade in the early thirteenth century. A number of Occitan writers, Nelli in the forefront, have created a new, twentieth-century Catharist myth, the fall of Catharism perceived as a turning point in history, an allegory for the fall of Occitania, the end of freedom, and the decline of humane values, under the boots of invading, colonizing hordes from Paris. At the heart of this fascinating medievalist phenomenon is to be found the arch-image of Montségur, the mountain citadel which held the remnant of Catharist resistance and was eventually stormed by the Count of Toulouse, who, perceiving on which side his *fouasse* was buttered, had joined the French.

Nelli refers a number of times to Montségur. His masterpiece in this line is an *Oda a Monsegur* (*Ode to Montségur*), composed in classical meter, a powerful, arcane evocation of the sacred mountain (Frye would call it a point of epiphany), the thunder and lightning which abide there, the Speaker's quest for enlightenment, his physical defeat, his spiritual and artistic victory, and finally his dialogue with an absent god from beyond the stars.

No less a masterpiece, in my opionion, is Nelli's playlet—*Beatris de Planissòlas*—one-third to one-half the length of a classical French tragedy, evoking the characters and issues we know best from Le Roy Ladurie's *Montaillou*.[8] Nelli reconstitutes, in noble blank verse, the confrontation between the châtelaine Beatrice, her erstwhile lover Peire Clergue, and the inquisitor Jacques Fournier, Bishop of Pamiers, who in 1334 became Pope Benedict XII. Beatrice speaks for courtly love, Clergue for catharist spirituality, and the bishop for Catholic dogma. When I read *Montaillou*, I thought the inquisitor the only sensible person in a universe of rustic psychotics. Nelli is more "politically correct" than I am, he gives the good lines to the adulteress and the heretic, and they are very good lines indeed. What might appear to be a symposium between three allegories is transmuted into a moving, heart-rending *dialogue de sourds*, three possessed yet vulnerable human beings who cannot communicate. Each goes alone to his end, chosen by him, willed by him, in the fire of the spirit.

Case history 4: Denis Saurat, like Nelli an intellectual, like Nelli a man on the margins of the French academic scene. Saurat spent much of his adult life teaching French in London. An eccentric, he published books on occultism and literature, Atlantis, and the esoteric religions of Blake and Hugo. Then, in his sixties, he composed a major corpus of verse in the Pyrenees dialect which he had had no contact with or use for since his teens. *Encaminament catar* (*Cathar Way*) and *Encaminament II: Lo Caçaire* (*The Hunter*) constitute a Catharist epic, narrative and didactic, grounded in genuine Catharist myth and doctrine (to the extent we can reconstruct them) plus present-day folklore of the Pyrenees and a bit of Jung and Atlantis.[9] Saurat claimed his very first pages were taken from a fourteenth-century manuscript. Alas, the Chatterton Complex is harder to pull off in our century than it once was. Charles Camproux wrote to Saurat at once, to praise the text but also to remind him that, on linguistic grounds, the language can be dated, at the very earliest, not much before 1938.[10] Saurat admitted the subsequent poetry to be his own but insisted that it was dictated to him in his sleep by a Voice. To their credit, the Occitan leaders corrected the spelling, edited the three volumes, and praised them for their aesthetic qualities, with only the most gentle smiles relating to the circumstances of authorship.

It is perhaps fair to say that *Encaminament catar* is the Catharist epic that Blake or Hugo would have written had it occurred to them to write one. The pure mythical creation is first class. So also is the conviction to create a medieval or medievalist epic in the most totally serious manner possible, destined uniquely for adults in the realm of high culture, yet without the ideological overlay (pro-Algerian Stalinism) we find in Aragon's *Fou d'Elsa*, for example. It is true that Saurat is not a genuine scholar in the sense that Nelli and even Aragon are. The Catharist reconstitution is good; it is also pure Saurat, with Saurat's dreams and obsessions, his personal need for and belief in a *gnosis* to which man can attain through esoteric teaching and esoteric rites of passage—set against modern reality and modern Christianity, and displaced onto its presumed historical source, the Middle Ages.

Case history 5: Bernard Manciet of Gascony, no doubt the greatest living poet of Oc. His masterpiece, *L'Enterrament a Sabres* (*Burial in Sabres*), published in 1988, a long lyrical epic or epic lyric, depicts the burial of la Dauna, an old lady in the village: the procession to the church, the traditional Catholic requiem mass, and the procession to the cemetery.[11] It is a simple, indeed trivial subject on the surface (*sermo humilis*), but to which Manciet brings the same gravity and *tremendum* that his forebears brought to the Battle of Rencesvals and the Fall of King Arthur. La Dauna, one-half a rustic notable, one-half the local witch, is the life and soul of the village and of traditional Gascon culture. The Gascon people are a flock of losers—drunkards, sluts, buffoons—yet they also embody the land and race, are the inheritors of centuries of history. Manciet brings to the two or three hours of the *erzählte Zeit* an intensity of *nunc stans* in *illud tempus*, an eternal present of sacred time when man speaks to God and God to man.

God reproaches la Dauna for having been a harlot on the roads; he threatens her and her people with judgment by fire, the Apocalypse. She then answers back, accusing him of never having been present, of (in Heideggerian terms) Being-ever-in-absence, a Transcendent Other who abandoned his people. We the little people have suffered more than you ever did on the Cross, she cries. You need us more than we need you! The central theme of *L'Enterrament* then is judgment: the Last Judgment, which itself forms part of the requiem mass, is anticipated in the lyrical outbursts of the dying Dauna and her dead friends: God's judgment of man, and man's judgment of God. It is at the end of time, and the end of civilization, that man turns away from the past, including the life of Christ, to the future, in Manciet's sardonic vision our only future as individuals, and as a race: *Dies irae, dies illa*.

Where is the medievalism in Manciet? First of all, in *sermo humilis* and the vision of death and judgment that I have just evoked. Also, behind the Dauna, the drunkards, the whores, and the mourners, fused in them, stands the history of Gascony, the kings and queens, dukes and duchesses, mercenaries and slave-traders. Especially prominent in this history is the Middle Ages, the last period when Gascons stood tall and mediated between great powers, when they determined the course of the West. Hence the pervasive influence of Eleanor of Aquitaine and of the soldiers of the Black Prince; hence a fierceness of rhetoric and thunder of discourse taken directly from Marcabru and Bertran de Born.

As with Delavouët, Manciet establishes an erotic register derived from *fin' amor* (and from the Song of Songs) where Eros presides at the core of the human experience and is the Way, the Truth, and the Life. In addition, as with Delavouët, Manciet renews the peculiarly medieval, typological sense of time, with la Dauna (we can translate her name as *Ma Dame* or Madonna) postfiguring both *Eva* and *Ave*, for, as Whore of Babylon, she perpetuates the worst of Eve, yet as intercessor for her people, the Chosen People of the Landes, she is the spiritual *figura* of the Mother of God. Love which is both Eros and Thanatos unites la Dauna and her creator: the Lord cherishes her in fire and sword, in breaking her and burning her. And she responds in fire of speech, denouncing him and demanding, instead of a soft death *à la Provençale*, death in ecstasy, to be torn apart by his lightning. Such is this allegory—Manciet's vision is powerfully allegorical, more in the spirit of Dante, Digulleville, and Langland than in romances about roses—the life and death of one frightful hag, who is also Gascony, the Gascon people, the Gascon language, and all of humanity, all the daughters of Eve and Mary.

What can we deduce from this? First of all, that the vision of the Middle Ages in contemporary Occitan writing is rich and varied, with allusions to, meditations on, or reconstructions of, the First Crusade, Henry II's wars with his sons, the Albigensian Crusade, the fall of Montségur, and the Hundred Years' War; courtly love and chivalry; Catharism and orthodoxy; individual troubadours and individual figures from Northern France, Roland, Tristan, and Perceval. The Middle Ages is celebrated as emblematic of authentic village life in the provinces, or as a cultural and historical high point which the Occitan people ought to revere, or as a time of lost opportunities, when the first reverses occurred in a long history of reverses. The medievalism is both public and private, for it treats of grand politics and history yet also of Eros and life at home; it reworks intertextually writers from the past and it creates new myths in the present. Ruled out emphatically are cultural nostalgia, *du folklore* and *du passéisme*. Also ruled out by these largely progressive and modernist writers is romantic political nostalgia, the myth of happy peasants interacting organically with their happy princes and bishops.

The Middle Ages is the most observable metaphor or structure of metaphors in Delavouët's and Manciet's imaginative reconstructions of the past. (As we head into the twenty-first century and almost nobody benefits any more from a truly classical education, will, in our popular culture, the Middle Ages stand for, metaphorically *be*, The Past?) However, Delavouët's and Manciet's respective imaginative worlds are that: imaginary, personal, mythical visions of a mythical, visionary past, with the result that the "action" in their poems can be assumed to have taken place at any time from the exploits of Astérix le Gaulois or the reign of Conan the Barbarian up to the usurpation of Danton and Robespierre. And rightly so, given that the village, these wonderful, beautiful villages in *la France profonde*, like Ireland, never knew a Renaissance and an Enlightenment, never detected a shift from mannerism to baroque or from classicism to rococo.

One result of this syncretism is that the writer in Occitan has a number of options in order to "negotiate the past." In the last ten years or so, the Baroque has emerged as a rival to the Middle Ages. Lafont, for example, composed the first *nouveau roman* in the annals of the South, in 1986. *La Festa*, in two volumes, a master work in all senses of the term, is situated chronologically partly in the twentieth century, partly in the sixteenth.[12] Lafont and others have launched the cultural myth that the Baroque, like the Middle Ages, is quintessentially southern, again in antithesis to northern French classicism.

The Middle Ages, and the past generally, occupy a more prominent place in contemporary Occitan literature than in, say, the literatures of French and English. The same is true for Breton. One explanation for the phenomenon is the special situation of a minority literature (some would

Medievalism in Occitan Literature 221

say a postcolonial literature) seeking cultural roots, seeking justification for its and its people's existence. A second explanation is that in modern Occitan, as in Breton and Lowland Scots, intellectuals write for other intellectuals, and teachers for other teachers. The modernist reforms, plus the enormous increase of literacy in the national language, have had one unfortunate, though perhaps inevitable consequence: that the literature is cut off from the shepherds, artisans, small farmers, and urban laborers who still speak the language (more or less) but cannot or do not read it. A museum culture, one might say, and a museum culture it is, in some respects though not in others; also for what it is worth, the literatures in classical Chinese, Japanese, Sanskrit, Arabic, and Persian retained aspects of museum culture for centuries and were no worse for it. A trait perhaps of museum culture, also perhaps of medievalism, is the omnipresence in Occitan of one theme—death: the dead king, metamorphosed into his own funeral stone, borne down the Rhone to be buried in Alyscans (Delavouët); the dying writer, going to seed in Clermont-Ferrand (Boudou); the martyrs of Montségur perishing in the flames of hate (Nelli); the old Dauna of Gascony perishing in the flames of love (Manciet). The metaphor, the allegory actually, is transparent: many believe that Occitan will, at some time in the not too distant future, cease to be a living language, that is no one will have *lingua di oc* as his mother tongue. That this could and will happen to the language of the troubadours has, for many of us, a tragic dimension. Fortunately, for them and for us, the writers of Oc "do not go gently into that good night . . . [they] rage against the dying of the light." And we can hear their rage and their swan song, and observe their Midsummer Night's fire with wonder and with love. That is also man's fate.

NOTES

This essay was originally delivered as a plenary address at the Eighth International Conference on Medievalism, held at the University of Leeds in 1993.

1. Leslie J. Workman, "Medievalism and Romantic Scholarship," *The Round Table* 7 (March 1992): 1-23.
2. Harold Bloom, *The Anxiety of Influence: A Theory of Poetry* (New York: Oxford University Press, 1973); see also other volumes of practical criticism by Bloom, as well as W. Jackson Bate, *The Burden of the Past and the English Poet* (Cambridge: Belknap Press of Harvard University Press, 1970).
3. William Calin, *In Defense of French Poetry: An Essay in Revaluation* (University Park: Pennsylvania State University Press, 1987), Chapter 7.

4. Roland Barthes, "Reflections on a Manual," in his *The Rustle of Language* (New York: Hill and Wang, 1986), 22-28.

5. Mas-Philippe Delavouët, *Pouèmo*, 5 vols. (Paris: Corti, 1971-77); Saint-Rémy-de-Provence, C.R.E.M., 1983-91). In my text I use the standard French spelling for these men's personal names. In the notes I follow their usage in publishing; they sometimes publish under a Provençal or Occitan spelling.

6. Joan Bodon, *La Grava sul camin* (*Obras complètas*, 3), "A tots" (Tolosa: Institut d'Estudis Occitans, 1978); *Lo Libre dels grands jorns* (*Obras complètas*, 5), "A tots" (Tolosa: Institut d'Estudis Occitans, 1978).

7. René Nelli, *L'Erotique des troubadours* (Toulouse: Privat, 1963); Renat Nelli, *Obra poëtica occitana*, "Messatges" (Montpelhièr: Institut d'Estudis Occitans, 1981).

8. Emmanuel Le Roy Ladurie, *Montaillou, village occitan, de 1294 à 1324* (Paris: Gallimard, 1975).

9. Denis Saurat, *Encaminament catar* (Tolosa: Institut d'Estudis Occitans, 1955); *Encaminament II: Lo Caçaire* (Tolosa: Institut d'Estudis Occitans, 1960).

10. Charles Camproux, *Histoire de la littérature occitane* (Paris: Payot, 1971), 243-45.

11. Bernard Manciet, *L'Enterrament a Sabres* (Garein: Editions Ultreïa, 1989).

12. Robert Lafont, *La Festa*, "Obradors" (Mussidan: Fédérop, 1983).

From *The Song of Roland* to the Songs of Arnaut Daniel: Chapbooks and Transcreations in Modern Brazilian Poetry

Roy Rosenstein

It is well known that Brazil, its people, and its literature have offered a receptive haven and on occasion a rich inspiration to the French tradition, from early published works by André Thévet (1575), Jean de Léry (1578), and Michel de Montaigne (1580) in the Renaissance to more recent personal visits by Paul Claudel and Darius Milhaud (1917-19), Blaise Cendrars (1924), Georges Bernanos (1940-45), and Albert Camus (1949) in our own times.[1] Rarely studied is Brazil's response to the Provençal writer Mistral, whose *Mireio* was translated into Portuguese, published in Rio de Janeiro and Paris in 1910, and commented upon in succeeding decades.[2] Still less often noted by medievalists and comparatists is the enduring presence of medieval literature, whether from the North or the South of France, in oral and written modern Brazilian poetry.[3] Yet in the twentieth century and on several registers, from the spontaneous to the contrived, from the popular to the academic, and from the epic to the lyric, from backlands retellings of the death of Roland and the Peers of France to carefully crafted, urbane versions of Arnaut Daniel's formal, hermetic lyricism, medieval strands are woven into the tapestry of both Brazilian folk literature and *belles lettres*. Roland and Arnaut: these are the hero and the poet on whom this essay will focus through a study of their latest incarnations in contemporary Brazil.

Studies in Medievalism VIII, 1996

Popular Brazilian literature affirms that Roland himself is alive and well, not just a distant memory. Two French travelers visiting Brazil independently in 1819, Pohl and St. Hilaire, and others since have noted in passing that the martyrdom of Roland was regularly renewed, whether as a tale recounted or as a performance reenacted *en plein air* in the Brazilian heartland.[4] In the early 1840s the American missionary Daniel P. Kidder traveled to the Northeastern village of Maceió and found a shop assistant at his counter reading a life of Carlos Magno.[5] This popularity of Carolingian themes is traceable to the many reprintings of the Portuguese prose version of the history of the Emperor Charlemagne and the Twelve Peers of France. In 1881 Teófilo Braga called it the most read book in Portugal ("o mais lido livro em Portugal"), and the same statement would still obtain through the early years of our century in Brazil.[6] The *História do Imperador Carlos Magno e dos Doze Pares de França* was regularly republished in São Paulo and Rio, a bit like a latter-day *Amadís* (which was itself Portuguese in origin). After the Bible, the *História* may be said to be the book which achieved the greatest penetration in the *sertões* or hinterlands of Brazil.[7] The original Portuguese editions of the *História* had been published in Lisbon in 1723, 1728, and 1789; it became available in various Brazilian imprints beginning with one in Bahia in 1820.[8] Its ultimate source, the *Conquête du grand roy Charlemaigne des Espaignes*, like the 1525 Spanish translation of the *Conquête*, has not enjoyed a comparable diffusion in subsequent centuries: in France, Roland and company play a lesser role, if any, in popular literature in modern times.[9] To be sure, in France there were *Bibliothèque bleue*, *imagerie d'Epinal*, and such *livres de colportage* versions of Carolingian figures, especially *Les Quatre fils Aymon*.[10] But only in Brazil were these narratives read aloud and commented upon as (or as if) contemporary. One Frenchman—perhaps Dean Raymond Cantel himself—visiting a remote northeastern village in Brazil was asked by an old man for news of Roland.[11] As Cascudo summarizes in the *Dicionário do folclore brasileiro*, "From the second half of the eighteenth century dates Roland's resounding career across the Brazilian collective memory. And it continues" ("Da segunda metade do séc. XVIII data a galopada sonora de Roldão pelas memorias brasileiras. E continua").[12]

Brazilian popular poets were expected to know the story of the Twelve Peers of France. It would have constituted "unforgivable ignorance" (*ignorância indesculpável*), says folklorist Cascudo, not to know it.[13] Had there been catalogs of the Brazilian hit parade like the ones that poets like Guerau de Cabrera or Guiraut de Calanson provided in their medieval *Ensenhamens*, Roland would have appeared at the top of the repertory expected even of such backwoods Brazilian bards. In the mid-twelfth century Guerau in "Cabra juglar" claimed that the great epic cycle of Charlemagne stories ("gran jesta de Carlon") was most important for a jongleur to know by heart, after the latest lyrics of Jaufre Rudel, Marcabru, and Ebles de Ventadorn but ahead of the classic *matière de Bretagne* or Arthurian legends. Thus Guerau mocks the *jongleur* Cabra: "Of Roland you know as little as of something that never existed": "E de Rollan,/ sabs aitretan/ coma d'aiso que anc non fon."[14] Clearly, for medieval European and modern Brazilian bards, Roland *did* exist. As in twelfth- and thirteenth-century southern Europe, so in nineteenth- and twentieth-century northeastern Brazil, the story of Roland was a must—perhaps even *le must*, as the French say today.

That the popularity of Roland survives down to quite recently is shown in reformulations by several modern Brazilian poets. Their retellings continue to find an unflagging readership among the people despite virtually total rejection on the part of the scholar. Thus Candace Slater hardly mentions pre-modern subjects in her excellent *Stories on a String*, entirely devoted to this popular form now called *literatura de cordel*.[15] While teaching in Brazil in 1992 I came across, among countless tales on post-medieval themes, one such update on Roland's demise, first in a dusty corner of the covered market at Teresina (Piauí) and later again at a lively kiosk in the open-air marketplace in Recife (Pernambuco). That text, reprinted in Juazeiro do Norte (Ceará) in 1978 under the title *A Morte dos 12 Pares de França* and listing as its author Marcos Sampaio, was still abundantly available at the two stands where I found such *folhetos*, or popular literature, essentially pamphlets and technically chapbooks.[16] A *folheto* is a gathering or quire, in the term of the English booktrade, designating the (in this case) eight-page unit (small quarto, that is to say, *quadras*) made by the printing of a single double-folded sheet, hence *folheto*, the standard name for the form. These little booklets, composed of groups of one or two, less often three or four quires, and rarely more (making eight, sixteen, twenty-four, or thirty-two pages respectively, up to fifty-six), are provided with a cheap cover, sometimes on colored paper and often with a naive wood-block engraving—much like the woodblock engravings that have adorned popular texts from the fifteenth-century incunabulum to the nineteenth-century Bibliothèque de Troyes volume. Like incunabula too, they sometimes feature a colophon that provides more publication data than the cover, which doubles as title page; on the other hand, while incunabula are foliated by quires, these *folhetos* are paginated or sometimes unpaginated, more like popular French literature of the last century.

A Brazilian folheto.

Marcos Sampaio is only one, but apparently the latest, of modern poets in the Northeast to have renewed the story of Roldão, as Roland is called in Brazilian versions.[17] Others include *A batalha de Oliveiros com Ferrabraz* by Leandro Gomes de Barros, and *O cavaleiro Roldão* by Antônio Eugênio da Silva.[18] The most recent edition of Sampaio's version I have seen is the one already mentioned, dated 1978; the Raymond Cantel collection lists a 1975 printing under the number M 193; the Casa de Rui Barbosa Foundation in Rio de Janeiro gives a 1941 printing in its catalog as number 18.[19] The same publishing house, José Bernardo da Silva (later succeeded by his daughters), had also given us Roland stories ascribed to other authors than Marcos Sampaio. These versions include those attributed to the publisher himself and to the popular and prolific Leandro Gomes de Barros, who died in 1918.[20] We know that around 1920 Barros's widow sold the rights of his work to yet another key *cordel* poet, João Martins de Ataíde (1880-1959), some of whose Rolandian material was later recycled, again by the same publisher, this time as his own work. As for our author (and one soon grasps with what caution the term should be applied), Sampaio himself signs the last stanza of his version in medieval fashion with an acrostic of his pseudonym, said to conceal one Moisés Matias de Moura.[21] As often happens with popular literature, it has so far been possible to unearth only scant data about and no other works by this latter-day

Turoldus, except to note again that his song of Roland is published under the same imprint as all the others mentioned above. Consequently, in examining his version of the story we must bear in mind that it is only one of many traditional reworkings and reprintings of a story outside copyright constraints and authorship issues. It might seem tempting to compare the authorship of this handful of poets, among whom Sampaio is only the most recent, to the authority of *La Chanson de Roland*, on which a long debate once raged over individual versus collective genesis, a discussion which we need not reopen today.

Sampaio's retelling is emphatically not the transcription of a performance by an illiterate poet before an illiterate audience, as might have been the case in 1819. It is a text written to be sold and read, addressed from its first lines to the Gentle Readers ("Amigos caros leitores") who are asked to listen to the story (*historia*) and meditate on its meaning. As for the audience of the *Chanson de Roland*, the story is presumably a familiar one: Roldão's *proezas* or prowess and Galalão's *traição* or treachery. Oliveiros and Carlo Magno (pronounced with an unwritten epenthetic vowel between *g* and *n*) make only cameo appearances here: protagonist Roldão and antagonist Galalão dominate the stage. The opening scene is set somewhere near Saragosa, as in the Oxford *Roland*. Indeed, from the outset Sampaio's version resembles nothing so much as Turoldus's, announcing Carlo Magno's intentions to send an embassy to Marcirio inviting him to forsake idolatry and embrace Jesus. The mission is entrusted to Galalão, but here the narrative (totaling only thirty-two pages, each of four and a half stanzas of six lines each, called *sextilhas*) becomes more schematic. No mention of the long war, of rivalry in the Christian camp, nor even of the traitor's motivations beyond avarice: leveling and immediacy characterize this abbreviated version. Instead, like a twelfth-century romance-writer such as Beroul in the earliest *Tristan*, for example, Sampaio abandons motivations in favor of denunciations and curses leveled at the evil baron Galalão who, though rich and of aristocratic blood, has sold himself and besmirched his honor. Like a medieval satirist, Sampaio animatedly compares Galalão's greed to that of Judas and Adam. As in other, earlier reductions of the feudal *Song of Roland*, its social dimensions are downplayed to highlight an individual, emotional choice motivated by avarice (as in the thirteenth-century *De Tradicione Guenonis*) set against (as here in our text, also variously subtitled or titled *Traição de Galalão*) a broad Christian backdrop.[22]

At Roncesvalhes, Roldão and Oliveiros will do battle against two armies of Turks. After defeating the first, Roldão now willingly blows his horn ("Roldão tocou a corneta") when he sees the second army loom large

228　　　　　　　　　Studies in Medievalism

on the horizon, then leads the attack with his own men "like rabid wolves"; English chapbooks would have said "as an egyr lyon."[23] Quite soon (by the next page, 9) Roldão alone is left alive with two of his fellows, the Duke Trietre and his own brother, Valdivinos: these two additional characters constitute the nominal innovations of intermediate Hispanic versions. A captured Turk points out Marcirio, who had bought Galalão, and Roldão with a vigorous *coupe épique* slashes his enemy down to the waist. Roldão ultimately collapses under a pine tree with no fewer than four fatal wounds, while Marcirio, showing astonishing recuperative powers, takes to the hills in anticipation of Carlo Magno's arrival.

Roldão's farewell to the world is addressed to his faithful sword Duridana: he eulogizes their shared exploits before trying in vain to smash it to pieces. After reopening his wounds by tooting his horn again, Roldão laments next his companion Trietre in a richly rhetorical complaint. Finally the hero prays to Jesus in Portuguese and Latin before succumbing. The author reports that at this point Archbishop Turpim, absent from the battle in this version, has a vision of the paladin's passion which he describes to Carlo Magno. The faithful Valdivinos returns with water to tend Roldão's wounds, only to find him dead: the elaborate *planctus* expected here will be pronounced instead by Carlo Magno, who arrives soon after. His lament shows traces of the intimacy between uncle and nephew and suggests an echo of medieval Hispano-Arabic and Galician-Portuguese women's songs of separation more expected from the mouth of *la belle Aude* than spoken by the great emperor Charlemagne: "Oh! meu amado Roldão . . . ! Ah! triste assim o que farei? oh! meu amigo Roldão . . !" (24-25).

After this long lament, the poet begs his readers to step back a moment from so moving a scene. Oliveiros's body is found and Carlo Magno vows revenge: he slaughters seven thousand Turks, and the soulless (*desalmado*, 29) Galalão, unrepentant, is quartered. Or rather, each of the four horses is said to drag off a *half* of his body. The Brazilian poet concludes with an *excusatio propter infirmitatem*, modestly asking his audience's indulgence for an artless tale and explaining that his verse stems only from the simplest inspiration.

Rather than dwell on any weaknesses of this avowedly reductive but nevertheless (at least minimally?) effectively narrated version, it may be useful to look at one representative detail. Mathematical improbability is a well known factor in such epic and mock epic texts, from Homer to the *Pèlerinage de Charlemagne* to Rabelais: here Roldão confronts ninety thousand enemy warriors (7). But Roldão also suffers from an otherwise unrecorded case of multiple fatal wounds disorder, lurching about with no

Brazilian Transcreations

fewer than four terminal wounds (*com quatro feridas mortais*, 9), perhaps intended to parallel the quartering of Galalão into four halves. The suspension of disbelief required here stretches the reader's tolerance to the limit. Is this a late addition, as it were, an exercise in epic *demesure* and in poetic overkill on the part of a poet who tries in vain to better by mathematical oneupmanship the legend he inherited? Perhaps. But by way of comparison it is useful to note how those multiple fatal blows can also be presented in a lyric mode by an anonymous popular poet, this time from Portugal, when in a ballad he tabulates strikingly the wounds of a fallen hero at Roncesvalhes:

> *Três feridas tinha no corpo, todas três eram mortal:*
> *por uma lh'entrava o sol, pela outra o luar.*
> *Pela mais pequena de todas, um gavião a voar,*
> *com as asas mui abertas, sem nas ensanguentar.*[24]

> Three wounds had he on his body, all three were fatal:
> through one passed the sunshine, by the other the moonlight,
> by the smallest of all, a sparrow-hawk flying
> with its wings wide open, without bloodying them.

The 1992 movie *Death Becomes Her* shows how a similarly gaping hole from a shotgun blast to Goldie Hawn's midriff provokes not horror but humor, thanks to the special effects which are the principal strength of this film. So too, this passage from the Portuguese ballad distances itself from the epic exploits of the Brazilian *folheto* version. The same chronic fatal wound syndrome, not invariably terminal in the case of a Hollywood character, can thus range, as in these three modern examples, from the ethereal Portuguese to the pedestrian Brazilian to the earthy Hollywoodian: that is, from the brilliant to the banausic to the bathetic, from the lyric to the epic to the celluloid. Indeed, the model for this scene of horrific wounds may just conceivably be traced ultimately to the *matière de Bretagne* or legends of Arthur, which France perhaps consciously sought to rival in developing its cycle of Carolingian material. According to the thirteenth-century *La Mort le roi Artu*, when Arthur ran his son Mordred through with his lance "l'estoire dit que aprés l'estordre del glaive passa parmi la plaie uns rais de soleil si apertement que Girflet le vit."[25] This double murder itself ratchets up the archetypal horror of the *Hildebrandslied* model of family reunion, in which the father will slay the son whom he does not know, by presenting now a father and son who deliberately deal each other ghastly death wounds. Mordred's peculiar perforation was

230   Studies in Medievalism

recalled by another poet when Dante the pilgrim hears of "him whose breast and shadow were pierced with a single blow from Arthur's hand" (*Inf.* 32. 61-62).[26] The Portuguese ballad of Roncesvalhes effectively expands on the Arthurian battle scene by tripling the puncture wound to accommodate not only a sunbeam but a moonbeam and even a low-flying sparrow hawk.

Our modern Brazilian version does not claim nor is it intended to rival the twelfth-century Oxford text or any of the intermediate retellings, such as the French romance or the Portuguese ballad. Sampaio's version evidently functions well enough independently, and continues to sell, in part because its audience is ready and suited for the current rewriting which by outdoing its predecessors might fulfill today's audience's anticipation—an audience perhaps by now raised on Hollywooden, Schwarzenegresco immortality. Are such movie heroes unkillable? Early cinemagoing audiences were shocked to see dead figures from the previous week's episodes resurrect intact in new roles and new movies; today no one is troubled that, unlike Tchen at the epicenter of Malraux's *La condition humaine*, a hero is virtually immortal, from Achilles to Roland to the Earp Brothers to Roldão.

That this reprint of Sampaio's *A Morte* should coincide with Gerard J. Brault's anniversary edition of *Roland* published by Penn State in 1978 seems to be no coincidence.[27] The periodic replaying of Roland's death between the event in the Pyrenees in 778 and its dodecacentennial commemoration at Roncevaux, University Park, and Juazeiro do Norte in 1978 is a long glorification of a heroic defeat, but not necessarily an ongoing degradation of the earliest and best version, the Oxford *Roland*. Still less would one maintain that vibrant medieval epic themes survive only in watered-down modern performance (or in *petit genre* or *grand écran* special effects). Epics are not at all composite versions of lyric fragments, as Gaston Paris had thought: the two genres can provide divergent perspectives on similar figures and themes. The epic version stresses the narrative dimension, the collective *événementiel*, and a birdseye overview of Roncevaux and of man against man in society, while the solitary soldier of the ballad provides instead the hawkeye perspective and private insight of the individual bard (and in this case, bird). As ever, in conventional poetry as elsewhere, there is room for the poet's (re)vision, original and inspired (as in the Portuguese ballad) or inherited and mechanical (as in the Brazilian chapbook).[28]

For a contrastive example we turn from heroics to poetics, in order to consider how medieval techniques may yet be respected, assimilated, perhaps surpassed by a contemporary poet. Popular poets in Brazil today

Brazilian Transcreations

231

are still called *cantadores* or *trovadores*, which is to say "singers" or "troubadours." The latter-day Brazilian troubadour is less likely to sing the legendary exploits of a Roland or a Perceval than tales of figures and events drawn from more recent international and local history. These have included the execution of American criminal Caryl Chessman, covered in ballads bearing comparison to Joan Baez's "Ballad of Sacco and Vanzetti," or the shooting of Lampião, the self-styled Bandit King whose glorious death with his wife, Maria Bonita, melds the martyrdom of a Roland and the massacre of a Bonnie and Clyde.[29] But today's poet may also on occasion admit and adopt the style of his distant medieval predecessors.

An appreciation for the twelfth-century Provençal troubadour Arnaut Daniel in modern Brazilian poetics shows how it is not just the building blocks or *Stoff* of medieval poetry but its techniques at their most difficult that may be admired and reintegrated in the twentieth century. Augusto de Campos (b. 1931) has championed Arnaut, rendering all of his eighteen lyrics of certain attribution into modern Portuguese poetic translations.[30] This is the *only* language, Romance or other, to offer the complete Arnaldian *oeuvre* in a poetic translation. There are three fundamental questions to be raised in reviewing Campos's Portuguese translations of Arnaut: why Portuguese, why Arnaut, and why and how Campos?

First, why Portuguese? Some years ago in an article on "Translating the Trobadors" I proposed a schematic typology of translations as exemplified through selected versions of the Old Occitan troubadours in English, French, and (modern) Occitan. In passing, the important translations into other Romance languages were also noted, including those, particularly interesting from a linguistic point of view, in Catalan and Romanian.[31] Omitted from that study were both the mechanical Spanish prose translations by the scholar Martín de Riquer and the inspired rhymed Portuguese versions by Campos, these last unmentioned also by Marcelle d'Herde-Heiliger in her virtually complete repertory of translations.[32]

Portuguese is in many respects unique among the Romance languages.[33] Aside from the functional prose translations by Segismundo Spina for his anthologies of medieval lyric and the poetic renderings by Campos, the troubadours are not at all available in Portuguese.[34] Yet Galician-Portuguese since the Middle Ages has been deemed better suited to lyric themes than to heroic narrative, reflecting a division in the Iberian peninsula similar to that in medieval Gaul and in classical Greece: *Francigeni ad bella, Provinciales ad amorem*. And even today, Portuguese is particularly well adapted not only to translation of sentiment but also to flexibility in structure. If it is often maintained that Provençal is syntactically the most supple of the Romance languages, Portuguese too shows certain striking archaisms in this respect. More than Old Provençal, Old Spanish readily tolerated the insertion of personal pronouns between verb forms in the future and conditional.[35] One remembers how the separation anxiety in the Cid's leavetaking from his wife Doña Ximena is reflected pronominally. "Ya lo veedes que partir *nos* hemos en vida. Yo irei e vos fincaredes remanida": *c'est la séparation dans la séparation.* Tmesis, lost to modern Spanish, remains an option in Portuguese alone among modern Romance languages: e. g., *fá-lo-ei* "I shall do it," *dir-te-ía* "I was going to tell you." The example is not arbitrary. Tmesis is often said to be the defining trait in e. e. cummings's poetry: his own favorite example may be his coinage *manunkind.* And it is precisely e. e. cummings who has been more successfully translated into Portuguese, by Augusto de Campos again, no less, than he has into French, for example, despite valiant attempts by sensitive fellow poets like the late D. Jon Grossman.[36] The Portuguese language, in the hands of Campos, is a particularly appropriate and adaptable medium for the rendering of foreign poetic models from twelfth-century Provence to twentieth-century America.

But why Arnaut? Augusto's translations from the Provençal do not constitute a comprehensive anthology of troubadour lyric but an entirely personal songbook reflecting the individual, eclectic, idiosyncratic readings and ambitions of a concretist poet. In addition to Arnaut, Campos has translated selected poems of troubadours Raimbaut d'Aurenga (also in *Mais Provençais*), the Count of Poiters, Marcabru, Bertran de Born, Bernart de Ventadorn, and Peire Cardenal (all in "Presença de Provença" included in his *Verso reverso controverso*). Missing from this honor roll, refreshingly perhaps for some, are the formally less innovative Jaufre Rudel and Guiraut de Bornelh, both of whom have been studied extensively in recent years, but not by Campos, for concrete and compelling reasons. As a concretist since the 1950s, Campos has always been keenly interested in formal constraints and creative wordplay, as is seen elsewhere in his admiration for cummings and his determination to render only what are the most difficult, and probably the least translatable, of cummings's poems. Similarly no doubt, according to Augusto's troubadour agenda, only the *trobar ric* of Arnaut will be essential reading for the poet of today. And only Arnaut is translated by Campos *in toto.*

If we care to examine closely one of the eighteen lyrics traditionally attributed to Arnaut, it is in some ways attractive to look at the technical *tour de force* that is Poem 1, in all editions except that of Wilhelm, who reverses the order of 1 and 18 to place "Lo ferm voler" at the beginning rather than at the other end of Arnaut's production.[37] It is precisely the nether end that is the subject of Arnaut's first poem, "Pois Raimons."

Brazilian Transcreations

This indecorous but formally elegant *sirventes* is Arnaut's response to the affair that confronted Lady Ayma, Bernard of Cornilh, and two other poets. As his surname evidently invited, Bernard weighed carefully the lady's playful but disconcerting demand that he blow her horn (*cornar lo corn*) as proof of his love. His refusal provoked a cycle of comments, including Arnaut's poem in support of Bernard's decision along with others which censured it. Wilhelm understandably considers this song to be of "questionable" attribution and taste, relegating it to the end of his edition. It is revealing to see how both Arnaut's "scurrilous" song (Wilhelm, xxix) and Campos's scrupulous translation (54-57) conform to Arnaldian poetic models, even in what is not the poet's most important lyric. Whatever the subject and tone, both Arnaut and Augusto provide intricately worked and richly rhymed lyrics. Indeed, the image of polishing one's work and the pearls that are to be attained constitute an Arnaldian trademark apparent even in this facetiously explicit, sexually charged poem, both in the first-stanza Occitan original (*grecs*, "pearls") and in its Portuguese translation (*bem se o esfregue*, "scrub it well"; cf. Arnaut's *lim* "I file" in 2:12; the erotic meaning of French *limer* dates only from Sade, according to Philippe Sollers).[38]

> *Pois Raimons e.n Trucs Malecs*
> *chapten n'Ayman e sos decs,*
> *enans serai vieills e canecs*
> *ans que m'acort en aitals precs*
> *don puosca venir tant grans pecs;*
> *c'al cornar l'agra mestier becs*
> *ab que.il traisses del corn los grecs;*
> *e pois pogra ben issir secs*
> *quel fums es fortz qu'ieis dinz dels plecs.*

> Since Raimon and Lord Truc Malec
> defend Lady Ayma and her orders,
> sooner would I be old and grey
> before I would agree to such requests
> from which might come such great shame;
> for in order to blow, beaks are needed
> with which to withdraw pearls from the horn;
> and then you might come out blind
> for the smoke is strong from within those folds.

234   Studies in Medievalism

Campos does not compose literal prose versions, unlike virtually all other editors and translators of the troubadours. His translations are what he calls transcreations (*transcriações*, 26), in which he hopes to have captured some of the form and spirit of a matchless original. This notion of transcreation (or creation through transmission) and the corresponding term exist also in English since Coleridge and have been employed most recently in discussing the wide diffusion of Visṇu Śarma's *Pańćatantra*.[39] Campos's sense of the translator's task and art coincides admirably with Pound's influential principle of creative translation. As accurately codified recently by Ronnie Apter, the poet-translator in order to "make it new" must accept intentional sacrifice to be able to achieve criticism by exaggeration and analogy.[40]

Pound may not have addressed himself to the complete works of Arnaut, attempting most (sixteen) but apparently not all (eighteen) poems then attributed to him.[41] "Pois Raimons" was first Englished by George Wolf only in 1972, then by James Wilhelm in his edition of 1981.[42] There are also prose versions in other languages, such as Nelli's in French and more recently Eusebi's in Italian.[43] Arnaut's Portuguese translator plunges into the difficult and forbidding task at hand with his customary concentration and brilliance—*Campos mentis*, as it were. This is certainly the right mindset with which to approach Arnaut's craft: however frivolous the subject of the lyric, his technique in it will invariably reveal the master artisan, Dante's *miglior fabbro*. Campos's version is a careful *poetic* translation, by a poet following closely in Arnaut's and Pound's footsteps and metrics.

How well has Campos succeeded in this task never undertaken by Pound or any other admirer of Arnaut? The *locus classicus* for the *topos* of troubadour untranslatability is old Emil Levy puzzling "Effery night when I go to bett" over *noigandres* in Arnaut, in Pound, *Cantos*, XX, as Campos well knows.[44] Martin de Riquer's scholarly editions and translations remain the indispensable tools for anyone who, like Campos, aspires to decipher the troubadours in the original, but they do not prepare the poet for the task at hand. A simple prose translation is already a perilous venture fraught with difficulties, even for the trained medievalist.[45] In this case, the model of Pound, the scholarship of Riquer, and the cautions of Levy can direct the inspiration and guarantee the fidelity of a poet-translator like Campos when he daringly undertakes for the first and to date only time to make the *dificilior* Arnaut Daniel speak yet another language. Augusto learns from the *miglior fabbro* and from the cautious scholar. Hovering over the exercise, from the choice of poet to the translation technique adopted, is old EP.

Brazilian Transcreations

235

All the poems in the Cornilh affair are composed according to the same metrical schema. Arnaut's has by far the most difficult rhymes: *ecs, utz, ais, ort, ilh.*[46] Campos's version follows the same pattern with no less difficult Portuguese rhymes: *eque, udo, ais, orte, ilho.* In general, the Provençal rhymes themselves have been preserved (*ais*) or translated (*utz/udo, ort/orte, ilh/ilho*). And in the third and again in the penultimate line of the first stanza, Campos has again outdone his original. With internal echo rhymes (*fique . . . seque; é que despregue*) Campos provides a different variety of mathematical oneupmanship, now in verbal virtuosity, from the kind seen in Sampaio's text:

> *Que Raimons ou Truc Malec*
> *de dona Aima se encarregue,*
> *mas antes fique eu velho e seque*
> *do que a tal prática me entregue,*
> *pois pra cornar preciso é que*
> *se tenha bico e bem se o esfregue*
> *pra que o corno náo descarregue,*
> *mas o mais certo é que despregue*
> *fumo tão forte que me cegue.*

> Let Raimon or Truki Maleki
> take charge of Lady Aima:
> sooner would I be old and dry
> before I would adopt such a practice,
> since to blow a horn it is necessary
> that one have a beak and scrub it well
> so that the horn not discharge.
> But most sure is that it sends off
> smoke so strong it will blind me.

Roldão tocou a corneta mas Arnaut Daniel não corna corno. Roland blew his horn, but Arnaut Daniel won't blow hers. Arnaut here echoes Roland's initial reluctance to blow the horn, though he too under certain conditions will reconsider his decision. Campos has also respected his model's choices: his poetic translation and artistic practice closely reflect at once Arnaut's lyric and Pound's technique. In sum, this is a translation perhaps worthy of Pound, but in Portuguese. It is accompanied by the appropriate Arnaldian passages from Dante and Pound which Campos has also translated as a supplement to his edition (though with some pardonable if puzzling changes: Arnaut's "Sovenha vos a temps de ma dolor" directed to Dante the pilgrim (*Purg.* 27.147) should surely be rendered as "relembrai a tempo a minha dor," not *para sempre*). Like many fellow poets and scholars, like James Wilhelm and George Wolf, Augusto discovered Arnaut through Ezra. And it is as a follower of EP that he promotes Arnaut as model for poetry and Pound as master of translation. It might be said that, like his teachers for Provençal and English poetry, Campos has played a parallel role in Brazilian lyricism.

Arnaut, the poet's poet, is privileged to speak not Tuscan but his own Provençal in *The Divine Comedy*. No other poet, Occitan or epigone, is granted the honor of speaking any vernacular but Italian in the *Commedia*. At eight centuries' distance, Arnaut now triumphs in Portuguese where he has never succeeded in mastering Tuscan: compare the disappointingly prosaic glosses in the Italian editions of Arnaut by Canello, Toja, Perugi, and Eusebi, or in the latest partial study by D'Agostino, or in the scatological anthology by Sansone (where it appears under the rubric "Variazioni posteriori").[47] As the Brazilian poet-publisher Cleber Teixeira writes of Augusto's translations,

> *Sobre o chão movediço desta*
> *minha Provença reinventada,*
> *onde Arnaut Daniel*
> *fala o português*
> *claro e belo*
> *de Augusto de Campos . . . .*[48]

> Upon the transplanted soil of this
> my reinvented Provence,
> where Arnaut Daniel
> speaks the clear and beautiful
> Portuguese
> of Augusto de Campos . . . .

As Segismundo Spina of the University of São Paulo wrote in 1956 in the historical introduction to the first edition and again in 1972 in the second edition of his anthology of medieval lyric, "A poesia lírica dos trovadores provençais não morria."[49] That is to say simply that the poetry of the troubadours was not dying (*ne mourait pas*), after the Albigensian Crusade in the thirteenth century, when Provençal lyric had taken root in neighboring countries. But this formulation would seem to admit the possibility that troubadour poetry might yet be extinguished. In Portuguese, the imperfect often takes on the meaning of the moribund condi-

Brazilian Transcreations 237

tional form, but the phrase as formulated in the imperfect indicative still leaves room for the poetry of the troubadours to disappear from the face of this earth at a later date. Rewriting in 1991, thirty-five years later, for the third edition of his anthology, Spina made a small but essential change. He corrected the earlier imperfect with the conditional, still not obsolete: "A poesia lírica dos trovadores não morreria," that is, "that troubadour lyric would not die"—presumably neither in the thirteenth century nor ever (ne mourrait pas). Between editions Spina's prophecy had been fulfilled with the publication of Campos's Mais provençais in 1980 and again in expanded form in 1987.

Like Roland, forever dying at Roncevaux but immortal in the popular imagination, so Provencal lyric has survived in Luso-Brazilian literature: not only in chronologically and geographically contiguous medieval Galician-Portuguese lyricism but also centuries later and half way around the world in far-flung modern Brazilian Portuguese poetic translation by Augusto de Campos, original poetry by Cleber Teixeira, and critical scholarship by Segismundo Spina.

In this way I hope to have demonstrated the enduring viability and visibility in Brazil of medieval narrative and technique from Northern and Southern France. Medieval literature remains present in the thematics of popular Brazilian poetry as it is in the poetics of learned Brazilian verse. In modern Brazil, Roland still blows his horn, and the voice of Arnaut is heard in the land, albeit no longer in their respective parlar materno.[50]

NOTES

1. André Thevet, Le Brésil et les Brésiliens, in Suzanne Lussagnet, Les Français en Amérique pendant la deuxième moitié du XVIe siècle (Paris: PUF, 1953); Jean de Léry, A History of a Voyage to the Land of Brazil, trans. Janet Whatley (Berkeley: University of California Press, 1990); Michel de Montaigne, "Of Cannibals," Complete Works of Montaigne, trans. Donald M. Frame (Stanford: Stanford University Press, 1958), 150-59. See Gilbert Chinard, L'exotisme américain dans la littérature française au XVIe siècle (Paris: Hachette, 1911); Pierre Hourcade, Testemunhos literários franceses sôbre o Brasil contemporâneo (Coimbra Editora, 1942); Alvaro Manuel Machado and Daniel-Henri Pageaux, Literatura portuguesa, literatura comparada, teoria da literatura (Lisboa: Edições 70, 1982); Francis Assaf, "The Specularity of Alterity: The Native Brazilians in André Thevet's Les Singularités de la France Antarctique," Romanische Forschungen 103 (1991): 244-52; Frank Lestringant, André Thevet, cosmographe des derniers Valois (Geneva: Droz, 1991), especially 94-95.

2. Gomes Júnior, trans., Mireio, poema provençal de Frederico Mistral: Tradução portuguesa, com texto provençal (Rio de Janeiro and Paris: Gomes Júnior,

livreiro editor, 1910), analyzed in a chapter of Luís da Câmara Cascudo, *Mouros, franceses e judeus* (São Paulo: Perspectiva, 1984), 49-64.

3.   See Zila Mamede, *Luís da Câmara Cascudo: 50 anos de vida intelectual, 1918-1968* (Natal: Fundação José Augusto, 1970); Sebastião Nunes Batista, "Carlos Magno na poesia popular nordestina," *Revista brasileira de folclore* 30 (1971): 143-70; Jean-Marie d'Heur, "Roland au Brésil: Note additionnelle," *Marche romane* 13 (1963): 85-95; Jerusa Pires Ferreira, *Cavalaria em cordel: O passo das águas mortas* (São Paulo: HUCITEC, 1979); Silvano Peloso, *Medioevo nel sertão: Tradizione medievale europea e archetipi della letteratura populare nel Nordeste del Brasile* (Naples: Liguori, 1984), 62-66; Peter Burke, "Chivalry in the New World," in Sidney Anglo, ed., *Chivalry in the Renaissance* (Woodbridge, Suffolk: Boydell, 1990), 257-58.

4.   Cascudo, *Mouros*, 45-46.

5.   Daniel P. Kidder, *Sketches of Residence and Travels in Brazil* (Philadelphia, 1845), 2:95-96; cf. Burke, 257.

6.   Cascudo, *Mouros*, 46.

7.   Batista, "Carlos Magno," 143.

8.   Cascudo, *Mouros*, 44.

9.   On literary versions, see Harry Redman, Jr., *The Roland Legend in Nineteenth-Century French Literature* (Lexington: University of Kentucky Press, 1991).

10.   Hans-Erich Keller, ed., *Jehan Bagnyon: L'Histoire de Charlemagne, parfois dite Roman de Fierabras* (Geneva: Droz, 1992), xxx-xxxi; Charles Nisard, *Histoire des livres populaires* (Paris, 1864; rpt. New York: Burt Franklin, n.d.), 2:396; *Les quatres fils d'Aymon* (Paris, 1838).

11.   Pierre Jonin, ed. and trans., *La Chanson de Roland* (Paris: Gallimard, 1979). Cf. Raymond Cantel, "La persistencia de los temas medievales de Europa en la literatura popular del Nordeste brasilero," in Carlos H. Magis, *Actas del tercer Congreso Internacional de Hispanistas* (Mexico City: Colegio de México, 1970), 175-85.

12.   Luís da Câmara Cascudo, "Roldão," *Dicionário do folclore brasileiro* (Brasília: Instituto nacional do livro, 1972), 770.

13.   Cascudo, "Mouros," 46.

14.   François Pirot, *Recherches sur les connaissances littéraires des troubadours occitans et catalans des XIIe et XIIe siècles. Memorias de la Real Academia de Buenas Letras de Barcelona* 14 (1972), 548 *et passim*.

15.   Candace Slater, *Stories on a String: The Brazilian Literatura de Cordel* (Berkeley: University of California Press, 1982).

16.   Marcos Sampaio, *A Morte dos 12 Pares de França* (Juazeiro do Norte: Filhas de José Bernardo de Silva, 1978).

17.   Batista, "Carlos Magno," 143-44; Cascudo, "Mouros," 45.

18.   Marlyse Meyer, *Autores de Cordel* (São Paulo: Abril, 1990), 72-75; *Literatura popular em verso: antologia/seleção* (São Paulo: USP, 1986), 1:467, 2:314-32.

19.   *Literatura de cordel: Collection Doyen Raymond Cantel* (Rennes: Université de Haute Bretagne, 1991), 128, 139; Peloso, 197.

20.   *Literatura popular*, 1:413, 417 (note 63), 2:577, and Sebastião Nunes Batista, *Bibliografia prévia de Leandro Gomes de Barros* (Rio de Janeiro: Biblioteca Nacional, 1971).

21.   Atila Augusto F. de Almeida and José Alves Sobrinho, *Dicionário bio-bibliográfico de repentistas e poetas de bancada* (João Pessoa: Universitária, 1978), 243, 187.

22.   Wiliam D. Paden and Patricia Harris Stäblein, ed. and trans., "'De Tradicione Guenonis': An Edition with Translation," *Traditio* 44 (1988): 201-51 (220).

23.   E. g., *Guy, Earl of Warwick*; see John Ashton, *Chapbooks of the Eighteenth Century* (London: Chatto, 1882), 139.

24.   Mário Cesariny, *Horta de literatura de cordel* (Lisboa: Assirio e Alvim, 1983), 44; J. Leite de Vasconcelos, ed., *Romanceiro português* (Coimbra: Universidade, 1958), 36-42.

25.   Jean Frappier, ed., *La Mort le roi Artu* (Geneva: Droz, 1964), 245.

26.   All quotations from Dante are from the edition by Charles S. Singleton, 3 vols. (Princeton: Princeton University Press, 1977).

27.   Gerard J. Brault, *La Chanson de Roland: Oxford Text and English Translation* (University Park: Pennsylvania State University Press, 1978).

28.   For useful remarks on the omnipresent theme of death in a popular literary tradition uninterrupted since the late medieval Dance of Death and transmitted via Holbein's engravings to contemporary Day of the Dead celebrations in Mexico, see Julian Rothenstein, *J. G. Posada: Messenger of Mortality* (London: Redstone, 1989); Elizabeth Carmichael and Chloë Sayer, *The Skeleton at the Feast: The Day of the Dead in Mexico* (London: British Museum, 1991); F. A. de Icaza, *La Danza de la muerte: Códice del Escorial* (Barcelona: Adiax, 1981).

29.   See Raymond Cantel, "La mort de Caryl Chessman et la littérature populaire du Nordeste brésilien," in *Homenaje. Estudios de filología e historia literaria lusohispanas e iberohispanas* (La Haye: Van Goor Zonen, 1966), 147-59; Billy Jaynes Chandler, *The Bandit King: Lampião of Brazil* (College Station: Texas A & M University, 1978).

30.   Augusto de Campos, *Mais provençais: Edição revista e ampliada* (São Paulo: Companhia das letras, 1987), and "Arnaut Daniel, o Inventor," in *Verso, reverso, controverso* (São Paulo: Perspectiva, 1988), 40-65.

31.   Roy Rosenstein, "Translating the Trobadors," *Yearbook of Comparative and General Literature* 37 (1988): 69-78.

32.   Marcelle d'Herde-Heiliger, *Répertoire des traductions de oeuvres lyriques des troubadours des XIe au XIII siècles* (Béziers: CIDO, 1985); Martín de Riquer, *Los trovadores: Historia literaria y textos*, 3 vols. (Barcelona: Planeta, 1975).

33.   Roy Rosenstein, "Ubicação e particularismo da língua de Camões," *Arquivos do Centro Cultural Português* 22 (1986): 243-62.

34.   Segismundo Spina, ed. and trans., *Apresentação da lírica trovadoresca* (Rio: Libraria acadêmica, 1956; *A lírica trovadoresca* (São Paulo: Grifo, 1972; USP, 1991).

240 Studies in Medievalism

35. Joseph Anglade, *Grammaire de l'ancien provençal* (Paris: Klincksieck, 1921), 262; Michel Bréal, "La science du langage (1879)," in George Wolf, ed. and trans., *The Beginnings of Semantics* (London: Duckworth, 1991), 127.

36. e. e. cummings, *40 poem(a)s traduzidos por augusto de campos* (São Paulo: Brasiliense, 1986); D. Jon Grossman, *E. E. Cummings* (Paris: Seghers, 1966). For the present author's experience teaching cummings in Brazil, see *Spring: The Journal of the E. E. Cummings Society*, n. s. 2 (1993): 96-97.

37. James J. Wilhelm, ed. and trans., *The Poetry of Arnaut Daniel* (New York: Garland, 1981).

38. Philippe Sollers, *Les Folies françaises* (Paris: Gallimard, 1988), 110.

39. Samuel Taylor Coleridge, *Literary Reminiscences* 4:166, quoted in the *Oxford English Dictionary*; Viṣnu Śarma, *The Pañcatantra*, trans. Chandra Rajan (New Delhi: Penguin India, 1993), xv.

40. Ronnie Apter, *Digging for the Treasure: Translation after Pound* (New York: Paragon, 1987).

41. Charlotte Ward, *Pound's Translations of Arnaut Daniel* (New York: Garland, 1991), ix, xiii; 129-31.

42. George Wolf, trans., "Pois Raimons e.n Trucs Malecs" by Arnaut Daniel, *The Columbia Review* 52.2 (Spring-Summer 1972).

43. René Nelli, ed. and trans., *Ecrivains anticonformistes du moyen-âge occitan: la Femme et l'Amour* (Paris: Phebus, 1977); Mario Eusebi, ed. and trans., *Arnaut Daniel: Il sirventese e le canzoni* (Milano: Pesce d'oro, 1984). Most recent is Martín de Riquer, ed. and trans., *Arnaut Daniel: Poesias* (Barcelona: Quaderno Crema, 1994).

44. Ezra Pound, *The Cantos* (London: Faber and Faber, 1957), 94.

45. Rosenstein, "Translating," 69, 77 (note 2).

46. István Frank, *Répertoire métrique de las poésie des troubadours* (Paris: Champion, 1953-57), #6, 1-4, vol. I, 3.

47. Alfonso D'Agostino, "Per la tornada del sirventese di Arnaut Daniel," *Medioevo romanzo* 15 (1990): 321-51; Giuseppe E. Sansone, *I trovatori licenziosi* (Milano: ES, 1992).

48. Cleber Teixeira, *Armadura, espada, cavalo e fé: Fragmentos 22, 23, 24* (Ilha de Santa Catarina: Noa Noa, 1991). On Teixera, see Alcides Buss, et al., "One Brazilian Poet: Cleber Teixeira," *Ilha do desterro* 4.9 (July 1983): 91-103.

49. Spina, *Apresentação da lírica trovadoresca*, 23; *A lírica*, 27.

50. This essay was essentially complete when I obtained, through the courtesy of Adovaldo Fernandes Sampaio in Goiânia, a copy of *Babariol, Babariol: Verso de Guilherme de Aquitânia traduzido por Virgílio Maia* (Fortaleza, 1993; reprinted 1994). This *folheto* is a rendering of "Farai un vers pos mi sonelh" with a short preface in which the contemporary Brazilian *trovador* explains how he made a popular adaptation (*cordelizou*) of the "best" of the first Provençal *troubadour*, effectively bridging the gap between the popular lyric forms of medieval Provence and modern Brazil.

Notes on Contributors

SUZY BEEMER teaches in the English Department at the University of Nebraska-Lincoln. Her research interests include early and contemporary Women's Studies, Renaissance Studies, and critical theory. She is currently a visiting scholar at the Belle van Zuylen Institute at the University of Amsterdam. Her work in progress includes a book manuscript, *"Assay the Power You Have": Compromised Subjectivities and English Renaissance Literary Women*.

ROBERT E. BJORK is Professor of English and Director of the Arizona Center for Medieval and Renaissance Studies at the University of Arizona, and he has recently become Director of the series Medieval and Renaissance Texts and Studies (MRTS). His publications include *Sources and Analogues of Old English Poetry II: The Major Germanic and Celtic Texts in Translation* (Boydell & Brewer, 1983), *The Old English Verse Saints' Lives: A Study in Direct Discourse and Iconography of Style* (Toronto, 1985), *Cynewulf: Basic Readings* (Garland, 1996), and translations of seven modern Swedish novels for the University of Nebraska Press. In 1987, he won the translation prize of the American-Scandinavian Foundation, and in 1989 he was awarded honorable mention for both a translation prize from the Translation Center of Columbia University and the John Nicholas Brown Prize of the Medieval Academy of America.

WILLIAM CALIN is Graduate Research Professor of French at the University of Florida. He works on medieval French and English literature, French poetry from the Renaissance to the present, and modern literature in Occitan and Breton. He has published nine books and seventy articles. *A Muse for Heroes* was awarded the Gilbert Chinard First Literary Prize for 1981; *The French Tradition and the Literature of Medieval England* was named by the American Library Association an Outstanding Book of 1995. His next project is *Minority Literature and Modernism: Scots, Breton, and Occitan 1920-1990*.

ALBRECHT CLASSEN, Professor of German Studies at the University of Arizona, has published books on Oswald von Wolkenstein, Wolfram von Eschenbach, autobiographical lyric poetry of the late Middle Ages, and the German "Volksbuch"; he is the translator of *Moriz von Cran* and of two textbooks. He is editor of *Tristania* and of *Synopsis*, associate editor of *Mediaevistik*, and book review editor for the *Journal of the Rocky Mountain Medieval and Renaissance Association*.

OTFRID EHRISMANN is Professor at the Institut für deutsche Sprache und mittelalterliche Literatur at Justus-Liebig-Universität in Gießen, Germany. His latest project is *The Myth of the Middle Ages: Medievalism in Germany*; his numerous publications on medieval literature and culture include *Das Nibelungenlied in Deutschland. Studien zur Rezeption des Nibelungenlieds von der Mittel des 18. Jahrhundert bis zum Ersten Weltkrieg* (München, 1975), *Nibelungenlied 1775-1920. Regesten und Kommentare* (Gießen, 1986), *Nibelungenlied. Epoche-Werk-Wirkung* (München, 1987); and most recently, *Der Stricker. Erzählungen, Fabeln, Reden* (Stuttgart, 1992).

MICHAEL GLENCROSS is a Senior Lecturer in French at the University College of Ripon and York St. John. He is the author of *Reconstructing Camelot: French Romantic Medievalism and the Arthurian Tradition* (D. S. Brewer, 1995). He has also published articles in a range of scholarly journals on his two main areas of research, early nineteenth-century French cultural history and representations of the Middle Ages in the Romantic period in France. He is at present working on a new book on culture and ideology in the July Monarchy, based on the study of illustrated magazines of the period.

WILLIAM CHESTER JORDAN is Professor of History and Director of the Shelby Cullom Davis Center for Historical Studies at Princeton University. His first book was *Louis IX and the Challenge of the Crusade: A Study in Rulership* (Princeton, 1979). He has also published books on French serfdom, on French royal policy toward the Jews, and on medieval and modern credit. His study *The Great Famine: Northern Europe in the Early Fourteenth Century* will appear this year, and he is editor in chief for a four-volume text, *The Middle Ages: An Encyclopedia for Students*, forthcoming from Scribner's.

ADAM KNOBLER is Assistant Professor of History at Trenton State College. He is currently writing a book on the Prester John mythologies in late medieval and early modern European imperial expansions, and he has also begun work on the place of the crusades in political culture of the nineteenth and twentieth centuries.

MARTHA L. MACFARLANE is a doctoral candidate in art history at the University of Chicago and an American Fellow with the American Association of University Women (1995-96). She is currently completing her dissertation on the history and historiography of medieval domestic architecture in southwestern France, "Constructing Cordes: The Idea and Invention of the Medieval House." Her architectural and historiographical research on the medieval house is enriched and informed by extensive study of the role of architectural imagery in medieval illuminated manuscripts, nineteenth- and twentieth-century architectural theory and practice, and urban and social history.

NILS HOLGER PETERSEN is Research Lecturer at the Center for Christianity and the Arts, Institute of Church History, University of Copenhagen. He has published work on medievalist aspects of music drama in Western Europe and on medieval liturgy and Latin music drama. His book on Mozart's *Idomeneo* and *Don Giovanni* in light of medieval liturgical and dramatic tradition is forthcoming from Edwin Mellen Press. He is also a composer of medievalist music and operas, including *A Vigil for Thomas Becket*.

ROY ROSENSTEIN is Professor of Comparative Literature at the American University of Paris. He has co-edited *The Poetry of Cercamon and Jaufre Rudel* (Garland, 1983) and *Etienne Durand: Poésies Complètes* (Droz, 1990). His work on medieval Occitan and Renaissance French literature has appeared in some thirty journals and collective volumes in Europe and the United States, and he has also published extensively on Luso-Brazilian and Spanish literature. Among his latest projects is a study of medieval literature in the French Resistance movement, forthcoming in the *Journal of the History of Ideas*.

RICHARD J. UTZ has taught at the University of Regensburg and the Pädagogische Hochschule Dresden and is currently at the University of Tübingen on leave from the University of Northern Iowa. He is the author of *Literarischer Nominalismus im Spätmittelalter* (1990), editor of *Literary Nominalism and the Theory of Rereading Late Medieval Texts* (1995), and co-editor of *"Realist" vs. "Nominalist" Semiotics: Shifting Paradigms of Literature* (1996); he is also co-editor, with Carol Poster, of the journal *Disputatio: An International Transdisciplinary Journal of the Late Middle Ages*. His article on Alfred Andersch appeared in Volume V of *Studies in Medievalism*.